Arming Japan

Arming Japan

Defense Production, Alliance Politics,
and the Postwar Search for Autonomy

Michael J. Green

Columbia University Press
New York

Columbia University Press
New York Chichester, West Sussex

Copyright © 1995 Columbia University Press
All rights reserved

Library of Congress Cataloging-in-Publication Data
  Green, Michael J.
      Arming Japan : defense production, alliance politics, and the post-
  war search for autonomy / Michael J. Green.
          p. cm.
      Includes bibliographical references (p.) and index.
      ISBN 0-231-10284-4 (alk. paper)
      1. United States—Military relations—Japan. 2. Japan—Military
  relations—United States. 3. Military-industrial complex—United
  States.   4. Military-Industrial complex—Japan. I. Title.
  E183.8.J3G69   1995
  355'.033552—dc20   95-19958
                                                                  CIP

Case bound editions of Columbia University Press
books are printed on permanent and durable acid free paper.

Printed in the United States of America

c 10 9 8 7 6 5 4 3 2 1

For N. S., D. H., and the other three M's,
and the City of Tokyo and Washington Pipe Bands

Sliante

Contents

Tables and Figures

Acknowledgments

This book has had several lives. It began in 1989 as an OP/ED piece I wrote for the Los Angeles Times with Nat Thayer about the Bush Administration's controversial plan to build a new support fighter with Japan—the FSX. Pundits in Washington were claiming that Japan would use the FSX to steal American aerospace technology and dominate world markets in yet another sector. At the time I was on a Fulbright Fellowship working in the office of Shiina Motoo, an internationalist in the Liberal Democratic Party, and I could see clearly the angst that FSX was causing for supporters of the U.S.-Japan alliance in Tokyo. I knew that the pundits in Washington were wrong. The United States and Japan were not about to replace the Cold War with a new war over technology. But I also knew how complex the interplay of technology and defense relations between the two countries was, and I wanted to tell the story in more detail. Nat Thayer and Shiina Motoo helped me get started on that task, and I will always be grateful to them for the insights they gave me into Japanese politics and the inner workings of U.S.-Japan alliance relations.

Later, in early 1990, I was approached by Richard Samuels and Michael Chinworth about publishing my initial research as a working paper for the MIT-Japan Program. That conversation inaugurated what would become a formal association with the program that resulted in four more working papers and numerous workshops, seminars, and lectures in both Cambridge and Washington. Dick and Mike have written their own books on Japanese defense and technology issues and have continually demonstrated the generosity and collegiality that characterize the MIT-Japan program and good scholarship in general.

In its most important stage this book was also a Ph.D. dissertation, completed in 1994 for The Johns Hopkins University School of Advanced International Studies. Professors Thayer and Samuels got another shot at my work at that point, but I was also helped a great deal by George Packard, Tom McNaugher, and Lyman Miller. In the years 1990–1994 my writing was also shaped by the comments of: Arthur Alexander, David Asher, Aburaki Kiyoaki, Paul Giarra, Gregg Rubinstein, Sheila Smith, Laura Stone, Tsuji Takuya, and Ezra Vogel. The next step was to turn the dissertation into a book, and here I was rescued by Murata Koji and Norio Endo, who helped me to correct some of my earlier mistaken assumptions about defense technology and the spelling of more obscure Japanese names. Finally, my manuscript would never have become a book without the hard work and important suggestions of my editors at Columbia University press: Kate Wittenberg, Chad Kia, Kerri Cox, and Ivon Katz. Their enthusiasm for the process of creating this book convinced me that my efforts to date were worthwhile. If the book works, it is in large measure thanks to the people I have listed above. Ultimately, of course, that judgment rests with the reader.

Acronyms and Abbreviations

ADI	Air Defense Initiative
AEW	Airborne Early Warning
ASDF	Air Self-Defense Force
ASM	Air to Surface Missile
ASW	Antisubmarine Warfare
AWACS	Airborne Warning and Control System
DPAC	Defense Policy Advisory Committee
DPC	Defense Production Committee
DSAA	Defense Security Assistance Agency
DSP	Democratic Socialist Party
GD	General Dynamics
FHI	Fuji Heavy Industries
FMS	Foreign Military Sales
FSX	Fighter Support Experimental
GHQ	General Headquarters (Occupation)
GSDF	Ground Self-Defense Forces
IHI	Ishikawajima Harima Heavy Industries
IRST	Infrared Search and Tracking
JDA	Japan Defense Agency
JMTC	Joint Military Technology Commission

JSDF	Japan Self-Defense Forces
KHI	Kawasaki Heavy Industries
LDP	Liberal Democratic Party
MD	McDonnell Douglas
MDAO	Mutual Defense Assistance Office
MELCO	Mitsubishi Electric Corporation
MHI	Mitsubishi Heavy Industries
MITI	Ministry of International Trade and Industry
MLRS	Multiple Launch Rocket System
MOF	Ministry of Finance
MOU	Memorandum of Understanding
MSA	Mutual Security Assistance
MSDF	Maritime Self-Defense Force
NDC	National Defense Council
NDPO	National Defense Program Outline
NSC	National Security Council
PARC	Policy Affairs Research Council
SAM	Surface to Air Missile
SDI	Strategic Defense Initiative
SSM	Surface to Surface Missile
S&TF	Systems and Technology Forum
TFT	Technology for Technology Initiative
TMD	Theater Missile Defense
TRDI	Technology Research and Development Institute

Arming Japan

Introduction

January 19, 1958. 11:00 A.M. It is a crystal-clear day at Fuji Heavy Industries' testing facility in Tochigi Prefecture. A group of officials from the Japan Defense Agency (JDA), the Air Self-Defense Forces (ASDF), and the Ministry of International Trade and Industry (MITI) are gathered around a swept-wing, two-seat training jet with a red hi-no-maru (rising sun) painted on the fuselage. This is the T-1, Japan's first jet aircraft indigenously designed and built during the postwar era.

Only three years have passed since the Japanese government committed itself to the development of the T-1, together with licensed production of the U.S. F-86 Saber Jet and its T-33 trainer version. The financial, technological, and political momentum for production of the F-86 and the T-33 followed from the Eisenhower Administration's decision to rebuild Japan's defense industrial base in the contest against international communism. Without this support Japan's defense and aerospace industries would never have emerged from the ashes of the Second World War. However, as all of the government and industry officials present today are fully aware, design and construction of the T-1 have been financed by Japan alone.

Two U.S.-trained test pilots board the jet and taxi it onto the runway. With a roar, the T-1's engine carries it 300 meters down the runway and up into the cobalt blue sky. The gathered dignitaries erupt in applause. Japan's postwar quest for autonomous defense production has begun.

No modern state is fully self-sufficient in the production of weapons of war, but those states with a high degree of autonomous production are often more powerful than those without it. Recognizing that a lack of self-reliance in defense production will inevitably create a condition of political and military dependence on the supplier of arms, many nations strive to achieve as great a level of domestic defense production as internal and international political and economic constraints allow. Thus small states such as Sweden, Israel, and South Africa design and build their own missiles, fighters, and tanks at great cost to their national treasuries.

This book explores the postwar history of Japan's search for autonomous defense production. *Kokusanka* (indigenization or, more accurately, national production-ization) has been well documented as an industrial policy theme in Japan's miraculous postwar economic recovery. Kokusanka has also been at the center of Japan's plans for postwar rearmament. Despite its "Peace Constitution" and close security ties to the United States, Japan designs and produces a seemingly impressive array of indigenous high-technology missiles, tanks, warships, and aircraft. Mitsubishi Heavy Industries' Type-90 tank, for example, is said to have the most sophisticated automation of any tank in the world. Kawasaki Heavy Industries T-4 jet trainer has been cited by U.S. aviation experts as a model of efficiency in design. Toshiba and Mitsubishi Electric have created a portable surface-to-air missile that they claim outperforms the famous U.S. Stinger. These weapons are testimony to Japanese technology and are powerful symbols of the potential for Japanese political and military self-reliance.

And yet, for all of its impressive hardware, Japan has not succeeded in developing an autonomous military industrial complex in the years since World War II. Today the defense industry in Japan accounts for less than 0.6 percent of total industrial production. Japan produces about 90 percent of its military equipment at home, but much of that is built under license from U.S. firms with a considerable amount of technology black-boxed (sealed so that Japanese engineers cannot understand the internal workings). Most of the big-ticket items in Japan's defense plans for the 1990s will be procured or built under license from the United States. These weapons include early warning aircraft, Aegis vessels, F-15s, and MLRS (multiple launch rocket system). Not included in Japan's list of new weapons are production of light aircraft carriers, an indigenous fighter, or any new indigenous training aircraft—all of which Japanese industry has been eager to design and build.

The absence of such indigenous weapons from Japan's new defense plans has not been the result of a lack of resources or productive capacity alone.

Instead, these weapons have been the victims of an intense forty-year-old policy debate over the merits of kokusanka itself. On one side, industrialists and conservative politicians in Japan have argued that autonomous defense production can strengthen national industries, improve military logistics, and bring greater freedom in national security planning. Their arguments follow the precedents of the Meiji Period modernization strategies, when the slogan "rich nation, strong army" (*fukoku kyōhei*) captured the notion that technological and economic strength was the surest means to insulate the national polity against the intrusions of a dangerous world.

The advocates of autonomy in defense production also react to a dilemma that smaller states have faced in alliances since the time of Thucydides. Aligning with a powerful state is necessary to deter powerful enemies, but the client state (in this case Japan) always faces the risk of either entrapment or abandonment.[1] Entrapment results when the state is dragged into conflict over issues that do not directly affect its national interest or when the larger power dominates the economic interests of the smaller ally. Abandonment results when the powerful ally abrogates the alliance or dealigns. The dilemma is that moving closer to the ally to avoid abandonment increases the chances of entrapment, while increasing independent policies and capabilities to avoid entrapment increases the risks of abandonment.

An independent capability to produce weapons protects smaller states against this dilemma by empowering them within the alliance while simultaneously providing a hedge against possible abandonment. The role of defense production has been a particularly important way for Japan to define its autonomy within the U.S.-Japan alliance, first because it embeds Japanese security within the goal of economic growth, and second because other hedges against entrapment and autonomy (a Gaullist independent nuclear capability, alignment with third countries, collective security arrangements, independent offensive capabilities) have all been politically or constitutionally problematic—if not impossible—for Japan.

However, indigenous defense production is no panacea, and the advocates of kokusanka in Japan have met strong opposition. There is, of course, the pacifist culture that surrounds Article IX of the Japanese Constitution. Many of Japan's technological and economic actors (in the universities, government, and industry) have consciously chosen to avoid association with defense production. Japan's policymakers have also discovered that the pursuit of autonomy in defense production can have the perverse effect of *limiting* the potential for independent political and economic action. When Japan's efforts to indigenize defense production have led to technoeconomic friction with the United States, for example, they have often *increased* the risks of abandonment (both military and economic). Similarly, when Japan's defense establishment has embarked on expensive domestic development programs, there has often been a heavy price to pay in terms of military efficiency, ironically increasing dependence on U.S. capabilities, and with it the risks of entrapment.

One might expect these costs of indigenous defense production to have declined with Japan's emergence as a technological and economic superpower, but that has not been the case. While Japanese industry has established a dominant global position in critical technologies such as advanced materials and microelectronics, systems integration (the ultimate goal in terms of military autonomy) has proven elusive as each succeeding generation of high-tech weaponry has taken revolutionary steps forward (one need only consider the decreasing frequency at which the United States has introduced new generations of weapons systems). At the systems level military technology has simply moved faster than Japan's ability to catch up, and this has made the opportunity costs of kokusanka no less troubling.

None of these complications were evident to Japanese or American policymakers when the two nations began rebuilding Japan's defense industrial base in the early 1950s. Japan was a nation extremely uncomfortable in alliance with the United States, but even less comfortable with the notion of abandonment. For the advocates of rearmament, kokusanka provided a simple linear formula for retrieving some degree of autonomy within the alliance structure. *How much* autonomy was still a moot point, since Japan had so far to catch up in technological and industrial terms. When Japan did begin to catch up two decades later, however, the question of *how much* autonomy began to matter a great deal. In theory the growth of an indigenous defense technology and industrial base should have freed Japan from dependence on the United States. Interestingly, Japan chose to *increase* military cooperation with the United States in the second half of the Cold War—even at times when detente was decreasing the external threat.

The story of Japan's postwar search for autonomous defense production is thus a story about the maturation of the larger U.S.-Japan security relationship. Japan's defense establishment approached each new generation of military systems armed with relative gains in indigenous technology and faced with new levels of relative decline in the American forward presence in Asia. At each stage of indigenization, however, Japan also confronted new complexities in military equipment at the systems level and expanding opportunity costs in terms of technoeconomic friction and geopolitical cooperation with the United States. While the successful indigenization of defense technology empowered Japan as a partner in the alliance, the failure of ambitious national projects on political, financial, and technical grounds also deepened interdependence with the U.S. Four decades in pursuit of kokusanka forced on Japan a new calculation of autonomy—a calculation in which indigenous capabilities would lead to greater influence *within* the alliance structure rather than escape from dependence on the United States.

It is with the evolution of Japan's internal debate over kokusanka that this book is most concerned, for that debate has helped to determine the parameters within which Japan's political elite will now attempt to calculate strategic choices for a post–Cold War world. The book takes an historical approach. The first chapter explains the prewar precedents for kokusanka and sets forth the arguments for and against autonomous defense production in postwar Japan. Chapters 2 through 6 then follow the path of indigenization of defense production and its impact on alliance relations from 1950 to 1994. Chapter 2 analyzes the establishment of Japan's defense industrial base in the 1950s and 1960s and the policy objectives and decision-making patterns set in motion by industry, government, and the National Diet in that period. Chapter 3 provides a detailed analysis of the 1970 Fourth Defense Build-Up Plan, in which Japan made a first bid for military and technological autonomy in anticipation of a U.S. withdrawal from Asia following President Nixon's Guam Doctrine. Chapter 4 explains the Japanese government's attempts to patch together closer alliance cooperation with the United States after the traumatic collapse of Nakasone Yasuhiro's Fourth Defense Plan. Chapter 5 explores the political explosion caused in the alliance by the Defense Agency's desire to develop a new indigenous support fighter, the FSX (fighter support experimental), and the efforts of the U.S. Congress and members of the Bush Administration to stop them. Chapter 6 focuses on how the FSX episode forced the Japanese government to reconcile its goals of autonomous defense production and closer alliance relations with the United States.

Chapter 7 analyzes the autonomy of the Japanese defense industry after the Cold War and assesses the potential for greater bilateral defense technology collaboration between the United States and Japan in new areas such as theater missile defense. In the concluding chapter the book suggests the implications of the history of kokusanka for the future of the U.S.-Japan alliance and Japan's own efforts to define a world role that balances military, technological, and economic power.

In the end, Japan's postwar debate over defense production demonstrates the divisive force that technonationalism represents in domestic and international politics. However, the history of kokusanka also suggests that shifting relative technological strengths between allies need not doom an alliance—even following the demise of a common enemy. Technological advancement creates as much complex interdependence as independence, with profound impact on the security policy of a nation like Japan.

1 | The Allure of Autonomy: Defense Production and Alliance, Defense Production and the Economy

The Historical Roots of Kokusanka

The goal of establishing autonomous defense production has been closely linked to the Japanese definition of national sovereignty since the middle of the last century. Any understanding of Japan's postwar kokusanka debate must therefore be set against the historical precedent established before the war.

After emerging from 500 years of isolation, the Tokugawa Shogunate was forced to sign unequal commercial treaties in 1858 and 1866 that exposed Japan's backward agrarian society to the dynamic industrial competition of the West. With extraterritorial rights and tariffs controlled by Europeans and Americans, Japan's leaders feared the dismemberment that had befallen China. As the young leaders of the Meiji Restoration fought to unify Japan, they borrowed Western arms and technology. "*Wakon yōsai*" (Western technology, Japanese spirit) was the rallying cry. Once the country was united in 1868, however, the Meiji government implemented policies that would at once reduce the reliance on foreign technology and stimulate the growth of Japan's political, economic, and military power.

The slogan "rich nation/strong army" (*Fukoku kyōhei*) would characterize these new policies for the restoration of national autonomy, and the pillar of the strategy was to "increase industrial productivity" (*shokusan kōgyo*)—a policy inspired by Germany's victories over France (the latter being the Meiji leaders' favorite model until 1870) and championed by the modernizers Ōkuma Shigenobu and Ito Hirobumi. The program to increase industrial productivity emphasized import substitution and the direction of overall technological and economic development through government guidance of the military industrial sector (even as most nonmilitary industries were, in fact, being privatized). As the historian E. H. Norman noted:

> This great expansion in the armament industries had the effect of stimulating the drive for self-sufficiency in Japanese industry. The military industries thus became a mold which shaped the pattern of Japanese heavy industry.[1]

By the turn of the century, this program had led to self-sufficiency for most wartime materiel (with the important exception of the Imperial Navy's capital warships which were primarily built in Great Britain) and had fostered the emergence of the great *zaibatsu* conglomerates. The debts incurred during the 1904–1905 war and by Japan's aggressive industrial promotion policies could have been devastating, but the Great War of 1914–1918 gave the Japanese economy a reprieve by rapidly expanding the demand for Japan's exports of manufactured goods while distracting potential trade competitors. Legitimized by this record of success, the basic tenants of "increasing industrial productivity" were further institutionalized with the passing of the Industrial Mobilization Law of 1918 (*Gunju kōgyo dōinho*), which gave the Government the powers to regulate industry in time of warfare.[2]

The drive for autonomous defense production was interrupted in the decade after the First World War by the instability of international financial markets. Hyperinflation caused by Japan's excessive specie reserves resulted in rice riots in 1918, which were followed by sudden deflation in 1920. Increasingly, the balance of power in the Far East was being determined not by military and political assets but by balances of payment and gold reserves.[3] When a new government under the *Minseitō* assumed office in 1929, its leadership determined to reestablish Japan's international prestige and exchange stability through a return to the gold standard and a policy of convergence with Anglo-American economic principles that would put an end to the industrialization-centered drive for autonomy of the previous five decades. Prime Minister Hamaguchi Osachi and Finance Minister Inoue Junnosuke slashed defense spending, forced rationalization on industry, and in January 1930 lifted the embargo on gold. The results, however, were calamitous. The worldwide depression and the sudden export of the nation's gold holdings caused Japan's export market to collapse.[4] The agricultural sector was in ruins and the militarists in near open rebellion. The stage was set for a return to the principles of autonomy inherent in the Meiji period's "rich nation/strong army" slogan.

In 1931 Finance Minister Takahashi Korekiyo reversed Inoue's policies and introduced a policy of monetary expansion and investment in munitions and heavy industries. As part of this program the government established a Kokusanka Promotion Council (*Kokusan Shinkō Iinkai*) to reassert the principle of import substitution, not just in military equipment but across the civilian economy as well. When Takahashi later attempted to rein in military spending, his authority to do so was openly questioned by the Army Minister. The military had taken a renewed interest in industrial policy since 1930 and asserted itself in economic issues increasingly throughout the decade. In 1937 civilian and military planners were fused into an economic "general staff" in the form of the Cabinet Planning Board. In 1938 the Army used its increasing political control to push through a National General Mobilization Law (*Kokka Sōdōin hō*), which effectively put the 1918 Industrial Mobilization Law into permanent effect. By the end of the decade, the industrialization and "rich nation/strong army" principles were distorted beyond what the Meiji leaders would have recognized. Instead of the military and industrial sectors working in symbiosis for the strength and autonomy of the nation, industrial interests had become almost entirely subordinate to the interests of the military clique that ruled the country. The result was the tragic disaster of the Pacific War.

In the aftermath of the war, the Japanese people blamed the militarization of the economy and society for the suffering they had been forced to endure. American Occupation authorities agreed and in 1945 banned the research, development, and production of weapons and aircraft. Those parts of the Japanese war-making machine that had not been pounded to rubble by allied bombing were dismantled, including the powerful zaibatsu (both the "new zaibatsu" that had grown in the war-oriented autarkic environment and the cosmopolitan older zaibatsu that had been reluctant converts to the militarists' cause). Article IX of the 1947 Constitution prohibited Japan from maintaining "war potential" and renounced the nation's "right of belligerency." Major architects of Japan's defense mobilization policies, men like Kishi Nobusuke (former Vice Minister of Commerce and Industry and future Prime Minister), were tried as war criminals.

In these early years of the Occupation, SCAP (Supreme Commander Allied Forces) and Japanese Ministry of Commerce and Industry (MCI) officials were unable to decide on a model for Japan's economic recovery. On the one hand, the MCI officials turned instinctively to the prewar model of promoting heavy industries through kokusanka. On the other hand, Prime Minister Yoshida Shigeru (who referred to MCI officials as "insects") and the Foreign Office feared the effects of a return to a planned central economy and preferred stable economic and social reconstruction based on the promotion of light industries.[5]

This debate over economic policy was effectively settled by the onset of the Cold War. By 1948 SCAP was restoring purged leaders to the political arena (including Kishi), and giving more thought to building Japan up as a military-industrial bastion in the Far East. With the outbreak of the Korean War the United States committed itself to reviving Japan's prewar heavy industries and created a *tokuju* (special demand) for war materiel that soon accounted for 70 percent of Japan's total exports. Heavy industry was given a further boost in 1952 when Occupation authorities lifted the ban on aircraft and defense production and in 1954 when the Mutual Security Assistance agreement provided financial and technological assistance for license production of a series of U.S.-designed tanks, ships, and jet aircraft.

Ultimately, Japan's postwar defense industry was not destined to play the same role that it had in prewar economic development. As the economy grew, defense demand took a decreasing share of total industrial output: from 1.20 percent in 1954 to 1.00 percent in 1960 to around 0.50 percent for the past three decades. Nevertheless, while weapons production declined in importance as the engine for economic growth, kokusanka became ever more important for those who sought a clear definition of Japan's relative technological and military autonomy from the United States.

Enthusiastic industrialists and hawks in the ruling Liberal Democratic Party began arguing in the early 1950s that establishing autonomy in defense production would enhance Japan's emergence as a postwar power by increasing leverage vis-à-vis the United States in the bilateral alliance and by strengthening Japan's competitiveness in important industries such as aerospace and shipbuilding. Opposition to this position emerged from the left but also, and more importantly, from within the conservative camp. The Ministry of Finance (MOF) and financial community, the Foreign Ministry, and those ideologically in support of the "Yoshida Doctrine" (economic strength with minimal remilitarization) did not object to the principle of indigenization of productive capacity per se but did argue that excessive autonomous defense production would cost too much, harm interoperability with U.S. forces, and eventually undermine the consensus at the base of the conservatives' successful governance of Japan throughout the postwar period. As Japan's technological and industrial power increased and the United States' relative military and technological leadership in Asia declined in the forty years after the Korean War, this debate intensified and accelerated. To an extent rarely appreciated, this struggle to define kokusanka shaped Japanese strategy in the postwar era.

But why autonomy in defense production? Before moving to the postwar history of kokusanka, it is important to first explain its allure—and its costs—in greater detail. From the first internal fight over licensed production of the F-86 Saber jet in the early 1950s through the political explosion of FSX in the 1980s and Theater Missile Defense in the 1990s, the debate over whether to import weapons or build them at home has come down to five issues: technonationalism; industrial policy; macroeconomic policy; alliance policy; and, of course, military capabilities.

Technonationalism

The drive for kokusanka can be explained first and foremost as a function of *technonationalism*. The term was first coined by Robert Reich in a 1987 *Atlantic Monthly* article, and scholars have yet to reach a consensus on what exactly it means. Nevertheless, the general notion that state-to-state relations are affected by nationalistic definitions of technology seems undeniable at the end of the twentieth century. It is also widely asserted that Japanese foreign and economic policy has been somehow driven by the idea that technology is an asset of national security.[6]

Richard Samuels, for example, has used "technonationalism" to describe what he identifies as a coherent ideology in Japan:

> Japanese military and industrial strategies have been built on a fusion of industrial, technology, and national security policies. This fusion, dubbed *technonationalism* [italics mine], has persisted in both the prewar era, when Japan used military means to achieve its national objectives, and in the postwar period, when its policies were more completely commercial.[7]

As Samuels explains in *Rich Nation/Strong Army: National Security and the Technological Transformation of Japan*, this technology ideology is "a set of coherent, even laudable, ideas," rather than "an irrational psychosis."[8]

The idea that governments might take a nationalistic view of economic policies (and an economic view of security policy) is not unique to Japan, of course. In fact, when Reich coined the term, he was describing U.S. economic policy.[9] In contrast to Samuels, however, who sees technonationalism as a rational framework for policy making in Japan, Reich points to the dysfunctional and irrational impact of nationalism on economic policy making (Reich explains, for example, how his students at Harvard would often express an irrational preference for low U.S. economic growth rates if that meant that Japanese growth rates would also be low).[10]

Ultimately, the technonationalism behind Japan's drive for indigenization of defense production encompasses all of the definitions that fall between Samuels's and Reich's: from the short-term emotional outbursts of nationalist politicians to the consistent normative patterns (or ideologies) of technology managers in industry and government. It is appropriate to begin with the irrational end of the spectrum.

The emotionalism behind the drive for kokusanka is best represented by nationalist politician and novelist Ishihara Shintarō, whose 1989 book *A Japan That Can Say "No"* became a bestseller in Japan and was eventually translated in the United States by DARPA, the Defense Advanced Research Projects Agency.[11] In *A Japan That Can Say "No"*, Ishihara lambastes Foreign Ministry officials and LDP politicians whom he accuses of sacrificing Japanese national interests and national pride by bowing to U.S. pressure to abandon plans for indigenous development of FSX. Ishihara's suggestion is that only the lack of development of fully autonomous defense production capabilities prevents Japan from becoming a great power. There is no question, according to his logic, that Japan could indeed turn its technological prowess into full autonomy in military production. In *A Japan That Can Say "No"*, Ishihara asserts that Japanese high technology is sufficient to build a far superior fighter than the U.S. F-16 and to potentially alter the East-West balance of power. The "Japanese must have confidence in their superior high-technology," he writes, "for then the Japanese could truly become an amazing race in the future."[12] Ishihara, in effect, links pride in technology to Japan's sense of nationhood, with pride itself the key to national strength, rather than the technological or economic advantages to be gained from autonomous defense production.

Ultimately, Ishihara's own influence on Japan's defense industrial debate has resulted in far more smoke than fire. Even his command of the issues is questionable, as evidenced by a 1989 interview in *The Wall Street Journal* in which he claimed that Japan could soon develop "air mines."[13] Nevertheless, Ishihara's 1989 book exposed a nationalist theme that resonates for many policymakers and industrialists in Japan and has driven defense industrial decision making in ways that were not previously appreciated in the West.

It is also worth noting that ill-placed pride in defense technology emerged in Japan well before Ishihara exposed "techno-arrogance" in the FSX debate. As early as 1958, senior officials of Mitsubishi Heavy Industries were arguing that Japan had the technology to build a fighter superior to the U.S. F-86, then being used by the Air Self-Defense Forces.[14] Amazingly, this came at a time when U.S. superiority in jet fighters was rivaled only by the Soviet Union and Japan had yet to produce a single jet aircraft. Similar claims have been made regarding aircraft since then. Over time these claims have come closer to reality. In a 1979 statement to the government, the defense industry declared that its companies had "attained the top levels of technology internationally."[15] Informed defense officials in Japan caution that the defense industry actually has many impressive technology "trees," but not the "forest of technology" that the United States has. Nevertheless, many in industry have long argued that the accomplishments of developing certain highly successful technologies alone demonstrate that Japan should adopt a policy of kokusanka across the board.

In short, technonationalism creates an impulse in Japanese defense industrial policy making that at once overemphasizes the potential strengths of Japanese technology while warning that Japan's very sovereignty is threatened by dependence on U.S. systems. Like a manic-depressive, Japan's defense technology management can swing from supreme confidence to complete crisis, but in either mode technonationalism creates a powerful force for kokusanka.

Industrial Policy

Samuels's definition of technonationalism includes both the emotionalism represented by Ishihara and the more rational economic planning instincts of officials in the government and industry. To understand the dissenting views on kokusanka within the Japanese political system, however, it is useful to separate the emotional from the rational. We consider next the rational dimension.

The potential importance of import substitution for national industrialization and economic growth was understood first outside of Japan, by Alexander Hamilton in the United States and Friederich List in Germany.[16] The concept was reintroduced to postwar academia by Joseph Schumpeter, who claimed that classical economic factors alone cannot account for economic growth and that nations can create comparative advantage through government intervention to establish technology trajectories.[17] This ability of government to choose "winners and losers" has been a point of debate in Japan just as it has in the United States, particularly when scarce government resources are at stake. But from the beginning of Japanese economic recovery during the Korean War, MITI and industry realized that defense production provided one mechanism for government targeting of industries and technologies that would not have to be justified by economic arguments alone.

The advantages of indigenous defense production to the civilian economy have changed for Japan as its industry has moved up the indigenization ladder. Initially, autonomous *licensed* production of U.S. defense systems played a central role in introducing technology into Japan. The brakes of the bullet train, for example, were based on the design of the brakes for the F-104 Starfighter, built under license by Mitsubishi Heavy Industries (MHI) in the 1960s. Autonomous production of the F-104, even though it was under license, also gave MHI engineers the know-how to develop the T-2, Japan's first indigenous jet aircraft.[18]

By the 1970s the patterns of technology diffusion and the role of the defense sector in the competitiveness of the Japanese economy began to change. Import substitution policies and severe restrictions on foreign direct investment had given Japan two decades of technology imports at bargain prices.[19] Eventually, experimenting with defense technology became more important than simply importing it. Engineers became as concerned with the know-why of defense-related technology as with the know-how. At the same time, the distinction between defense technology and civilian technology began to blur worldwide with the growth of smart weapons. Policy-

TABLE 1.1
Climbing the Indigenization Ladder

1. Servicing and repair of imported weapons systems.
2. Overhaul of imported weapons systems.
3. Local assembly of imported subassemblies.
4. Limited licensed production; assembly with some locally-made components; locally-made components sold to licenser.
5. Some independent licensed production, but important components are imported.
6. Local licensed production of less-advanced arms; r&d on improvements and derivatives.
7. Local licensed production for most weapons; limited r&d for advanced arms; r&d and production for less-advanced arms.
8. Complete independence in r&d and production.

Source: United Nations Institute for Disarmament Research, 1988.

makers in Japan soon came to realize that they could derive benefits not only from technological spin-offs from defense production, but also from taking civilian technology and spinning it onto defense systems. Erasing the artificial distinction between defense and civilian technology, they recognized, would improve Japan's overall technology base, to the benefit of both industry and the military. As the Director of the JDA's Technology Research and Development Institute (TRDI—the JDA's R&D arm) indicated in an interview in 1990: "there is no black versus white, military versus civilian technology. All technology is just different shades of gray. It becomes military or civilian in application."[20]

With these new patterns in technology diffusion, autonomous development became more important than autonomous *production* for Japanese industry. Autonomous development of weapons systems allows companies to spin-on more civilian technology to defense, utilizing their highest value-added resources in technicians and equipment at the Defense

TABLE 1.2

Ratio of Domestic Procurement to Total Procurement (Kokusanka Ratio)

Year	Kokusanka Ratio
1950–1954	34 percent
1955	30
1960	75
1970	91
1975	95
1976	95
1977	93
1978	85
1979	85
1980	88
1981	80
1982	87
1983	90
1984	91
1985	91
1986	91
1987	91
1988	91
1989	90.4
1990	89.1
1991	90.0
1992	92.2

Source: Japan Defense Agency

Agency's expense. Autonomous development also allows industry to leave behind the know-how advantages of licensed production and move toward the next step—the know-why experience of developing a system from beginning to end.

This point is particularly true for Japan's aircraft industry, which has traditionally relied on the JDA for 80 percent of its market and for what are often, in effect, subsidies to experiment with systems integration—a skill the industry will never develop as a subsystems supplier to Boeing or McDonnell Douglas. MITI decided on the autonomous development of the T-1 and T-2 jet trainers in the 1950s and 1960s, for example, to give industry its first experience in autonomous systems integration even though the ASDF already had trainer versions of the F-86 and F-104 to work with—a fact that has prompted many ASDF pilots to call the T-2 "a trainer for industry, not pilots."[21]

However, experimenting with spin-on technologies and systems integration in kokusanka projects can in turn cost industry a great deal, if the systems do not graduate from the R&D phase to full production. R&D project funding from the TRDI comes in lump sums and is rarely more than seed money, covering only a portion of actual R&D costs.[22] Japan's defense industry has consistently lobbied for "design-to-cost budgeting" and a larger budget for TRDI in order to counter this problem, but with only minor results. One of the only ways for companies to recoup losses incurred in R&D, therefore, is at the production phase—either by hiding the costs in production or taking them out of the 5 percent profit margin provided by the JDA. This can only be done, however, when companies can control production cost projections themselves—something quite difficult under FMS (Foreign Military Sales from the U.S. government) or licensed production, where many cost projections are already established. This fact further strengthens industry's resistance to imported weapons and licensed production and explains one of the reasons for the strong preference for bringing autonomously designed weapons systems to the production phase. As a 1974 policy assessment by the Defense Production Committee of Keidanren (The Federation of Economic Organizations—the political headquarters of big business in Japan) states:

> High quality technicians and productive workers are necessary for weapons production, but the current stop and start method causes these technicians and workers to be repeatedly reassigned. Not only does this disrupt production plans in other areas, it creates undesirable redistribution problems as well.[23]

For industry and the designers of industrial policy in MITI, a consistent policy of kokusanka—uninterrupted by imports—also brings extra momentum to the development of competitiveness in related industries such as aerospace. Competition for defense contracts among domestic manufacturers is minimal in Japan. With jet fighter aircraft, for example, Mitsubishi Heavy Industries (MHI) almost consistently wins the lead contract, with Kawasaki Heavy (KHI) and Fuji Heavy (FHI) as the principal subcontractors; Ishikawajima Harima Industries (IHI) usually builds the jet engines. When companies know that they will be designing and manufacturing the successor to a system already under production, it allows them to take a long-term view of systems development and capital investment. They gain the freedom to invest in technologies or manufacturing capacity that may not yield truly economical results for a generation. The Defense Production Committee's 1974 report explains why:

> A policy of autonomous production of certain weapons systems results in the accumulation of technologies and the skill to develop those technologies which has a positive long term effect on the future acquisition of weapons. When a system is imported, however, this effect is—if not lost—at least significantly reduced.[24]

Based on receipts of income alone, defense contracting is rarely profitable in Japan. With kokusanka, however, there are often other advantages: expanded resource utilization, experimentation with spin-on applications of tech-

TABLE 1.3

Growth in Japan's R&D Spending (TRDI Spending)

Year	Ratio to Defense Budget (percent)	Amount (100 million yen)
1968	2.01	85
1976	1.21	183
1985	1.84	578
1986	1.95	653
1987	2.08	733
1989	2.21	818
1990	2.35	921
1991	2.50	1032
1992	2.60	1140
1993	2.80	1259
1994	2.90	1360
1995	3.00	1396

Source: Japan Defense Agency (*Nihon no Bōei*, 1995)

nology, systems integration experience, and momentum in technology development.

It is important to remember, however, that the trajectory of Japan's technology development did not end in the 1970s. The economic arguments for kokusanka that made sense in the 1950s became more difficult to justify as Japan took an ever larger role in the global economy in succeeding decades. In the 1980s Japan moved to the top of the international technology hierarchy, faced growing diversity internally in its high-technology firms, and saw a growing diffusion of international technology assets. In this new environment external pressure for technology reciprocity and internal pressure to share risk and knowledge with foreign firms raised the opportunity costs of kokusanka. In many areas the Japanese government has begun demonstrating a less nationalistic view of technology. For example, MITI's June 1992 *Issues and Trends in Industrial/Scientific Technology: Towards Techno-Globalism* asserted that:

> technological innovation is a series of interactions cutting across national boundaries, in which various technological elements are incorporated dynamically. In most cases, the development of a practical product or technology involves the gradual accumulation of inventions and improvements realized in more than one country. . . . Whether a company intends to devel-

TABLE 1.4

Ratio of Defense Production to Total Industrial Output

Year	Ratio
1954	1.20 percent
1955	1.00
1965	0.50
1975	0.40
1980	0.36
1981	0.35
1982	0.46
1983	0.50
1984	0.48
1985	0.51
1986	0.55
1987	0.58
1988	0.54
1989	0.54
1990	0.57
1991	0.55
1992	0.57

Source: Japan Defense Agency

op and produce a product or whether a country intends to reinforce a field of industry, it will be increasingly difficult both technologically and economically to develop and own industrial/scientific technology in an independent and exclusive manner.[25]

How broadly and deeply MITI and industry have embraced the new religion of technoglobalism will be a point of debate for years to come. There is no question that the goal of technological advancement is untarnished. However, the history of kokusanka also gives evidence of MITI officials' growing recognition that the excessive pursuit of indigenous development can isolate Japanese firms from global partnerships and defeat the ultimate goal of technological advancement. Technology strategies have had to change with trends in technology flows. Increasingly, microelectronics manufacturers have grown in importance relative to heavy industry and systems integrators in Japan's defense industrial base. For these electronics companies, the value of engaging in defense production is the ability to understand rapid changes in technology that occur in *both* the civilian and the defense sectors (particularly since the distinction between the two is now gray). These companies need interaction with foreign defense firms as much as they need protection from those firms. Even heavy industries, traditionally the most conservative and nationalistic in Japan's defense industrial community, have been forced by economic realities to move away from large national aerospace projects and toward increasingly profitable subcontracting work for Boeing, McDonnell Douglas, and other U.S. companies.

While these trends do not suggest that Japan is about to spread its technological wealth around the world, they do reveal that, in terms of the nation's technology advancement alone, there are growing opportunity costs

TABLE 1.5
Ratio of Defense Production to Total Output by Industry, 1987

Shipbuilding	8.26 percent
Aircraft	79.56
Vehicles	0.09
Weapons/ammunition	99.93
Communications	0.67
Petroleum products	0.68
Coal	0.03
Clothing	0.09
Medical equipment	0.13
Foodstuffs	0.13
Other	0.08

Source: Japan Defense Agency

to pursuing autonomous defense production. Indigenization strategies offer important advantages to nations playing rapid industrial and technological catch-up, but there is nothing permanent or universal about these advantages. Economies grow and change and so too must industrial and technology strategies. These strategies can change at the level of the firm, the industry, or the nation. It should not be surprising then that at times during the postwar pursuit of kokusanka, divisions arose between MITI and industry; between electronics firms and heavy industries; and within the ranks of even the most committed defense contractors.

The instinct of technonationalism represented by Ishihara may prove an enduring element in Japanese defense policy making, but as a matter of rational industrial policy, kokusanka has a point of diminishing returns.

Macroeconomic Policy Implications

It is also important to recall that the microeconomic strategy of kokusanka can only take place within policy parameters set by other economic planners in Japan. While MITI and industry have looked at defense production for its sectoral impact, the Ministry of Finance (MOF) and Japan's major financial institutions have considered the question from a macroeconomic perspective. They have generally shown a lack of enthusiasm for indigenous defense production based on three considerations.

The first of these considerations stems from the fact that defense production has contributed relatively little to overall Gross National Product (GNP) growth in Japan. The exception to this occurred during the Korean War, when defense industrial production helped to spark Japan's economic recovery. Demand caused by the Vietnam War may also have contributed as much as one billion dollars per year to exports, but this was recognized as a temporary stimulus that had little to do with Japan's capabilities for *autonomous* defense production.[26] As noted, in the two decades after the Korean War, defense industrial production accounted for less than 0.5 percent of total industrial output, climbing only gradually to its 1988 level of 0.55 percent.[27] In 1992 Japanese military aircraft production was only three times larger than the bicycle industry's production, and the total military sales of Mitsubishi Heavy Industries, Japan's largest defense contractor, amounted to only one-fourth of the military sales of McDonnell Douglas.[28] Given the limited appetite of Japan's own forces for military equipment and the 1967 Japanese Cabinet decision to ban the export of weapons, macroeconomic policymakers have seen little prospect that autonomous defense industrial production could ever realistically provide a major stimulus to GNP growth again.

The pursuit of autonomous defense production also threatens to disrupt the macroeconomic benefits to Japan of alliance with the United States. Under the alliance system, the United States has sponsored Japanese membership in the OECD, the General Agreement on Tariffs and Trade and other international economic organizations. It also has secured foreign markets for Japan, most importantly in the United States itself. In exchange, Japan has had only to respond to demands for incremental increases in burden-sharing. This has kept annual Japanese defense spending below, or close to, 1 percent of GNP. According to Hugh Patrick and other scholars, this low level of defense spending may have contributed as much as 2 percent per year to GNP growth in Japan (a stark contrast to the lack of potential economic stimulation offered by defense production).[29] These macroeconomic benefits make Finance Ministry officials wary of kokusanka strategies that threaten to disrupt the alliance system and Japan's secure place in the global economy.

Finally (and certainly not surprisingly), the Ministry of Finance is frequently in opposition to kokusanka for budgetary reasons. Indigenously designed and developed weapons usually cost more per unit than imports do. The small size of Japan's defense market and the ban on arms exports have deprived the Japanese defense industry of the economies of scale that Western arms producers enjoy (the appreciation of the yen has not helped

TABLE 1.6
Japan's Defense Budget, FY1955–FY1993

Fiscal Year	Budget (billion yen)	Budget/GNP Ratio
1955	134.9	1.78
1965	301.4	1.07
1975	1,327.3	0.84
1980	2,230.2	0.90
1985	3,137.1	0.997
1986	3,343.6	0.993
1987	3,517.4	1.004
1988	3,700.3	1.013
1989	3,919.8	1.006
1990	4,159.3	0.997
1991	4,386.0	0.954
1992	4,551.8	0.941
1993	4,640.6	0.937
1994	4,683.5	0.948

either). For example, in the mid-1960s, Japan's T-2 jet trainer was projected to cost three times its American competitor and eventually was completed at twelve times the cost. These budgetary concerns have not been the MOF's alone. The high cost of indigenous weapons draws scarce financial resources away from other areas in the defense budget such as personnel, base support for U.S. forces, and readiness—areas that each have their own important constituencies in the JDA and Japan Self-Defense Forces (JSDF).

Technonationalism and the sectoral concerns that define Japan's technology trajectory clearly drive the kokusanka debate at one level, but the resources available to MITI and industry's strategy are determined at the level of national economic planning and finance dominated by the MOF and Japan's financial institutions.

Security Policy and the Alliance

The kokusanka debate is also driven by its profound implications for Japan's security. In the twentieth century Japan has consistently defined its role in the international system as a function of alliance with the world's hegemonic power. In the first part of this century, that power was Great Britain. During the Second World War, Japan joined the Axis and allied with the German Third Reich. In the postwar era Japan has aligned itself with the United States, through the 1952 and 1960 Security Treaties. The first two alliances ended in tragedy. The durability of the current alliance depends in large measure on Japan's willingness to accept dependence on the United States—particularly in the area of defense industrial capabilities.

At one level, military dependence on the United States is not unattractive for Japan. The Yoshida Doctrine built a domestic consensus around the premise that Japan would focus on economic development while the United States relieved it of having to play a major security role in the postwar system. At another level, however, such dependence was extremely uncomfortable for a nation that joined in its previous two alliances with the specific aim of developing greater independence in addressing the security affairs of East Asia.

At issue with kokusanka is not whether to end the U.S.-Japan alliance, but how to escape the entrapment-versus-abandonment dilemma Japan faces within the alliance. The advocates of kokusanka claim that autonomous defense production will give Japan greater independence of action within the alliance. Not surprisingly, the opponents of kokusanka claim just the opposite: that a lack of defense industrial autonomy gives Japan greater independence in Asia.

On the surface, the advocates of autonomy have a simpler argument to make. The logic follows that Japan's capacity for autonomous foreign policy (*jishu gaikō*) or autonomous defense (*jishu bōei*) is directly proportional to the nation's ability for autonomous development of weapons (*buki no jishu kaihatsu*). As the Defense Agency notes in its 1970 Basic Policy on Equipment Production and Development: "Autonomous defense production is crucial to autonomous defense."[30] And autonomous defense, in turn, is crucial to autonomy in foreign policy, as the Defense Production Committee of Keidanren notes in its 1974 policy study:

> at the very least, [a policy of relying on imports of weapons] prevents a nation from adopting hostile activities towards the supplier of its weapons. And even if one accepts that a country would not go as far as taking such hostile action, that country would still be unable to take action which opposes the intentions of its supplier.[31]

But here the advocates of autonomy run into trouble. Article IX of the Japanese Constitution renounces the right of belligerency. And as Nagai Yōnosuke claims in his probing 1967 treatise on Japan's foreign policy, *Heiwa no Daishō* (Compensation for Peace), Japan would only increase its insecurity and vulnerability by choosing a Gaullist-type autarky through the independent possession of nuclear weapons (though the technological possibility exists).[32] As Nagai points out, this political reality means that "the first principle of [Japan's] foreign and defense policies must be to never allow the United States to become an adversary."[33]

This principle holds for the advocates of kokusanka as well, as the 1974 Keidanren Defense Production Committee report sheepishly concludes: "It is not necessarily the case, of course, that a country loses *all* sovereignty when it does not develop weapons autonomously" [italics mine].[34] The argument for the advocates of kokusanka (and the Defense Production Committee forms their core) is over the *degree* of autonomy Japan should have within the alliance. In this there is overlap with U.S. policy; the term *autonomous defense* originated with Americans calling for more burden-sharing from Tokyo in the early 1970s.

Autonomous defense, kokusanka, and even nationalism are all quite different from militarism, then, which is seen as inherently antidemocratic in Japan. The advocates of kokusanka cannot argue against the alliance, but they can argue that autonomy in defense production capability leads to equality in alliance by providing Japan the ability to defend itself if necessary and to contribute to the maintenance of the alliance on an equal footing, rather than as a technology-dependent junior partner. Morikawa Hiroshi, the director of Keidanren's Defense Production Committee until 1990, captures this sentiment:

> In a real crisis can a nation expect to fight using only equipment imported from abroad? A nation has to have at least an R&D base capable of developing the weapons it needs to defend itself. . . . And we need to improve our own technology base in order to foster cooperation and joint development projects. In the future we expect international cooperation to increase. As you know, these international consortia involve much give and take. If we do not have technology ourselves, we can expect nothing from our partners. Isn't it natural, therefore, for Japan to spend 5 percent [of its defense budget] on R&D [as opposed to the current 2.5 percent] when even West Germany is spending over 6 percent!35

The guardians of the U.S.-Japan alliance in Tokyo, led traditionally by the Ministry of Foreign Affairs, usually argue the opposite line. They maintain that while some degree of autonomous defense production must be tolerated for practical reasons, an aggressive effort to build import substitutes for every U.S. weapons system will eventually undermine the alliance. They see the advocates of kokusanka at their most benign as enthusiastic industrialists and at their most malevolent as dangerous militarists. In either case, they view kokusanka as a force which threatens the delicate domestic and international consensus behind the course that Yoshida Shigeru set for Japan.

Like the advocates of kokusanka, those whose interests have been threatened by kokusanka return to the original issue of autonomy-versus-alliance to argue that close defense ties with the United States actually create greater autonomy for Japan. Japan's leadership in Asia, their argument goes, depends on the reassuring presence of the U.S.-Japan alliance. As Vice Minister of Foreign Affairs Kuriyama Takakazu noted in a 1990 interview with the *Asahi Shimbun*: "Japan should contribute to political stability and economic development in the Asia-Pacific region in nonmilitary ways. And if Japan is to pursue such contributions there is no realistic alternative to the security treaty."36

Under this view, the direction of Japan's weapons policy should not be toward more autonomy in defense production but toward greater interoperability and interdependence. As one senior Foreign Ministry official (Nogami Yoshiji, Director of the Foreign Ministry's Institute for International Relations) remarked in a September 1990 edition of the influential opinion journal *Chuo Koron*:

What is important for both Japan and the U.S. in terms of the security rela-
tionship is to recognize the benefits to each side of interdependence.
Establishing weapons interoperability is one way to build interdependence.
Both nations should have a mature security concept and consider that we
exist as a security community. Only then will it be possible to reexamine the
U.S.-Japan security relationship.[37]

This official's final sentence is telling. Under the alliance framework, he suggests, interoperability is a mechanism for developing greater equality under
the alliance framework, rather than greater subservience. Japan's ability to
lead in the articulation of the common goals of the alliance emanates from
its contribution to the fulfillment of roles and missions in the alliance.
Integration of U.S. and Japanese systems, operations, and planning empowers Japan as a "constituent" of the alliance.

Greater autonomous defense production has the opposite effect, according to the opponents of kokusanka. First, they maintain, import substitution
of weapons destroys the concept of a common security community by rais-
ing the costs of deterrence for the alliance as a whole. Furthermore, in the
process of designing indigenous weapons systems, Japan (or any country)
inevitably develops indigenous mission requirements as national economic
and technological constraints channel development programs in unique
directions. This complicates interoperability and increases competition
between national industries. When bilateral competition becomes a greater
force than bilateral collaboration, then the alliance becomes a trap for Japan;
a mechanism for containing Japanese economic strength rather than foster-
ing the development of a more equal partnership with the United States.

The possibility of a transformation of the alliance in this way has been a
frightening prospect to those constituencies in Japan that favor a strong
defense policy most, including both the advocates and the opponents of
kokusanka policies. The kokusanka debate is, after all, a debate *within* the
defense policy-making community, where the question is not *whether*
Japan should have weapons but *what kind* of weapons Japan should have.
The question of whether Japan should have weapons was settled for the
conservatives by the alliance with the United States. With each new degree
of bilateral defense cooperation, the pro-defense constituency has grown
stronger and entered further into the mainstream: Yoshida's 1952 treaty
formed the basis for the creation of the Self-Defense Forces. The 1960 treaty
brought the business community and the Liberal Democratic Party (LDP)
behind expanded rearmament. The 1976 National Defense Program
Outline and the 1977 Guidelines for U.S.-Japan Defense Cooperation led to

the growth of a pro-defense *zoku* (caucus) within the LDP with membership from every faction.

The kokusanka debate represents a dagger aimed not only at the center of the emerging national consensus behind defense spending but at Japan's entire domestic political arrangement. As historian and Yoshida Shigeru biographer John Dower notes: "The reconsolidation and recentralization of conservative authority during the Yoshida era was inseparable from the strategic settlement reached between the United States and Japan."[38] The Yoshida Doctrine was, in fact, not a "doctrine" but a "compromise" among the advocates of disarmed neutrality, unilateral rearmament, and disarmed economic (and technological) alliance with the United States—all of whom had to fit under the conservatives' ideological tent in order to achieve the political stability necessary for economic reconstruction.[39] Only alliance with the United States would allow the accommodation of all three views, and the stability of the conservative leadership of Japan today is still based on that strategic settlement. Indeed, even the Socialists eventually bought into this consensus as a condition for forming a joint coalition with the LDP under Murayama Tomiichi in July of 1994.

This is the baseline to which the opponents of kokusanka return. Unbridled kokusanka, they maintain, is a threat not only to the alliance, but to the delicately crafted consensus behind Japan's defense community itself. The advocates of greater autonomous defense production cannot ignore this argument. Ultimately, they are unable to separate their agenda for autonomy from Japan's strategy for alliance.

Military Capabilities

In most nations, the military establishment has a powerful voice in decisions of defense production, but the political and legal constraints associated with Article IX of the Japanese Constitution have rendered the JDA and JSDF comparatively weak bureaucratic players on such issues. For most of its history, the Defense Agency has been effectively "colonized" by Bureau and Division Directors seconded from other, more powerful, ministries. As a result, the defense bureaucracy has been a sounding board for all of the technonationalistic, industrial, macroeconomic, and political factors examined above. It would be a mistake, however, to assume, as many observers of the FSX episode have, that Japan's military professionals do not influence the framing of the kokusanka debate or its outcome based on an assessment of the military capabilities required for the JSDF mission. In fact, the JDA and JSDF have gradually established a degree of institutional integrity that has allowed them to bring increasing military realism to the question of weapons development and procurement. To some degree this realism has brought into sharper focus the autarky-versus-efficiency dilemma (indigenous systems can end up costing more and working less) that military establishments face in most other advanced industrial nations.

In part, the military establishment's growing confidence and credibility in procurement issues have resulted from the passage of time. The Self-Defense Forces were formed in 1954 out of a national police reserve force, with primary responsibility for preserving domestic stability, and have only developed external (but defensive) missions as an extension to U.S. military strategy in the Pacific. Bureaucratically, the JDA has been dependent on the National Police Agency or the Finance Ministry for filling the top bureaucratic post of Administrative Vice Minister, with the Procurement Bureau led by a MITI official, the Accounting Bureau by an MOF official, and the Counselor for International Affairs by an MOF official.[40] It took some time for the agency's own officials to rise through the ranks to the level where they might become Administrative Vice Minister; the first was in the 1980s (Nishihiro Seiki). It also took time for the agency to begin developing its own agenda and institutional continuity.

In the process of establishing this bureaucratic identity and integrity, however, the civilian officials of the JDA (the *naikyoku*) have been bullied to the point that they are often extremely cautious on politically sensitive kokusanka questions. At times the JDA has taken an aggressive stand on procurement issues under the direction of forceful leaders such as Nakasone Yasuhiro, Director-General in 1970, or Nishihiro, in the late 1980s. But when these strong personalities have left the scene, the agency has invariably seen its budget and mission attacked by the concealed knives of other more powerful ministries. In the kokusanka debate this has led the JDA to pursue positions that leave it the least vulnerable to attack, sometimes eager for autonomy, sometimes fearing it.

The uniformed services, in contrast, have developed a sharper focus on defining the military rationale for weapons development and procurement as they have established more credibility and integrity in the political system. The source of this credibility has been twofold: first, they have a comparative advantage in understanding the growing complexity of modern weapons systems; and second, the division of roles and missions between the U.S. and Japanese forces in the 1980s has allowed the JSDF to become, in effect, proxy lobbyist for the U.S. military in Japan's budget process. Given the political pressures from the United States for burden-sharing, this latter element has been particularly important. On the other hand, the JSDF also has much closer ties to industry than do the JDA civilian officials. The major defense contractors usually have between them more than 120 recently retired field-grade officers and admirals as advisors (in the practice of *amakudari* [descent from heaven]).[41] As a result of this connection, the JSDF have often focused on developing autonomous defense technology, in contradiction to the services' parallel focus on interoperability. Predictably, these conflicting demands on the JSDF from industry and from the United States have led to inconsistent policies on kokusanka.

The services are also divided by some of the same rivalries that characterize their American cousins. While the Air, Maritime, and Ground Self-Defense Forces all draw officers from a single defense academy (as well as from private and national universities), they retain many of their prewar traditions and share different levels of interoperability with U.S. forces (the MSDF being closest to the U.S. Navy and the Ground and Air Self-Defense Forces somewhat more distant from the U.S. Army and Air Force). The result is poor interoperability among the three Self-Defense Force branches, frequent redundancy in procurement, and different perspectives on the kokusanka question. Each service must pay a price for autonomous development of weapons in terms of efficiency not only compared with potential adversaries but also vis-à-vis the other services of the Self-Defense Forces.

Particularly damaging for the advocates of defense industrial autonomy in the JSDF has been the fact that Japanese weapons have never been tested in combat. The experience U.S. defense systems have had in the Third World conflicts of the Cold War has given U.S. contractors information and testing on a scale Japan can never approach. Differences in testing and evaluation budgets between the United States and Japan are also striking: in any given year, U.S. test and evaluation budgets for one missile are usually greater than the JDA's entire testing and evaluation budget.

To the extent that the uniformed services have developed a sharper focus on the efficiency-versus-autarky dilemma of weapons procurement, they have frequently done so in terms of logistical sustainability, not combat efficiency. A focus on combat efficiency would sink industry's aspirations for autonomy, since U.S. equipment would clearly be superior. And the political constraints on operational planning make the maintenance focus more logical for the JSDF. The most traumatic crises of the JSDF have been the 1963 *Mitsuya Kenkyū* incident,[42] in which the JSDF Joint Staff Office was attacked in the Diet and the press for engaging in wartime planning and threat assessment that was too explicit, the 1970 collision of an ASDF fighter with an All Nippon Airways (ANA) airliner, and the 1989 collision of the MSDF submarine *Nadashio* with a recreational fishing boat. Each of these incidents has reinforced the JSDF's focus on making equipment work safely and on time, and not just on how it will perform in combat.

In terms of logistical sustainability, the JSDF has found considerable ground for arguing in favor of kokusanka. The 1989 White Paper on Defense states that kokusanka

> facilitates the procurement of equipment most suitable to Japan's unique environmental features, postdeployment improvements on the equipment in accordance with domestic technological developments, as well as the maintenance of equipment and the supply of spare parts over a long period.[43]

The JDA argues, accurately, that Japan's "exclusively defensive defense" mission (*senshu bōei*) necessitates different kinds of weapons. Imported U.S. systems can have operational capabilities that are unnecessarily costly or even unconstitutional for Japanese forces. In addition, the JDA and JSDF's concern with maintenance and spare parts is real. Increasingly, the United States has "blackboxed" sensitive software for fire control systems, missile guidance, and flight control in aircraft. In order to repair such software, Japan's Self-Defense Forces must remove hermetically sealed boxes and send them to the United States for repairs, where the equipment has usually received the lowest priority (after NATO countries and Middle East allies).

Senior JDA officials first began emphasizing the dangers of relying on the United States for maintenance and supply during the Vietnam War. A 1982 JDA report suggested that relying on the United States was not only militarily risky but a major budget problem as well:

> Due to the U.S. military expansion program, the lead time for obtaining weapons imported from the U.S. has lengthened to 3 to 4 years, causing great confusion in industrial management. If JDA does not reevaluate the contract term, industry will have great difficulty with financial management, exchange rate fluctuations risk and equipment maintenance.[44]

Thus cost effectiveness has been used as an argument for kokusanka as well as against it.

Studies of one of Japan's earliest experiences with domestic production, the F-104, suggest that a direct off-the-shelf purchase from the United States would have cost 10 percent more than producing the jet under license, as Japan eventually did.[45] This price differential was due in part to Japan's lower labor costs in the 1960s and to inexpensive transfers of technology for engine and software components. Both of these inputs have risen dramatically in cost over the intervening decades, erasing some of Japan's comparative advantages in production. On the other hand, the average 5 percent in royalty fees on the F-104 established a cost input that has not changed much. Japanese industry also claims higher efficiency in production. Moreover, when negotiating licensed production agreements through the U.S. Defense Security Assistance Agency, Japan has had to pay a 3 percent fee and sign a detailed Memoranda of Understanding that must be renegotiated if Japanese contractors are to initiate even the slightest changes in the terms of the licensed production.[46] Finally, many in the JDA suspect that U.S. companies are unfairly using Japanese purchases to pass on certain R&D costs that the U.S. Government will not pay for.[47]

Ironically, then, as the United States has called for increased burden-sharing and division of roles and missions with Japan, and the JSDF has developed greater (though still limited) institutional integrity within the Japanese political system, the services have used their new platform to focus on the inefficiencies of procuring weapons from the United States. These arguments have considerable impact, but the same political constraints that prevent the JSDF from arguing too explicitly about the combat efficiency of systems also prevent them from arguing too openly against interoperability with their most important bureaucratic allies—the U.S. defense establishment.

Technonationalism, industrial policy, macroeconomic policy, alliance relations, military capabilities . . . these concerns intersect at the question of defense production. Major procurement decisions in Japan have thus taken on the character of a proxy war for the more significant debate over the direction of Japanese security policy, industrial development, and relations with the United States. The next six chapters detail the growth of Japan's defense industrial base and the evolution of that debate.

2 | "On Sea, on Land, and Then On to Space!": The Growth of the Defense Industry's Political and Technological Base, 1950–1969

The Roots of the Kokusanka Debate, 1950–1954: Rearmament, the F-86, and the First Defense Plan

It is difficult to say when the leaders of Japanese industry began their quest for autonomous defense production in the postwar period because few ever considered defense production completely dead. Even after MacArthur's September 1945 Directive Number 3 banned civil and military aircraft research, development, and production, aircraft engineers from the cluster of companies that would re-form as Mitsubishi Heavy Industries in 1963[1] were corresponding with one another while they honed their skills on the production of bus bodies, farm machinery, and cooking pots.[2] Meanwhile, the bureaucracies responsible for disarmament of the navy were quietly building a small naval force for Japan.[3] And through Operation Roll-up, a pool of skilled Japanese workers was created in 1947 to repair used U.S. equipment left over from the Pacific War.[4]

But a few enthusiastic engineers writing letters and building buses cannot create the political, financial, and technological momentum necessary for the development of an indigenous defense industrial base. Industry had been flattened by U.S. bombing and the majority of the Japanese people,

(*Umi ni Riku ni, soshite uchu e*—from the title of the Mitsubishi Heavy Industries' official company history)

exhausted and resentful of war, were happily embracing the process of demilitarization. Without a jolting shock to the international system, the defense industry may never have moved beyond the production of light machinery.

That shock came in June 1950 with Kim Il Sung's reckless attack across the thirty-eighth parallel. The Korean War turned the Cold War into a "hot war," and led the United States to view Japan in a completely new light. Suddenly, the creation of Japanese industrial and military capacity was vital to the containment of the communist threat across the Tsushima Strait, and U.S. policy changed accordingly. To support the war effort in Korea, the U.S. spent

TABLE 2.1

Japan's Major Military Aircraft Development Programs

Aircraft/ Contractor	Principal Year Ordered	Funding/ kokusanka
T-33A TRAINER JET (FOR F-86 PILOTS) KHI	1955	Knock Down/ Licensed Production 67 Percent U.S. Funding 60 Percent Domestic Production
F-86F FIGHTER	1955	Knock Down/Licensed Production 67 Percent U.S. Funding 60 Percent Domestic Production
*T-1 TRAINER (First Autonomously Developed Jet) FHI	1956	100 Percent Domestic Production. Engine Imported Until Development of Domestic J-3 Engine
P2-V7 ASW Plane KHI	1958	52 Percent U.S. Funding/ 50 Percent Domestic Production
F-104J/F-104DJ (Lockheed Corp. Chosen Over Grumman F-11F)	1960	27 Percent U.S. Funding/ 85 Percent Domestic Production
*YS-11 Prop Plane (First and Only Commercial Kokusanka Passenger Aircraft)	1964	50 Percent Funding by Government 23 of 182 Ordered by JDA
*MU-2 MHI	1964	100 Percent Domestic Production

more than 700 million yen reviving seventy-four of Japan's devastated prewar heavy industries. In order to deter future communist threats against Japan, MacArthur recommended the creation of a national police reserve for Japan in 1950, the predecessor to the current Self-Defense Forces. And on March 8, 1952, GHQ rescinded its ban on aircraft and ammunition production. By 1952 the newly energized Japanese defense industry had productive capacity, legal status, and domestic and U.S. customers. Indeed, Korean War–related production, or tokuju, had stimulated the entire economy to the point that the government declared defense production a "national policy area."[5]

TABLE 2.1 *(Continued)*
Japan's Major Military Aircraft Development Programs

Aircraft/ Contractor	Principal Year Ordered	Funding/ kokusanka
F-4 EJ MHI	1969	90 Percent Domestic Production
*C-1 TRANSPORT KHI	1970	100 Percent Domestic Production
*T-2 TRAINER JET MHI	1970	100 Percent Domestic Production
*FST-2 (Based on T-2) Base for the F-1 MHI	1971	100 Percent Domestic Development and Production
*F-1 (Based on T-2) MHI	1977	100 Percent Domestic Development and Production
P-3C ASW Plane (Chosen Over KHI- Designed Kokusanka PXL) KHI	1978	License Produced
F-15J MHI	1981	70 Percent Domestic Production 155 Ordered
*T-4 TRAINER JET	1984	100 Percent Domestic Development and Production 93 Ordered
FSX (Joint Development Based on F-16)	1989	60 Percent Domestic Production/Joint Development

*Autonomously developed, subsystems may be imported or under license.
Source: Various *Jietai sobinenkan.*

As important as the special demand of the Korean War was, however, policymakers and businessmen realized that it could not last forever. For the defense industry to play a continuing role in the economic recovery of Japan, there would need to be a substantial commitment of political will in Tokyo and financial and technological assistance from the United States. The United States, for its part, seemed ready to make that commitment. As early as 1950, John Foster Dulles had decided that Japan could become the military-industrial linchpin of Asia.[6] The U.S. Occupation authorities also supported the idea. In 1950, for example, MacArthur's deputy, General Charles Willoughby, formally rehabilitated the purged Hattori Takushirō, previously of Tōjo's general staff, and 400 of his associates to assist with the formation of the new police reserve, knowing that they would push for expanded defense capabilities.[7] Then in December 1952 the State Department prepared a report expressing the view that Japan should enlist 325,000 to 350,000 troops, along with air and naval forces, by 1955. In this same period, the U.S. military began openly discussing with Japanese industry the possibility of producing major U.S. weapons systems under license in Japan in the future.[8]

These developments led Japanese industry to the realization that the United States represented a better ally for reestablishing defense production than any political force inside Japan. The key for industry would be building a coalition in support of defense production that pulled the U.S. government into Japan's domestic political debate. Industry organized itself for that task.

The headquarters for aspiring defense industry was Keidanren (the Federation of Economic Organizations), which had been formed in 1946 from the Federated Committee of Economic Organizations (*Keizai Dantai Rengō Iinkai*). The Federated Committee had itself been made up of a number of organizations, including several, such as the Council on Key Industries (*Jūyō Sangyō Kyōgikai*) and the Japan Economic League (*Nippon Keizai Renmei-kai*), that had had explicitly military-industrial objectives only the year before. (Keidanren would soon become the headquarters for industry as a whole, although through this period the organization often followed the lead of the industry organization Nikkeiren on broader economic issues.)

In the winter of 1951 Keidanren formed a "Working Group on U.S.-Japan Economic Cooperation" (*Nichibei Keizai Teikei Kondankai*) and distributed a report to both governments calling for sustained U.S. economic assistance and the establishment of a limited Japanese military capability.[9] Later this working group was divided into three formal Keidanren committees: the General Policy Committee, the Committee for Asian Development and, most importantly, the Defense Production Committee (*Bōei Seisan Iinkai*).

The Defense Production Committee would take the lead as the principal lobbying arm for the defense industry, a role it fills to this day. The committee's emergence from a group mandated to foster U.S.-Japan economic cooperation was not insignificant.

Parallel developments were occurring outside of Keidanren in other parts of industry as well. In September 1952 the Occupation-period Japan Technology Production Cooperative Association (*Nihon Gijitsu Seisan Kyoryokukai*) shed its deceptively peaceful name and reformed as the Japan Ordnance Association (*Nihon Heiki Kogyokai*), predecessor to the current Japan Defense Equipment Industry Association (*Nihon Bōei Sobi Kogyokai*).[10] By 1952 the organization had 138 members and 200 researchers working for it. Between the Defense Production Committee and the Japan Ordnance Association, industry had established by 1952 the forces it needed for a sustained push for expanded autonomous defense production.

With political organization in place in Japan, industry moved from the broad theme of the Working Group on U.S.-Japan Economic Cooperation toward the specific task of securing U.S. military security assistance for Japan. Across industry and government, there was consensus that the country needed the economic assistance that the United States was now willing to pay in order to bolster Japan as a pillar of economic strength in the Pacific. The members of Keidanren recognized that the main interest of the U.S. Government was in assisting *military* industrial production in Japan, and that was precisely the sector which the new Defense Production Committee would use to hook U.S. support for their agenda.

The Defense Production Committee presented this position to the U.S. and Japanese Governments in its first policy paper in July 1953. The paper called upon the United States to continue procuring weapons from Japan for the Pacific Region and stressed that security assistance was vital for the economic base of Japan and the rest of free Asia as well.[11] Helping Japan replace the U.S. demand of the Korean War, the report stressed, would turn Japanese industry into a pillar of American deterrence in Asia.

The Defense Production Committee's proposals resonated in at least one important branch of the Japanese Government: the Ministry of International Trade and Industry. MITI officials saw clearly the advantages to be gained in industrial development from a massive injection of technological and financial assistance from the United States. But MITI's approach to defense production differed from the defense industry's in two important respects. First, where industry had been eager to build on U.S. demand during the Korean War, MITI had grown alarmed at the expanding influence of the U.S. military on Japan's industrial development and wanted greater control of the future of strategic planning for the defense industry. Thus, while MITI supported industry's position in 1952 by officially declaring defense production an area of "national importance" (*Jūyō Sangyō*), the ministry also put industry on notice with the passage of the National Aircraft Manufacturing Enterprise Law of July 1952 (*Kōkūki Seizohō*) and the Weapons Production Law of August 1953 (*Buki Nado Seizohō*)—two pieces of legislation that brought defense production under strict government regulation.[12]

The second difference between MITI's agenda and the defense industry's was in the emphasis MITI policy placed on moving away from defense-oriented demand as quickly as possible. MITI officials generally had their eyes on the broader goals of Japan's industry as a whole: creating demand, introducing technology, and earning foreign exchange through export promotion. Over the long term, most MITI officials had far more interest in the creation of civilian aircraft and shipping industries than in nurturing defense production. The arms industry was viewed by senior officials as only an intermediate step toward such legitimate "peace industries," which would be acceptable to the Diet, the media, and financial sectors and would have large export markets.[13]

In order to establish defense industrial production as an intermediate step toward broader industrial development, MITI needed jurisdictional control and fiscal investment. The first was claimed when the 1952 Aircraft Manufacturing Enterprise Law shut the rival Ministry of Transport out of the airplane building business. Control of aircraft development was then cemented in 1954 with the establishment of an Aircraft Division within the Heavy Industry Bureau (predecessor to the current Aircraft and Ordnance Division, Machinery and Information Bureau).

MITI had considerably more difficulty, however, in securing fiscal investment. Ambitious plans to introduce tax rebates, subsidies, and other financial incentives to support the Aircraft Manufacturing Enterprise Law were blocked by another powerful bureaucratic actor: the Ministry of Finance. The MOF Budget Bureau director threw cold water on MITI's enthusiastic planning in December 1952 by telling the *Yomiuri Shimbun* that the government *had no plans* for remilitarization and would be unable to give special treatment for the military aircraft industry alone.[14] Major financial institutions, such as the Industrial Bank of Japan and the Japan Development Bank, were equally ambivalent about subsidizing what they viewed as politically unhealthy plans for a defense industry and fiscally unwise plans for an aircraft industry. In 1953 a number of leading bankers announced that they would not extend refinancing terms to firms that planned to commit more than 20–30 percent of output to defense products.[15]

MITI and the defense industry each found similar reluctance to embrace kokusanka on the part of Japan's nascent military forces as well. The National Safety Agency (*Hoanchō*) was established in August 1952 as a replacement for the National Police Reserve created by MacArthur during the Occupation. In order to keep a close eye on the new agency, Prime Minister Yoshida left the position of administrative vice-minister empty, filling many of the duties himself for the first year.[16] The Finance Ministry, meanwhile, maintained direct control over the agency's budget through officials seconded to the NSA, men who were hardly prepared to assist MITI in the creation of a commercial aircraft industry through what was intended to be a strictly constrained budget.[17] Thus despite the Defense Production Committee's formal request in 1953 that the new agency develop propeller aircraft domestically in preparation for its first major acquisition program, the NSA rejected the idea of kokusanka and turned instead to what MOF officials saw as superior U.S. aircraft. Indeed, there was considerable disagreement within the NSA regarding the need for any air arm at all well into 1954.[18]

Japan's political leadership proved equally unenthusiastic about kokusanka in this period. When Prime Minister Yoshida dispatched Ikeda Hayato (and his protégé Miyazawa Kiichi) to negotiate the terms of the Mutual Security Assistance agreement with the U.S. State Department in 1953, the Liberal Party Government's aim was specifically to *avoid* becoming the arsenal of Asia.[19] Yoshida's main concern throughout the MSA negotiations was to receive as much economic aid from the U.S. with as little commitment to militarization as possible. In this he had the support of much of his Liberal Party and the Foreign Ministry. As John Dower explains:

> Where Yoshida, viewing the situation largely from the perspective of the national budget, concluded that Japan could not afford extensive domestic rearmament, business leaders, who thought more in terms of technological and industrial stimulation, as well as the potential export market for Japanese military products, argued that Japan could not afford not to move rapidly into military production.[20]

MITI and the industrialists were not entirely isolated, however, for despite the tepid and even hostile reaction to autonomous defense production displayed by the NSA, the Liberal Party, and the financial world, the

United States continued to fan the embers of kokusanka in the MSA negotiations. Wherever possible, industry used this *gaiatsu* (foreign pressure) to advance its aims. When the NSA deemphasized kokusanka in its procurement plans, for example, the Defense Production Committee countered with a plan of its own based on the expansive defense build-up envisaged by the Department of Defense planners the year before. The DPC's plan (the *Ichishian*) called for 3,750 aircraft at a total cost of 29 trillion yen—all based on surveys of various companies' estimates of their own potential for expanded capacity and supported by early planning prepared by the U.S. Government.[21]

Industry's efforts to lock the United States into Japan's early defense debate finally came to fruition in 1954 with the signing of the U.S.-Japan Mutual Defense Security Assistance Agreement. The injection of capital and technology represented by U.S. security assistance was something Japan's financial and industrial leaders could not refuse. And U.S. security assistance in turn allowed Japanese industry to bypass the Ministry of Finance in efforts to broaden the defense industrial base and gave MITI an alternate source of funds for the development of an aircraft industrial policy.

But U.S. security assistance was also a double-edged sword for Japan. With U.S. funds came U.S. defense industries eager to expand their business in Asia. Japanese industry could not compete with these advanced companies and feared permanent relegation to an inferior position as a repair and assembly shop for the massive U.S. defense industrial complex. Autonomy in defense aircraft production, it became clear, could only result from greater autonomy in defense capabilities. As a result, the pro-kokusanka faction in Japan began a paradoxical ritual that would be repeated throughout the postwar history of U.S.-Japan defense technology relations. With one hand, industry used the MSA framework to approach U.S. industry and the Pentagon directly to lobby for specific investment and technology transfer to assist in establishing production lines for the F-86 jet fighter in Japan. With the other hand, the Defense Production Committee urged the Japanese government to emphasize defense production, not for the sake of replacing special demand but for the sake of now promoting Japan's "self-defense."[22] "U.S.-Japan Economic Cooperation," Keidanren's theme for the previous two years, had served its usefulness with the securing of U.S. financial and technical assistance in the MSA agreement. Industry now had new religion.

The F-86 and the First Defense Build-Up Plan

The centerpiece of industry's plans for creating an autonomous defense industrial base was the F-86 Saber jet. Two years of overhauling and repairing this jet during the Korean War had taught Japanese engineers just how far behind the United States their jet aircraft technology had become after years of neglect dating back to the Second World War. There was no question; moving beyond the repair and overhaul stage to full production could only be achieved through licensed production, and the F-86 was the most promising candidate for license. Even as the domestic debate over MSA and kokusanka brewed in 1953, therefore, Mitsubishi took its case to directly to Washington.

The Pentagon proved to be an enthusiastic partner. In the winter of 1953 Deputy Assistant Secretary of Defense Irving Ross circulated a memorandum in the U.S. government calling for the development of a military aircraft industry in Japan and proposing that Japan produce 300 F-86 fighters under license to help get the industry started. This was followed in April of 1954 by the dispatch to the U.S. of a joint survey team from the Japan Ordnance Association and MITI to examine methods for transferring the appropriate military production skills and technology to Japan.[23]

Before technology and funds could be transferred under the MSA agreement for F-86 production, however, the Japanese government was required to prepare a national defense plan. Since 1952 the Defense Production Committee had been pushing its agenda for expanding indigenous defense production on the National Safety Agency's long-range defense planning committee (the *Seido Chōsa Iinkai*).[24] The DPC urged the government committee to accept industry's massive defense build-up plans and the deputy director of the NSA and his uniformed colleagues, now briefly unfettered from MOF control by the MSA agreement, followed that expensive model. Putting forward the premise that the United States and the Soviet Union might begin a Third World War by the year 1960, the NSA planning committee prepared a draft plan that called for Japan to establish a military establishment of 300,000 troops, a 450,000-ton fleet, and 6,700 aircraft at a total cost of 9 trillion yen over twelve years.[25]

The Finance Ministry clamped down, however, and when the NSA was transformed into the Defense Agency by the Diet in 1954, the 9 trillion yen plan was rejected. Industry—undeterred—worked with supporters inside the new Defense Agency and the newly established Self-Defense Forces to retain as expansive a plan as possible. In the end, after a dozen redrafts, a five-year plan was announced to the Diet in November of 1955 by JDA Director-

General Sunada Shigemasa. Sunada called for a force of 180,000 troops, a 124,000-ton fleet, and 1,300 aircraft. While not at the scale originally proposed by the Defense Production Committee, Sunada's proposal nonetheless represented a victory for industry. The equipment required for Sunada's mobilization left plenty of room for expanded defense production. The DPC's 1953 plan had been based on total potential capacity and not political reality. Capacity could be met and then expanded on again in the future, when political circumstances allowed.

Most important of all, the Sunada plan contained commitments for the first procurement of an eventual 300 F-86F jet aircraft and another 210 T-33A jet trainer aircraft. The United States offered to finance 52 percent of the costs of production and allow Japan to produce 60 percent of the component parts domestically (MHI received 1.5 billion yen from the United States for the F-86 and Kawasaki Heavy Industries [KHI] received 800 million yen for the T-33). Because of its effective lobbying in Washington, Mitsubishi won the primary contract—consequently, it won the political and economic leadership of the jet fighter industry and of the Defense Production Committee for decades to come. With the licensed production of F-86 and the establishment of the JDA's First Defense Plan, the baseline for the expansion of domestic development and production of weapons was set. So too, however, were the contours of the debate over how far kokusanka should go.

First, in the 1950–1955 debate, the U.S.-Japan security relationship emerged as a clear yardstick for defining Japan's arms production needs. Without the *gaiatsu* of the Pentagon, MITI and the Defense Production Committee would not have won support for domestic production. A future U.S. political role in defense production in Japan was further entrenched by the 1954 Mutual Defense Assistance Agreement itself, which implicitly encouraged the continuation of licensed production of weapons beyond the F-86 (and with its "mutual" definition established the precedent that U.S. policymakers would use to encourage the flowback of technology from Japan to the United States in the joint production of the FSX three decades later).

Second, the Ministry of Finance found itself trying to balance its own fiscal considerations with the demands of the U.S. in deciding budgetary questions related to weapons production. MOF was opposed to spending funds on autonomous production, but ironically the ministry found itself lobbying Yoshida's ruling Liberal Party for an increased defense budget in 1954 out of concern for the impact of the party's antidefense attitude on the MSA negotiations. In later years MOF's opposition to extensive investment in an autonomous defense industrial base would again be undermined by such burden-sharing issues.

Third, MITI and industry were internally divided by the high political, budgetary, and resource costs of developing a military aircraft industry. The failure of MITI's early attempts to establish the fiscal investment necessary to move from defense production to aircraft production put industry and the ministry on parallel tracks, and the goal of kokusanka was held with equal conviction. But as the costs of achieving autonomy rose, so too would division between those who viewed autonomous defense production as an end and those who viewed it as a means.

Fourth, the goal of creating an export market for weapons—with Japan as an "arsenal of Asia"—was still-born. Keidanren's Defense Production Committee sent an ambitious study team to Southeast Asia under Doko Toshio in March of 1956, but the team concluded that the market was too unstable (despite U.S. government prodding). Some small arms were eventually sold, but exports never became significant, and when demand did grow for weapons in the region in the 1960s, the domestic political controversy associated with weapons sales led to Japan's arms export ban of 1967. Japanese industry was stuck with what demand it had at home.[26]

Finally, the Safety Agency and the JDA, the consumers of Japan's weapons, were created in the midst of controversy and were unable to develop an authoritative voice in the debate over weapons production. With procurement personnel seconded from MITI and senior administrative personnel generally from the Finance Ministry or National Police Agency, the JDA had confused priorities. Only the Technology Research & Development Institute (TRDI), which was created in its first form in 1952 as the NSA Technology Research Center (*Hoanchō Gijutsu Kenkyujo*), had a clear agenda in the early 1950s: the strengthening of Japan's military technology base through the licensing of technology from the United States.[27] Over time, however, the entire JDA and JSDF would gradually develop a significant, but limited, degree of authority over procurement decisions.

Setting the Stage for Political Intervention, 1955–1960: The P2V-7, the F-104 Decision, and the Second Defense Plan

Throughout the kokusanka debate of the first half of the 1950s, one important part of Japan's iron triangle was missing: the politicians. As prime minister, Yoshida was not particularly interested in creating a promilitary establishment within his Liberal Party. The atmosphere changed somewhat when

Hatoyama Ichirō's Democratic Party formed a cabinet in December 1954. One of Hatoyama's goals was to enact constitutional reform which would have, among other things, fully legitimized the new Self-Defense Forces and opened the way for further remilitarization. But hopes that constitutional reform would be achieved by the merging of Hatoyama's and Yoshida's parties into the Liberal Democratic Party in November of 1955 were dashed when the opposition won control of more than one-third of all seats in the following election in February 1956. What remained was an LDP too large to be ideologically consistent on the question of remilitarization and an opposition with the ability to block forever the creation of a fully legitimate constitutional setting for defense spending.

One mark of the Hatoyama Cabinet was its desire to achieve some distance for Japan from the United States. Had constitutional reform succeeded, the defense industry would probably have profited from the new diplomatic autonomy. But the conservatives' plans for constitutional reform failed, and industry's problems were compounded by the U.S. government's announcement shortly afterward that defense assistance had peaked and would be gradually reduced. The possible consequences of a lack of domestic political support coupled with declining U.S. support for defense production became apparent in 1957 when the Finance Ministry took its scalpel to Sunada's proposal for the First Defense Plan. Where JDA had been anticipating an annual growth rate of 30 billion yen in the defense budget, MOF began insisting that the increase be no higher than 20 billion per year. MOF also went after the JDA's plans for licensed production of the Lockheed P2V-7 antisubmarine plane, funds for which had been promised by the U.S. government through MSA in 1956.[28]

TABLE 2.2

Postwar Defense Plans

1958–1960	The First Defense Build-up Plan
1962–1966	The Second Defense Build-up Plan
1967–1971	The Third Defense Build-up Plan
1972–1976	The Fourth Defense Build-up Plan*
1976	The National Defense Program Outline
1980–1984	Midterm Defense Program Estimate
1983–1987	Midterm Defense Program Estimate
1986–1991	Midterm Defense Program Estimate
1991–1996	Midterm Defense Program Estimate
1994–??	Review of the National Defense Program Outline

Initially called by JDA Director General Naksone Yasuhiro the "New Defense Plan."

It was clear that industry's fight for kokusanka could not end within the JDA. Nor could the United States be relied on as a primary source of financial support. A broader political and budgetary base was required, and the new Liberal Democratic Party had to be the target for building that base.

Beginning in 1955, LDP politicians came into the kokusanka debate at two levels. First, a small group of prodefense Diet members became vocal supporters of kokusanka within the Party's policy-making organ, the Policy Affairs Research Council (PARC). They rallied around a former naval staff officer named Hori Takushiro and soon came to dominate the Defense Division of the PARC. With nominal responsibility for approving the Defense Agency's budget and legislation, the members of this prodefense group developed close ties to the defense industry. Industry was further helped in its political expansion when Funada Naka, a faction leader and champion of kokusanka, became director-general of the LDP from 1955 to 1956. Under this benevolent umbrella, the Defense Production Committee organized the Defense Liaison Committee (*Bōei Renraku Kyōgikai*) in 1955 to link the JDA, MITI, industry, and the LDP's Defense and Industrial Divisions. Industry would build on this network to win support for kokusanka of major systems several times over the next decade.

The second arena for political intervention that emerged in the late 1950s was the prime minister's office. Although initially a welcomed development, the increasing interest of Japanese prime ministers in the procurement debate eventually led to major political problems for industry.

The prime minister's office derived its influence in procurement questions from 1954 legislation establishing the National Defense Council (*Kokubō Kaigi*—currently the *Anzen Hosho Kaigi*, or Japan National Security Council) to provide oversight to the Defense Agency created in the same year. The National Defense Council, modeled in part on the U.S. National Security Council, was chaired by the prime minister and included several key ministers of state but no military personnel. The NDC has often been dismissed as a mere rubber stamp for Defense Agency decisions, and this characterization has been accurate in many instances. But because the NDC represented the first and last arena for cabinet-level debate on procurement questions, it played a crucial role in the ongoing kokusanka debate. Kokusanka decisions arrived at by the Defense Agency and MITI's Aircraft and Ordnance Division are subjected to new interministerial and international pressures at the cabinet level. Conversely, the NDC (and the current NSC) can also be used by the JDA to increase its leverage vis-à-vis the Ministry of Finance.

It was in this latter mode that the NDC was first activated in 1957. In May of that year the NDC approved the Basic Policy for Defense (*Kokubō no Kihon Hōshin*), which set forth the premise that in the event of aggression against Japan, the nation would rely on its defense structure with the United States until the United Nations could be mobilized to end the conflict.[29] The next month the NDC settled the fight over the P2V-7 and the JDA's budget, determining that the annual growth rate of defense spending would be 25 billion yen (exactly midway between the JDA and MOF proposals—a pattern that would be repeated), and that the P2V-7 would go into production. In short, the JDA, industry, and MITI received an unexpected reprieve when the budget questions of the First Defense Plan were elevated above the level of MOF control.

The most striking characteristic of the NDC's 1957 decisions, however, was the influential role played by the prime minister. As chairman, Prime Minister Kishi Nobusuke pushed the NDC to accelerate its decision on defense spending and the P2V-7 so that he would have a powerful souvenir to give President Eisenhower during his visit to the United States in the middle of June.[30] All of the NDC's decisions were made under the pressure of this deadline, which guaranteed that they were made in the context of the U.S.-Japan relationship. In debates within the NDC and the cabinet, Kishi (like most Japanese prime ministers) was only a first amongst equals in many respects—at best an arbitrator of the various factional and institutional interests. On the eve of a state visit, however, he was able to assume the aura and responsibility of head of state, and as such had increased leverage vis-à-vis other factions and ministers within his cabinet. In the case of the P2V-7, this heightened authority in the prime minister's office was of great benefit to industry.

LDP intervention in procurement decisions did not always benefit the defense industry's cause of kokusanka, however. The year after Kishi saved the P2V-7, he allowed his half-brother, Minister of Finance Satō Eisaku, to orchestrate a reversal of the JDA's decision on the replacement for the F-86, which dealt a major blow to the members of the Defense Production Committee.

The ASDF had begun reviewing candidates to replace the F-86 in 1956, after the LDP's Defense Division voted to include a major jet fighter program in the Defense Agency's First Defense Build-up Plan. Five aircraft were initially considered: Grumman's F-11 F1, Lockheed's F-104A, and North American's F-100D, N-156F, and F-102A. After two high-level missions to the

United States in 1957 and 1958, the Air Self-Defense Forces and Defense Agency recommended to the NDC that the Grumman F-11 F1 would be the safest and easiest aircraft to maintain. Their decision received tentative approval from the NDC in April of 1958.

Had the decision to purchase the F-11 ended with the NDC's tentative approval in April, the JDA and JSDF would have been well on their way to establishing military professionalism and bureaucratic authority in procurement decision making. Industry had expressed a strong preference for the F-100 because it offered the greatest potential workshare for the Japanese side.[31] The JDA had successfully rejected industry's first choice in order to meet its own mission requirements.

In the end, however, the professional opinion of the ASDF and the Defense Agency proved insufficient to sustain the F-11 decision against pressure from Lockheed's supporters in the LDP. Through Kodama Yoshio, the most notorious kingpin in postwar Japanese history, the Lockheed Corporation had been channeling funds to certain LDP politicians in support of its marketing effort.[32] Two figures in particular were sympathetic to Lockheed because of their relationship with Kodama: Finance Minister Satō Eisaku and Policy Affairs Research Council Chairman Kōno Ichirō. Prime Minister Kishi also had links to Kodama from their days together as prisoners in the Sugamo Prison (indeed, Kodama was present when Kishi signed an agreement with Ōno Bamboku and Kōno creating the Kishi administration). Almost immediately after the NDC's tentative decision, Finance Minister Satō began openly questioning the validity of the F-11 decision. Within the ASDF, Deputy Chief of Staff Genda Minoru (chief tactical planner for the attack on Pearl Harbor in 1941) also went public with criticism of the decision to go with Grumman. In August PARC Chairman Kōno formally asked the JDA to reexamine its decision.

By June of the following year, the momentum had swung fully against Grumman. The NDC reversed its decision and ordered a reassessment of the FX (next generation fighter) decision. In August Genda was promoted to ASDF Chief of Staff (most likely with Sato's approval, given the MOF's continued influence on personnel decisions). After a third fact-finding mission to the United States, Genda formally recommended licensed production of the upgraded D version of the F-104. The NDC concurred in November.[33] Genda later resigned and was elected as a member of the Satō Faction to the Diet, dominating the Defense Division of the LDP for almost twenty years afterwards and assuring that all former SDF personnel running for the Diet (there are usually two in the Upper House at any time) would run with the support of the Satō faction. Tanaka Kakuei, who inherited the Satō faction in the 1970s, was later indicted for receiving bribes from Lockheed while prime minister.

The reversal of the Grumman decision was the clear result of political intervention at the highest level. It demonstrated the continuing weak bureaucratic position of the Defense Agency and Self-Defense Forces in high-visibility decisions even after the establishment of the Defense Agency. The F-104 decision also highlighted the NDC and prime minister's office as the most effective points for external pressure against procurement decisions pushed by pro-kokusanka factions inside MITI and the JDA. This lesson would be repeated by Lockheed in the case of the P-3C a decade later and again by the United States in the case of FSX. Finally, the F-104 decision revealed how isolated the defense industry's own political constituency really was. Not only was industry's choice of the F-100 eventually rejected but the political conflagrations over the Grumman-Lockheed scandal delayed production of the F-104 by over a year,[34] almost jeopardizing the original consensus for domestic production over imports.[35]

When F-104 production did finally begin, it marked a new level of maturity in Japan's military industrial relationship with the United States. In preparation for production of the F-104 J (F-104D) AND F-104 DJ (two-seater) the United States and Japan signed an agreement in April 1960 for the first time for "coproduction" of weapons. Industry relied on the United States for only 27 percent of financing, and Japan increased its level of kokusanka to 85 percent (up from 60 percent with the F-86).[36] Notwithstanding these accomplishments, however, it was clear in the case of the F-104 that industry had serious political weaknesses it had to address to assure stable domestic production. Industry's ultimate goal was not coproduction, after all, but rather the indigenization of all stages from development through production. After almost a decade of political maneuvering, industry and MITI had still not succeeded in asserting control over their own technoeconomic trajectory and industrial destiny.

This task was made more complex in many ways by the signing of the U.S.-Japan Treaty of Mutual Cooperation and Security in 1960. The treaty represented a victory over the left in Japan (which was a good thing for defense industrialists, of course), but it also assured that the advocates of autonomous production would have to deal with new pressures from alliance politics. The impact of the new treaty on kokusanka policies became immediately apparent with the planning for the Second Defense Plan (1962–1966). Under Director-General Akagi Muneo, the JDA had proposed in 1959 to spend 2 percent of GNP on defense, with an emphasis on air and sea components, including the introduction of a helicopter carrier for the Maritime Self-Defense Forces (MSDF). This plan was rejected by the NDC in January 1961, because it was not consistent with sharing of defense roles implicit in the new U.S.-Japan Security Treaty. Instead, the NDC agreed upon spending 1.62 percent of GNP on defense and the postponement of any decision on carriers for the MSDF. The Second Defense Plan thus became the first budget statement on defense to assert that Japan would secure the equipment it needed "under the U.S.-Japan Security Treaty system."[37] The twin pillars of "self-defense" and "alliance" behind Japanese defense planning were now set. The relative weight of the two would be determined through the kokusanka decisions of the next two decades.

Industry would not enter this fight empty-handed, however, for contained within both the First and Second Defense Build-Up Plans was language to assure that the nation's industrial and technological base would enter into the consideration of all defense planning. The First Defense Plan stated, for example, that "effort will be put into R&D to the extent necessary for self-defense." This led to the establishment of the JDA's current R&D center in 1958: the Technology Research and Development Institute (TRDI), which would concentrate on the development of new systems and not just experimentation with old U.S. technologies.[38] The Second Defense Plan strengthened the language on R&D further, declaring that "in order to *increase* defensive capabilities, research and development will be promoted" [italics mine].[39] While these statements were not as obviously in favor of domestic development as were the policy statements industry would later obtain, they were certainly a start. By the adoption of the Second Defense Plan, the domestic content of defense procurement had risen from 40 percent (in the First Plan) to 80 percent. R&D amounted to 1.3 percent of the budget, still a small ratio, but one increasing nonetheless.

Meanwhile, between 1958 and 1962, in which politicians fought primarily over competing U.S. systems, MITI and industry were moving to establish legislation and kokusanka projects that would strengthen Japan's autonomous jet aircraft production base. Mitsubishi Heavy Industries's original goal had been to develop an autonomous successor to the F-86 based on spin-offs from licensed production of the jet. MITI and the JDA discouraged this, however, considering the country's defense industry not quite mature enough to attempt autonomous development. In the interim, industry was given the opportunity to hone their jet production skills on the autonomous development of a jet trainer instead, the T-1A, and its J-3 engine.

Then in 1958 MITI drafted and passed through the LDP a new piece of legislation, the Aircraft Industrial Promotion Law, which explicitly linked the development of a commercial aircraft industry to the defense industry and established kokusanka as the goal of Japan's industrial policy toward aircraft.[40] Based on the 1958 law, MITI and industry launched their most ambitious effort to date: the design and development of a fully autonomous transport plane for both civilian and military use: the YS-11. Keidanren had endorsed the expansion into civilian production and the YS-11 in a 1957 report claiming that commercial aircraft exports could be built on the back of the defense industry.

First, however, industry had to achieve autonomy in development and production of weapons, and this required autonomy in decision making.

Expanding the Kokusanka Coalition: The T-2, the YS-11, and the Third Defense Plan

To achieve its goal of autonomy, the defense industry and its supporters in government and the Diet acted in the early 1960s to put an end to the unstable political intervention and production interruptions that had characterized the F-104 decision. Great strides had been made in technology development in the First and Second Defense Plans, but because the JDA was still often a pawn in its own procurement policy debates, reliable long-range planning was becoming extremely difficult. Without this planning, the benefits of defense production to overall technological and industrial development could not be realized. In the wake of the F-104 decision, therefore, the leaders of the defense industry set about to strengthen the political coalition for kokusanka and to lobby for greater stability in the defense market. By the end of the decade, their efforts would bear fruit.

The Defense Production Committee began laying the groundwork for a broader kokusanka coalition by organizing the Defense Equipment Kokusanka Consultation Committee (*Bōei Sōbi Kokusanka Kondankai*) in 1961. This committee moved beyond the earlier Defense Liaison Committee, boasting a broad-based membership, comprised not only of defense industry representatives and MITI and JDA officials but also vice-ministers from the Ministry of Transport and the Science and Technology Agency, senior executives from nondefense industries, and members of the LDP. Through the group's membership, the defense industry succeeded in giving the impression of broad political support for its goals. In fact, the name list was misleading, as most of the actual staff work and drafting of policy statements was conducted by the Defense Production Committee itself. Nevertheless, through its connections to the LDP's Defense Division, the Committee allowed the defense industry to increase considerably its leverage on the government.[41]

The versatility of the Defense Production Committee's new political coalition was clearly demonstrated in 1963, when the Kokusanka Consultation Committee was used as a front to lobby for extended production of the F-104. The production run of the F-104 at MHI's Nagoya plant had been scheduled to end in January 1965 and industry could expect no new orders to replace that steady demand. MHI had experienced empty production lines when the F-86 production run ended in 1960 and had no intention of repeating the experience, particularly given the fact that in 1961 the company had committed itself to sinking massive funds into the development of the YS-11 and the MU 2 business jet. During this same period U.S. military assistance was being cut back, further increasing MHI's financial exposure in the defense aircraft market. Stability of demand became a primary political goal not only for MHI, but for the defense industry as a whole.

Thus in May of 1963 the Defense Production Committee issued a policy statement urging the government to order 100 new F-104s, even if that meant creating new fighter squadrons. The Defense Agency immediately objected that it did not require any new squadrons. Undeterred, the Defense Production Committee submitted its requests to the members of the Kokusanka Consultation Committee and the LDP's Defense Division. Pressured from the prodefense Diet members of the LDP and from MITI, the Defense Agency's director-general eventually agreed to request funds for the production of an additional fifty F-104s through 1967. In budget negotiations with the Finance Ministry, this amount was eventually reduced to thirty aircraft.[42]

After assuring the extended production of the F-104, the Defense Production Committee turned its attention to winning LDP and government support for four policies that would further lock the Defense Agency into a smooth pattern toward future kokusanka: developing Japan's first supersonic jet; increasing the R&D budget; developing an indigenous early-warning radar system; and introducing a rolling-budget system for weapons development and production. From 1964 to 1966 the committee submitted policy statements through the Kokusanka Consultation Committee to the LDP's Defense Division and the Defense Agency urging adoption of these policies.

The Defense Production Committee also renewed its calls on the government to take necessary diplomatic measures that might allow greater arms exports to Southeast Asia. The JDA Equipment Bureau agreed, but the decision had powerful implications for Japan's foreign policy and remained off the agenda until it was finally contained by the Satō Cabinet's "Three Arms Export Principles"—an effective ban on all exports of weapons.

Throughout this period, the political and economic environment in Japan was improving for the goals of the Kokusanka Consultation Committee and the defense industry. Defense production in the early 1960s accounted for over a tenth of heavy industrial production, prompting the government of Ikeda Hayato to insist that defense planning be done in the context of the Economic Planning Agency's overall strategic planning for Japan.[43] This guaranteed that the arguments for strengthening the industrial base through kokusanka of weapons would have a hearing outside of MITI. In addition, the termination of U.S. military assistance, while presenting some budgetary problems, did give the JDA a new degree of freedom in preparing defense plans.

The JDA exercised its new flexibility in November 1966 when, as part of the Third Defense Plan, it agreed to proceed with domestic development of a supersonic jet trainer, the TX (later called the T-2). Originally the JDA had considered importing the T-38 directly from the United States, but when MITI won Ministry of Finance support for autonomous production, the JDA opted to change its operational requirements and upgrade the F-86F in order to give industry time to develop the T-2.[44] The element of industrial policy was undeniable. Generally, when nations develop supersonic jet fighters, they later produce modified versions of the same jets as trainers. Japan was doing the opposite—developing a supersonic jet as a trainer first, in order to later build a jet fighter based on its trainer design (the T-2 eventually was modified and used in developing the F-1, Japan's first jet fighter, hence the popular quip in MITI and the JDA that the T-2 was "a trainer for industry, not pilots"). Parallel to the TX decision, industry and MITI were winning support for an array of other autonomous aircraft and defense projects, including the C-1 transport, the Tan-sam short-range surface-to-air missile, and the YS-11.

The JDA's organization and guidelines for defense planning began to reflect this new emphasis on self-sufficiency. Under the Third Defense Plan, the Defense Agency agreed to "promote R&D, modernize weapons and pursue *kokusanka as appropriate*" [my italics].[45] Then in 1969 the Finance Ministry agreed to examine a rolling-budget system for the Defense Agency that would further promote long-term indigenous development of defense systems.[46] Finally, in September 1969 the Defense Agency restructured its Procurement Bureau into a Development Planning Division and Procurement Demand Division in order to "strengthen the autonomous structure" of Japan's defense production base.[47] ⫻

The Japanese government's new level of investment in autonomous defense production in the *Third Defense Build-Up Plan* was also the result of subtle changes in the U.S.-Japan relationship that had not yet received broad attention in either country. For one, the end of U.S. Mutual Security Assistance to Japan had given MITI and industry much more freedom to push their kokusanka agenda in procurement planning. At the same time, United States involvement in the Vietnam War was changing the Japanese defense establishment's attitude toward dependence on U.S. weapons systems. The priority given to weapons for use on the battlefields of Southeast Asia meant that Japan's Self-Defense Forces and companies producing U.S. weapons under license often received equipment that was "late, over cost, and below expected quality standards," in the words of a 1966 report by the Japan Aircraft Industry Association.[48] The reputation of licensed production arrangements with the United States fell even further in 1967, when U.S.-Japan negotiations over licensed production of the Nike Hercules and Nike Hawk antiaircraft missiles stalled over Pentagon insistence on R&D royalty payments from Japan.[49]

At the same time that dissatisfaction with U.S. systems was spreading in Japan and the end of MSA was freeing the Japanese government to pursue more autonomous development projects, bilateral macroeconomic imbalances were providing the first hints that the government could not pursue kokusanka in isolation from the overall trade relationship with the United States. In a 1967 summit meeting with Prime Minister Satō Eisaku, for example, President Johnson requested that Japan act to reduce its holdings of dollars by $500 million. Following the meeting, the Finance Ministry brought pressure on the Defense Agency to increase procurement of imported weapons from the United States. Industry reacted strongly. In a December 1967 policy paper to the government, for example, the Japan Ordnance Association wrote:

It has been recently reported that the United States is requesting that Japan increase its imports of weapons as one form of cooperation in defending the dollar. If the government is considering changing its basic policy of kokusan-ka enunciated in the Third Defense Build-up Plan and increasing weapons imports or decreasing the level of kokusanka, this would touch upon the fundamental policy of autonomous equipment and freeze the enthusiasm for defense production which exists in the private sector.[50]

Concern within industry was understandable. Hopes that defense production could be made more profitable through eventual arms exports were dashed by a 1967 Cabinet resolution banning military exports to communist countries, countries in conflict, or countries in danger of entering conflict (a decade later, Prime Minister Miki Takeo would extend this ban to *all* nations). This left industry completely dependent on domestic demand. Moreover, despite the technical, economic, and political momentum behind kokusanka in the 1960s, the government had still not committed itself to a basic policy of kokusanka, as the Japan Ordnance Association claimed in its policy statement. In fact, the Defense Agency did no more in the *Third Defense Build-Up Plan* than commit itself to "kokusanka as appropriate" (*tekisetsuni*). The political coalition for autonomous defense production was still incomplete. This would change at the end of the decade, however, when profound shifts in America's global strategic position coincided with changes in the leadership of Japan's Defense Agency to bring the defense industry as close as it would come to receiving a full commitment to kokusanka from the Government.

3 | "Self-Defense to the Fore, Alliance to the Rear!":* The Nixon Doctrine, the Fourth Defense Plan, and the Political Zenith of Kokusanka, 1970–1976

When Nakasone Yasuhiro became Defense Agency director-general in the third Satō cabinet in January 1970, a recognition spread among JDA officials, SDF personnel, and industry leaders that this unconventional new politician would bring significant change to Japan's defense policies. For starters, the food on bases began to improve. Where once the Ground Self-Defense Force recruits had eaten simple meals of watery rice and vegetables, they now were being served a variety of meats and fish, with fresh fruit for dessert. Industry began to anticipate a richer diet as well. Executives who had worked with Nakasone in his previous position as director-general of the Science and Technology Agency knew that he had been an enthusiastic supporter of an autonomous rocket program for Japan. The JDA offered an even larger pot for a politician interested in developing the nation's aerospace technology, the budget for precision-guided missiles alone being larger than the Science and Technology Agency's entire budget for space development.

On the other hand, Nakasone also presented something of an enigma to the traditional members of the defense constituency in industry, the LDP, and the government. He had never been actively involved in the prodefense efforts of Funada, Hori, and other hawks in the PARC. He was known to have

Asahi Shimbun headline on the announcement of the JDA's draft Fourth Defense Plan, March 19, 1970

strong views on alliance relations with the U.S. and was particularly noted for the black tie he once wore in protest of Japan's "subjugation" to America and for his opposition to Prime Minister Yoshida's early policies. But then Nakasone's ideological opposition to the Yoshida Doctrine was surpassed by his pragmatic opportunism, and until 1970 that opportunism had prevented him from fully committing his political resources to the defense debate.

Events in the late 1960s refocused Nakasone's attention on defense. In Japan and the rest of Asia, political observers sensed that America was no longer willing to "bear any burden" for the security of the region. On the defense-industrial side it showed in the haphazard way weapons systems were being marketed and in the poor quality and long delays involved in foreign military sales to Japan during the Vietnam War. President Johnson, in his last summit with Prime Minister Satō in 1968, embodied American exhaustion and overreach in Asia. The president's emphasis on the need for Japan to develop a stronger defense posture gave industry in Japan "even more hope than expected for the build-up and modernization of defense equipment," in the words of one Defense Production Committee policy paper.[1]

When an informal briefing President Nixon gave to reporters at an officers' club in Guam on July 25, 1969, was trumpeted in the press as America's statement of withdrawal from Asia, the Japanese political establishment received its strongest notice yet that the time was ripe for defense autonomy. With the Guam statement formalized into the Nixon Doctrine shortly afterward, the U.S. call on Japan to contribute to the security and stability of East Asia was clear.[2] It took more concrete form in Satō's November 1969 summit with President Nixon, which resulted in the formal agreement to return Okinawa to Japan. This then opened the debate in Tokyo over the need for greater SDF force projection capabilities to defend the newly reacquired islands.

The entire debate that surrounded the Nixon Doctrine and the return of Okinawa in turn provided a tremendous boost to Satō and the LDP domestically. The Nixon Doctrine and the reversion of Okinawa fed the appetite for autonomy in Japan, but the Nixon administration's professed desire for greater cooperation also promised closer U.S.-Japan ties at the same time. There was something for everyone in the conservative camp with the reversion of Okinawa, and it caused nothing but confusion for the opposition. As a result, Satō and the LDP swept to an unexpected level of victory in the December 27, 1969, Lower House election. At the point of greatest change in the international system since the end of the war, the conservatives in Japan had a mandate for bold action.

Enter Nakasone Yasuhiro. Nakasone had fought in the 1969 election as the leader of his own faction for the first time since defeating Mori Kiyoshi in a 1967 leadership battle that followed the death of Kono Ichiro, the faction's previous leader. Nakasone did well in the 1969 election, and his search for a rampart on which to plant his new faction's battle flag led him to the Defense Agency. Trends in the nation's defense policy suited his ideological temperament, and the promise of a significantly expanded defense industrial constituency suited his political needs. Nakasone wanted a forum to demonstrate dramatic change. In 1970 the JDA seemed ideal for that purpose.

The previous year Nakasone's predecessor at the Agency, Arita Kiichi, had begun the process of preparing Japan's Fourth Defense Plan to reflect a reduced U.S. conventional-arms presence in East Asia. Nakasone, however, was far more hawkish and ambitious. Arita's planning represented a continuation of past defense thinking, not the sort of radical change Nakasone sought. Several months into his position, therefore, Nakasone initiated a policy review of Japan's 1957 *Basic Policy on Defense* (*Kokubō no Kihon Hōshin*) with the aim of shifting the priorities in Japan's security policy formation away from the maintenance of the U.S.-Japan Security relationship (*Anpo*) and toward the development of autonomous defense (*jishuboei*).[3] One passage in particular in the 1957 *Basic Policy on Defense* targeted for elimination was Section 4, which declared that Japan would "deal with external aggression on the basis of the Japan-U.S. security arrangements, pending the effective functioning of the United Nations in the future in deterring and repelling such aggression."[4] Instead, Nakasone proposed to replace this concept with the phrase "to supplement Japan's defense with the Japan-U.S. security arrangements."[5]

This shift in emphasis was profound and when Nakasone floated the idea at his first (and last) meeting of the National Defense Council on July 24, 1970, Foreign Minister Aichi Kiichi and PARC Foreign Affairs Research Commission Chairman Kosaka Zentarō publicly attacked the plan. Eventually, Nakasone's effort to rewrite the *Basic Policy on Defense* went nowhere, but the aggressive director-general was able to disregard the opposition within the LDP and proceed with the general thrust of his new defense concepts nonetheless. The political constellation surrounding defense policy had changed by 1970. For one, the director-general of the agency was the leader of his own faction and, as such, was able to establish a new level of integrity and autonomy for the agency within the government. Under Nakasone the JDA published its first white paper and established its first "wisemen's commission" ("The Group to Diagnose the Defense of Japan, the

JDA, and the JSDF"). These public relations moves did much to reinforce the integrity of the JDA under Nakasone. Moreover, the devastation of the left and the opposition in the 1969 election appeared to give the conservatives a broad new mandate. The internal contradictions in Japan's interpretation of the Nixon Doctrine were simply not yet clear. And, of course, there was a decade and a half of momentum for autonomy now behind the defense establishment. Perhaps most important of all, however, was the profound shift in the business community's assessment of Japan's defense posture and defense industrial base.

The proportion of Japan's industrial output accounted for by defense (in terms of sales) decreased from just over 1 percent to 0.5 percent between the creation of the JDA in 1954 and the time Nakasone took over the agency in 1970. However, this quantitative reduction masked important qualitative changes that were occurring in the defense industry as the growth of smart weapons increased the value of defense R&D and brought new companies and new executives into the leadership of the defense industry. Keidanren's own figures tell the story. In 1967 MHI topped the list of defense contractors with a total of 20 billion yen in sales. Two years later MHI still topped the list with an increase of about 55 percent to 33 billion yen in sales. But Tōshiba, by comparison, went from twentieth place in 1967 with 1.15 billion yen in sales to third place in 1969 with over 12 billion yen in sales—a more than tenfold increase! The pattern repeats with the other electronics firms; MELCO (Mitsubishi Electric) moved from fifth place in 1967 with 2.25 billion yen in sales to second place in 1969 with 33 billion yen in sales! Over the same years the increase in sales of the metal-benders and systems integrators such as Kawasaki Heavy Industries and Ishikawajima Harima Heavy Industries increased only incrementally and their rankings fell accordingly.[6]

In the same period, defense R&D took on a far more important role in all high-tech companies. This fact was reflected in a 1970 Defense Production Committee survey of eighty-eight member companies, which demonstrated that R&D for indigenous defense technologies (as opposed to experimenting on imported technology) increased on average from 20 percent of companies' total R&D activities in 1965 to over 30 percent in 1969.[7] TRDI's funding of this research increased from 31 percent on average per company in 1962 to 50 percent in 1968. This expanded R&D effort was going toward a whole array of new weapons: the BADGE radar system, avionics for the F-104, Nike/Hawk SAMs, surface-to-surface missiles. These were all R&D intensive systems, which—in the words of the Defense Production Committee's report—"represented a new age for industry."

This new age of high-tech weapons translated directly into a new and broader constituency in industry for autonomous defense production. In the same year that Tōshiba rose to become the third-richest defense contractor, its chairman, Doko Toshio, became the chairman of Keidanren. Doko was an engineer by training and was a strong advocate of increasing Japan's indigenous technology base. He was also a keen observer of international politics and, along with a growing number of his peers in Keidanren, began expressing doubts about the reliability of American deterrence under the Nixon Doctrine—something which until then most businessmen had taken for granted. In his address to the Annual General Meeting of Keidanren in 1970, for example, Doko noted that:

> With the U.S. military withdrawal from Asia, South East Asian security has become a major problem. . . . Japan must increase its autonomous defense capabilities and be able to work for the collective security of Asia.[8]

Similar messages were repeated in business forums throughout 1970.[9] In an influential economic report prepared by an advisory committee for the Minister of Finance, for example, senior business executives strayed from their macroeconomic policy message to urge the Ministry of Finance to support an expanded budget for autonomous defense and to work for the repeal of Article 9 of the Constitution.[10]

Rival agencies to the JDA were caught off guard by the shift of their constituencies toward a reevaluation of the U.S.-Japan defense relationship and the need for greater autonomous defense production. Nakasone charged straight into these ministries at the height of their confusion in June of 1970, by issuing a Defense Agency policy statement endorsing a policy of fully indigenizing defense production. Nakasone's *Basic Policy on Equipment Production and Development* moved well beyond all previous policy papers regarding kokusanka, stating that:

> From the standpoint of autonomous defense, it is desirable for Japan to be defended with equipment developed and produced by Japan alone. *From this point on, the development and production of military equipment will be limited to Japanese industries as a matter of principle.* (emphasis mine)[11]

The policy paper also confirmed that the JDA would promote "planned equipment procurement," "increased R&D," and "utilization of technologies developed in the private sector"—three of the defense industry's political goals throughout the previous decade. (The one area of the report that was not in response to the defense industry's lobbying was a proposal for the introduction of free competitive bidding for defense contracts, a proposal which did not last long.) As the delighted director of the Defense Production Committee noted: "The Nakasone position was a great departure from previous defense production policy."[12]

Indeed, industry found itself having to catch up to the enthusiastic Nakasone. Following the JDA's *Basic Policy on Equipment Production and Development*, the Defense Production Committee released a paper promising to increase its own capital investment in defense R&D and production, in exchange for long-term bundle contracts to assure the future of kokusanka.[13]

The *Basic Policy on Equipment Production and Development* was only Nakasone's prelude to the preparation of a gargantuan defense build-up plan that would secure the budgetary resources necessary for a rapid expansion of the defense industrial base. To signify the departure from past incremental defense increases, Nakasone dropped Arita's "Fourth" Defense Plan title, and set the JDA bureaucrats to work on what he termed a "New" Defense Plan. They did so with instructions to studiously avoid the National Defense Council, the main conduit for other cabinet members (and faction leaders) to exert their influence on defense planning.[14] In fact, during Nakasone's tenure at the JDA, the NDC met only once, in spite of a series of pressing policy issues such as the renewal of the Security Treaty and the determination of a force posture for Okinawa. JDA officials recognized that Prime Minister Satō was simply not interested in defense issues, and other cabinet officers and faction bosses were not willing to risk political capital interfering with Nakasone's running of the Defense Agency—at least not yet.

Throughout the process of preparing the New Defense Plan, Nakasone not only approved the procurement requests of the three services but often went beyond their needs to encourage projects whose attraction lay solely in terms of industrial policy. An expensive example of this was Nakasone's inclusion of development and procurement funds for an Airborne Early Warning (AEW) aircraft. Under the Third Defense Plan, TRDI had looked at putting phased-array radar on the C-1 transport jet. The conclusion of both that institute and the ASDF was that this was technically feasible but probably entailed too many variables to be cost-effective. Besides, they noted, the threat did not justify the development of AEW domestically. Acting on these recommendations, the JDA halted the program. Nakasone, however, reversed this decision, because, according to observers in the agency, he saw the lack of an immediate threat-based need for AEW as the perfect opportunity for experimenting with the system without having to worry about its actual effectiveness.[15]

Nakasone released the New Defense Plan to the press in April 1971. It was the first and last plan to be issued without approval from the NDC. And it was unprecedented in its scale. Under the new plan (or the "Nakasone Plan" as it was referred to almost immediately), the JDA proposed to increase the defense R&D budget by 350 percent, to build 900 aircraft, 200 naval vessels, and 1,000 tanks—a budget increase of 220 percent over the previous defense plan. The defense industry would obtain funding for the domestically developed C-1 transport aircraft (including R&D on an AEW version), T-2 jet trainer, and the FST-2 ground support fighter (based on the T-2 frame) and R&D funds for developing the HX helicopter (3 billion yen) and the PXL antisubmarine aircraft to replace the American-designed P-2 (17 billion yen).[16]

Reaction from the rest of the political world was immediate. The Finance Ministry declared the plan "fiscally impossible." For their part, the opposition parties decried the creation of a new militaristic state. And yet Nakasone had read his audience well. The momentum toward autonomy from the 1960s was strong, and the growth of Japan's GDP to the number-two rank in the free world that same spring did much to encourage grand thinking. Within the LDP and the business community there was strong political momentum for autonomous defense—particularly in defense production. The *Nakasone Plan* was submitted to the NDC for deliberation in May of 1971.

"Nixon-Shocked" Away from Autonomous Defense

In July 1971 the trend toward autonomous defense in the New Defense Plan was brought to a screeching halt by the combined "Nixon shocks" of U.S.-Chinese rapprochement (July 15) followed by the free-floating of the U.S. dollar (August 15). Nakasone had read his domestic audience well, but he had no way of knowing external factors might change so dramatically. Suddenly, rapprochement with China removed one of the primary threats used implicitly to justify the defense build-up of the 1960s. The collision of an ASDF F-86 with an All Nippon Airways jetliner on July 31 further decreased the Japanese public's tolerance for weapons production. At the same time a free-floating dollar made imported weapons cheaper than weapons produced domestically and created a political demand for Japan to use the dollars it held. Washington ratcheted-up political pressure on Japan to import U.S.-made weapons in a July visit by Secretary of Defense Melvin Laird to Tokyo and during bilateral economic consultations between Secretary of State William Rogers and Foreign Minister Fukuda Takeo in

September.[17] Without understanding the consequences, the Nixon administration had upset the momentum for kokusanka that it had unintentionally created two years earlier with the Guam Doctrine.

On July 5, 1971, Nakasone had left the JDA to become Secretary-General of the LDP as a part of the third reshuffling of the Satō administration. As Secretary-General, Nakasone might have had enough clout to protect his former agency's agenda, but that would have been uncharacteristic for any LDP politician, particularly one with ambitions as high as Nakasone's. Instead, Nakasone was replaced by three different JDA director-generals in a six-month period (Masuhara, Nishimura, Ezaki), none of whom had the time, power, or inclination to stand up for Nakasone's plan. Support within industry also contracted. The prospect of normalized relations with the PRC created business possibilities that far outweighed the advantages of kokusanka to all companies, even many that had been putting greater energy into defense production in the late 1960s. Doko himself was chairman of the China-Japan Businessmen's Council. And all businessmen were well aware of the PRC's strong opposition to the New Defense Plan, thanks to extensive reporting (and soliciting) of statements by PRC leaders on the part of the liberal newspaper, the *Asahi Shimbun*.

The JDA lay open and exposed. The Finance Ministry struck first by proposing a postponement of the plan because of changes in the international political economy. Sensitive to the proceedings of the Diet and the demands of the Finance Ministry, the Defense Bureau of the JDA split with the uniformed personnel over the size of the defense build-up.[18] Within the LDP, the liberal Miki and financially conservative members of the Ōhira factions faced off against the politically conservative Satō, Kishi and Nakasone factions.[19] Finally, in the fall of 1971, unable to sustain the momentum it had built previous to the Nixon shocks, the Defense Agency announced that it was examining a significantly reduced Fourth Defense Plan in which annual growth in defense expenditures would fall from the 18.8 percent originally proposed by Nakasone to the 15 percent levels of the previous defense plan (it would eventually fall by even more).[20] Shortly thereafter, Defense Agency Director Nishimura Naohiro announced his intention to increase imports during the Fourth Defense Plan by $200 million.

The defense industry panicked. Despite open reassurances from Nakasone's successors that the Defense Agency would maintain the principle of kokusanka established in the 1970 Nakasone Plan, the Defense Production Committee issued warnings to its members that kokusanka was in peril. Industry had good reason to worry. Personnel expenses accounted for half of the defense budget, and the Defense Agency made clear statements that it would not reduce the personnel budget. This forced each arm of the SDF to explore reductions in equipment, particularly in the numbers of aircraft and ships. Such reductions would further weaken the already poor economies of scale of domestic military aircraft manufacturers. Industry's competitiveness was already hurt by the "dollar shock." Moreover, the U.S. Department of Defense was stepping up its demands that Japan utilize American-designed weapons in its Fourth Defense Plan.

In October 1971 the defense industry's worst fears were realized when the Defense Agency announced that it would reduce its target ratio for kokusanka in the Fourth Defense Plan to 87 percent of all procurement—a level comparable to the Third Defense Plan. Then in February of 1972, the NDC passed a new amended outline to replace the original Nakasone Plan. Conspicuously absent from this outline were any references to kokusanka or increasing R&D funds, the two areas that had formed the pillars of Nakasone's *Fourth Defense Plan Outline* and the 1970 *Basic Policy on Equipment Production and Development.*[21]

When the new administration of Tanaka Kakuei entered into deliberations over the specific force levels for the Fourth Defense Plan in the autumn of 1972, the political and economic trends toward autonomous defense and autonomous weapons development seemed dead. The February *Outline for the Fourth Defense Plan* offered the defense industry no more promises of kokusanka than had existed in the previous decade. And the political environment for defense production was still degenerating steadily. Japan normalized relations with the PRC in September and in the Diet the Government was under pressure from the opposition to reduce spending on military aircraft programs. MITI and the Finance Ministry were also under severe pres-

TABLE 3.1

The Fourth Defense Plan

Item	Nakasone Plan	JDA Plan under Masuhara	Final Gov't. Proposal
F4EJ PHANTOM	76	52	46
RF4E	18	14	14
FST-2	126	96	68
C-1 TRANSPORT	30	30	24
T-2 TRAINER	80	73	59
P2 J ASW PLANE	45	43	43
PXL	R&D funding	R&D funding	postponed
AEW	R&D funding	R&D funding	postponed

sure to increase imports in order to reduce excessive holdings of U.S. dollars amidst the first signs of U.S.-Japan trade friction. In the September 1972 Hawaii Summit, Tanaka had promised Nixon a $320 million emergency aircraft import program, including the P3-C.[22] In desperation, MHI's chairman proposed in a press conference afterward that Japan pay U.S. $2 million as a "nuclear umbrella tax" rather than import weapons that would interfere with kokusanka. MHI officials conceded that their Chairman's proposal was "personal" and not likely to be adopted by the government.[23] Defense Production Committee officials began to speak of a new ice age.[24]

The T-2, FST-2, and PXL—Test Cases for Kokusanka

In the wake of these setbacks, the defense industry fought to save the budgets for the kokusanka of its "jewels," which had been approved under Nakasone's initial defense plan: the T-2 jet trainer, the FST-2 ground support fighter (based on the T-2, this would later become the F-1), and the PXL antisubmarine plane.[25] In the defense industry's view, these three production programs were the keys to the technological and commercial base for the development of a world-class military aircraft industry in Japan by the twenty-first century and had to be preserved, no matter how the overall budget was reduced. The president of the Japan Aircraft Industry Association called the T-2 and FST-2 "matters of life and death for the future of Japan's aerospace industry" and KHI's president maintained that PXL development was vital to "improving Japan's industrial technology base."[26]

The decisions on these systems would define the future of Japan's efforts at autonomous defense production. In the end, kokusanka of the T-2 and the FST-2 survived, while the PXL did not. Continuation of the autonomous T-2/FST-2 line led directly to the decision to develop the FSX autonomously fifteen years later. The decision is therefore an important link in the chronology leading to the FSX explosion. The debates over these systems, and the different decisions that resulted, are also important for the insights they offer into the nature of the support for kokusanka within Japan's defense constituency. A pattern is clear in the T-2/FST-2 and PXL decisions, traces of which were evident in the earlier decisions on the F-104. In both cases, consensus for production of a system at the industry-JDA-MITI level was reversed as the decision came under the pressure of competing inter-ministerial agenda at the higher political level. Unlike the F-104 decision, however, the FST-2/T-2 and PXL decisions pitted indigenous systems against U.S. imports. Increasingly, therefore, the procurement debate was becoming one not only of industrial and defense policy, but also international trade and alliance policy—a trend that would reach a climax with FSX. The sharpening of the alliance versus technoeconomic autonomy debate would significantly complicate the aerospace technology trajectory anticipated by industry.

Industry first suspected that the T-2/FST-2 might be in trouble when JDA Director-General Nishimura announced his intention to increase weapons imports in the fall of 1971, but Nishimura's successor, Masuhara Keikichi, included ninety-six of the FST-2 and seventy-three of the T-2 in his budget proposal to the Ministry of Finance in October of 1972. The battle for the FST-2 and T-2 was therefore joined between the JDA and the MOF in the period of October 7–9, 1972. At meetings between the two agencies' administrative vice ministers, MOF argued that building the T-2 and FST-2 would cost a third more than importing comparable aircraft from the United States, proposing specifically that the ASDF import Northrop's F5B Trainer and F5E Ground Support Fighter. The JDA's administrative vice minister responded (with very little evidence, since the jet was not yet built) that this would be unacceptable since Mitsubishi's FST-2 was a far superior aircraft in combat. However, MOF remained insistent. The ministry's negotiators clearly felt that political momentum was on their side. The opposition parties had specifically mentioned in the Diet the T-2 and FST-2 as projects that should be cut. Moreover, the International Bureau of the ministry was pressuring the Budget Bureau to reduce its holdings of U.S. dollars by procuring equipment from the United States. Indeed, MITI itself had formally requested that the Defense Agency increase its procurement from abroad in order to transfer dollars back to the United States.[27]

By the end of these negotiations, the Defense Agency side retreated to a compromise in which it would import a portion of its trainer jets in order to help the Ministry of Finance spend dollars but would proceed with a limited production of the FST-2. Again MOF remained adamant. It would not appropriate funds for the FST-2 as long as Northrop's F5E could be imported for less. The meetings ended with the press predicting that at the next day's National Defense Council Meeting, Prime Minister Tanaka would "consider the demands of the opposition" and the "strong feeling of consensus for importing (the F5E) amongst the government's top officials" and agree to the Ministry of Finance's proposal.[28]

The next day Tanaka did no such thing. In fact, he ignored the Defense Agency's own offer to compromise and announced full kokusanka of both the T-2 and the FST-2. The *Asahi Shimbun*, attempting to explain its earlier inaccurate predictions, attributed the Tanaka decision to strong pressure from Defense Agency Chief Masuhara on the eve of the decision. Chief Cabinet Secretary Nikaidō Susumu offered the explanation that the government had decided that the FST-2 had "superior technology" and would allow the "ASDF to fill a variety of missions with one type of aircraft (the T-2)" and that this was "more important than reducing dollar holdings."[29] Neither explanation offered much insight into the actual dynamics of the final Tanaka decision.

Unfortunately, what occurred in the twenty-four hours between the government's development of a compromise and Tanaka's decision will never be clear. What is clear, however, is that working level consensus for the import option was diffuse, while the kokusanka faction had its vital interests at stake. In terms of political opportunity costs, Tanaka had sufficient flexibility to decide against his own government's consensus decision, no matter what his own motives may have been, and the kokusanka faction took advantage of this flexibility.

The kokusanka faction was able to argue that production of the T-2 and FST-2 was of vital importance to the national interest on several levels. First, industry had committed itself to considerable investments in R&D and plant modernization for the production of the T-2 and FST-2 several years earlier and had done so with the political commitment of the Defense Agency and MITI. In fact, MITI and the JDA had considered including the T-2 in the Third Defense Plan but had opted to SLEP (service-life-extension-program) the F-86-F instead in order to buy time until the T-2 would come on line. As John Campbell and other scholars of Japanese budget politics have found, it is very difficult for the government to suddenly withdraw funding from an industry to which it has committed its support.[30] While the Defense Agency and MITI had made only limited budgetary outlays to industry for the T-2 and FST-2, implicit in support for industry-funded R&D was an eventual return on investment through budgetary outlays for production. Moreover, the T-2 and FST-2 were in the direct kokusanka line of evolution that extended from the T-1, Japan's first autonomous jet, to the F-1 and on to the FSX. For the defense industry, losing out on eventual production of the T-2 and FST-2 would have meant destabilization of its production base and an end to the kokusanka route that had already been opened with the T-1.[31]

A senior executive at Mitsubishi Heavy Industries was no doubt aware of this when he warned immediately after the Tanaka decision that "straying from the basic policy of kokusanka for the T-2 projects (including FST-2) would have caused immediate damage to the more than 500 companies involved in the contract." An official from Fuji Heavy Industries, the second

contractor, echoed this warning when he claimed that "temporarily importing aircraft instead of the T-2 would have closed down production lines and
put over 250 people out of work." Thus, as these executives explained to the
press in the wake of Tanaka's decision, it was "natural that the government
stand by its commitment to the FST-2 and T-2."[32]

The motives of the import faction, in contrast, were less focused. The goal
of reducing dollar holdings was important on a macroeconomic level, but
kokusanka of the FST-2 and T-2 was of immediate importance to the future
development of Japan's jet fighter industry. MITI's request to the JDA that it
increase procurement from abroad was fulfilled on a political level by the
Defense Agency's plans to license produce the Phantom F-4. And for the
Ministry of Finance, not importing the R5E meant the loss of an opportunity to use only several tens of millions of dollars in foreign exchange. This was
primarily a symbolic amount, not worth a fight with the Prime Minister.
Finally, there was no focused pressure from the U.S. side for importing the
F5E. Ultimately, Tanaka was able to ignore *gaiatsu* with impunity.

The circumstances and the result were different in the PXL decision.
Despite a considerable investment of time and money by TRDI and KHI dating back to 1964 and an official decision by the National Defense Council for
kokusanka of the PXL on October 2, 1972, the NDC announced on October 8
that it would temporarily cut funds for future research on the aircraft and
would reexamine whether to develop the PXL or import Lockheed's P-3C.[33]
This subjected the PXL kokusanka decision to a prolonged political debate,
during which diffuse external pressures concentrated to defeat the kokusanka faction's narrower agenda. Most significantly, PXL became a clearer test
case of the autonomy versus alliance trade-off.

The official explanation given by the Maritime Self-Defense Forces for
the postponement of a production decision on PXL was that an autonomously developed aircraft would take too long to bring to production
(nine years from the initial R&D stage).[34] This was no doubt a factor, but not
a convincing argument in itself, as KHI was already well into the R&D stage
and withholding funds one year would only delay production further. There
were other factors as well. One was poor politicking by the defense industry.
As the director of the Defense Production Committee confessed in an interview several years later: "the Defense Production Committee viewed production of the T-2 and FST-2 as the most vital issues for the future of Japan's
aircraft industry" and simply "neglected lobbying (*nemawashi*) for the PXL."
The fact that the chairman of the Defense Production Committee was from
MHI lends some additional credence to this point. There was also what the

Defense Production Committee staff viewed as the Maritime Self-Defense Forces' "strong attachment to the U.S. and the P-3C."[35]

Ultimately though, the most important factor in the move to delay a decision on funding for the PXL was timing. The PXL was under development for the Fifth Defense Plan and involved a much longer-term financial commitment to kokusanka than had the T-2 or FST-2. The fact was that cabinet-level consensus still did not exist for a long-term commitment to kokusanka. As a result, when the NDC established an Expert Committee in August 1973 to review the advantages of kokusanka versus importing, it in effect created a forum for interministerial debate on not only the PXL decision, but on the future of kokusanka itself. Brought to the national stage and subjected once again to international pressures in this way, the kokusanka debate entered a realm where the defense industry's coalition atrophied.

The Expert Committee's twelve members deliberated over the merits and demerits of kokusanka for over a year, reflecting the priorities of their home agencies. The defense industry experts generally favored kokusanka of the PXL, arguing that it had superior speed and ASW software to the P-3C. The Maritime Self-Defense Force Command Staff, reflecting its close operational ties to the U.S. Seventh Fleet, argued that importing the P-3C would be preferable from the standpoint of interoperability with U.S. Forces. The MSDF was particularly concerned about Japanese industry's inexperience in designing the necessary ASW software. The Defense Agency's Internal Bureau, while generally in favor of kokusanka as a principle, was highly sensitive to pressure from the Ministry of Finance to procure from abroad and was concerned that the 1973 oil shocks (following the OPEC embargo) would temporarily push up personnel and logistical costs. They argued for delaying kokusanka until future programs.[36] The Ministry of Finance was strongly opposed to investing any more financial resources in aircraft development of any kind, particularly after it became clear that the YS-11 passenger aircraft project would not be economically competitive and would go deeply into debt.[37] It was MITI, however, that the defense industry identified as the pivotal vote.[38]

In order to bring the Expert Committee around to the kokusanka faction's position, the Defense Production Committee circulated two documents in the government and LDP under the titles, *Proposals for the Development and Production of* PXL and *Security Policy and Equipment Procurement*. These documents, aimed primarily at MITI, argued that the R&D experience and technological spin-offs to be gained from kokusanka of the PXL were vital not only to the defense industry but to the future growth of Japan's high-tech industry as a whole. Relying on the United States for defense technology, they maintained, would form a structural barrier to the growth of all of Japan's high-tech industries.[39] In particular, industry executives were concerned that the postponement of PXL development would be acutely damaging because joint production of the 250-passenger YX aircraft with Boeing had been indefinitely delayed.[40]

But by 1973 MITI was facing new pressures in international trade policy that conflicted with the Aircraft and Ordnance Division's narrower agenda of promoting the aircraft industry. U.S. and European companies had initiated aggressive export promotion campaigns aimed at Japan's potentially huge arms market in the midst of growing pressure from the Nixon administration for Japan to use its excess dollars in government procurement.[41] In itself this might not have been enough to push the ministry against kokusanka, but growing friction in negotiations with the United States over steel export restraints in 1974 tipped the balance. Just before the Expert Committee was to announce its recommendations in December of 1974, MITI came down squarely against the option for kokusanka of the PXL. The final report from the committee announced that it was impossible at such an early stage to find a decisive point in favor of either importing or domestic production. Damned by faint praise, the PXL option was effectively dropped from that point on. In December 1977 the JDA officially submitted a request to the NDC for procurement of the P-3C.

Throughout the PXL debate, U.S. government and industry exerted various forms of pressure on the Japanese government. Though this pressure was neither consistent nor systematic, it ultimately proved decisive in moving the procurement decision to a political realm beyond the control of the defense industry, thereby condemning the PXL to extinction. Prior to 1972 the U.S. Navy had been unwilling to lease its brand-new ASW plane to Japan. The JDA, however, felt a strong need for new ASW capabilities to counter growing Soviet submarine activity in the Sea of Okhotsk—capabilities that the aging P2V7 did not have. This situation led the MSDF to give partial endorsement to KHI's PXL design, in spite of the service's preference for interoperability. A month before the experts' committee convened, however, the U.S. side announced that it would be willing to lease the P-3C to Japan after all, a decision that considerably weakened the MSDF's support for the PXL within the committee.[42]

In addition to causing the SDF to change its position on PXL several times, U.S. actions altered the political context of the PXL decision. Particularly important was the behavior of Lockheed, the maker of the P-3C. Shortly after the JDA's decision to import the P-3C, Senate hearings in the United States

revealed that the Lockheed Company had offered a bribe through an inter-
mediary to Prime Minister Tanaka in exchange for support of the procurement of the Lockheed Tristar aircraft and possibly the P-3C as well. Whether
the bribery case extended to the P-3C or not, Lockheed clearly *was* successful
in creating the impression in Japan that their executives had persuaded fellow Californian Richard M. Nixon to lobby Prime Minister Tanaka to buy
the P-3C during their summit at San Clemente in 1972.[43] Whether the
impression was accurate or not, it was reported in the press and led the
members of the Expert Committee and the JDA and MITI to view the PXL
decision as a bilateral political issue.

The cloud of possible bribery or backroom deal-making in San Clemente
makes the task of analysis more difficult. Nevertheless, the patterns in interministerial decision making revealed in the FST-2/T-2 and PXL decisions still
offer important insights. The first of these patterns was the strong political
intervention through the office of the prime minister. Japanese prime ministers are often dismissed as weak compared to their European counterparts,
but as chairmen of the NDC, both Kishi and Tanaka exercised considerable
influence on procurement decisions that had reached deadlock at the ministerial level. It is important to note, moreover, that these prime ministers'
actions cannot be attributed to their narrow ambitions in political financing alone.

As prime ministers each had a broader perspective on how the alliance
relationship and defense production interacted. Kishi, for example, wanted
to bring Japan back on the world stage through the U.S.-Japan alliance. This
led him to push for procurement of the P2V7 as an *omiyage* before his summit with Eisenhower in 1959. Tanaka also sought a larger role for Japan, this
time in Asia through normalization of relations with China. To that end, he
needed to have defense relations with the U.S. that were as smooth as possible, including, if necessary, the abandonment of the PXL project and even
kokusanka itself. Where Kishi had to consider what buying U.S. weapons
would do for the bilateral relationship, Tanaka had to view how defense production would affect Japan's position regionally. The counterintuitive idea
that defense technological autonomy could hinder diplomatic autonomy
was not lost on Tanaka—and emerged as a central consideration to defense
planning in the wake of the Fourth Defense Plan.

A second pattern that became increasingly important after 1970 was
MITI's move against kokusanka when the ministry was embroiled in larger
trade issues. Although MITI had reaffirmed its dedication to developing an
aircraft industry in the 1970 MITI vision, the ministry's support for kokusan-

ka faced new limits. Indigenous development of the FST-2 and the T-2 was of central importance to the maintenance and possible nurturing of the domestic aerospace industry. Importing the F-5E offered too negligible a reward (it possibly would reduce the trade imbalance by a mere $200 million) to justify reversing a commitment made a decade earlier to the T-2 line of systems. PXL, on the other hand, came at a time of increased trade friction with the United States, was clearly a target of the U.S. Department of Defense, and had not yet built enough momentum to survive. Thus, while defense experts in both the United States and Japan have complained that the inviolate "Chinese Wall" between trade and defense issues was suddenly broken down in 1988 by the FSX spat, in fact, trade had clearly been a major consideration in Japan's procurement decisions since the early 1970s. A failure to recognize this trend has been at the core of both governments' and legislatures' overreactions to FSX.

It is intriguing to note that industry was so alarmed by the growing link between kokusanka and bilateral alliance and trade relations that the Defense Production Committee commissioned a study in 1974 to quantify the potential impact of international political and economic affairs on Japan's kokusanka policy in the future. The study, *Bōei Sōbi Kakutoku hōhō no Sentaku* (Choices in Equipment Acquisition Methods), used PACAGE methodology (Policy Assessment and Choice through Appraisal of Global Elements) but failed to come up with any conclusions other than the fact that Japan's domestic constituency for kokusanka was still heavily influenced by the international environment and that the government (no surprise here) had to make an even stronger commitment to the principles of kokusanka enunciated in the 1970 *Basic Policy on Defense Production*.[44]

Finally, the increasing relative influence of the JSDF in procurement decisions must be singled out as an important feature of the PXL and FST-2/T-2 decisions. It may seem logical that as the users of weapons systems, the uniformed personnel would have some decision-making powers, but when compared to the F-104 decision, in which the ASDF was completely ignored by the politicians, the T-2 and PXL decisions revealed increasing reliance on JSDF experts by the nonuniformed defense establishment (i.e., the Defense Agency Internal Bureau, the Ministry of Finance, and MITI). To a large extent the SDF's new realism resulted from the practical demands placed on the services by the need to defend Okinawa—a strategic requirement that moved the services beyond their previous narrow gendarme-like focus. Changes in the SDF's status also can be traced to closer operational ties to U.S. forces that resulted from this new mission.

However, the SDF's growing voice in procurement decisions did not nec-essarily mean that the services would support the generally-less-expensive import option in the future. Indeed, the MSDF's difficulty in deciding whether or not the U.S. Navy would even permit licensed production of the P-3C contributed to the ongoing reexamination of the nature of Japan's dependency on the U.S. for defense technology. In particular, the MSDF struggled with the PXL decisions because of Japan's weakness in ASW soft-ware design for the aircraft. The JDA considered various options, including using the U.S. Navy's antisubmarine EPDS software on KHI's platform. But ultimately, as long as the United States had the technology required to make the PXL an effective ASW platform, Japan's ability to design and build the *hardware* indigenously did not matter. As one senior JDA official noted in an internal postmortem on the PXL decision:

> If you recognize that our loss in the Second World War was in the area of mil-itary technology, then it was certainly on the side of electronics. And yet, in the postwar period we have again neglected electronics and invested defense technology in aircraft development.[45]

Military planners were beginning to recognize that greater defense auton-omy required greater autonomy in the integration of software and hardware. The elevation of electronics companies on the Defense Production Com-mittee's rosters in the late 1960s assured that at least some in industry real-ized this as well. And yet the outcome of the Fourth Defense Plan and the PXL and AEW decisions led industry to focus instead on how to compensate for the sudden loss of new airframe projects. The Defense Production Committee issued a company-wide survey in 1977, for example, that stated that because of "the drastic reductions in procurement from the original Fourth Defense Plan" "maintenance of Japan's defense industrial base would be very difficult."[46] And in 1976 the SJAC (the Society of Japanese Aerospace Companies, previously the Japan Aircraft Industry Association) wrote that because of the failure to develop the PXL and YX "Japan remains only a parts supplier to the European and American industries—nothing more than a local village factory to the world."[47]

To some extent the government was able to respond to industry's concern by avoiding a clear statement on kokusanka in the PXL decision. The NDC's final report noted that while the time required for developing an effective PXL made importing the P-3C appropriate in that particular case, "kokusan-ka is still desirable" as a general rule.[48] Indeed, through kokusanka of the T-2 and FST-2 the government had committed itself to the autonomous development of support fighter aircraft. Industry would pin all of its hopes on the development of this line of systems in the future. As TRDI's deputy director noted in retrospect two decades later:

> With the T-2 and F-1 we were feeling the pinch of U.S. pressure. With direct import or license production, there would have been no advantage in terms of aerospace technology. In that sense, we were lucky to preserve the kokusanka line. The T-2 and F-1 were crucial for the technology that blossomed to help develop the FSX and move us on to the 21st Century![49]

In the meantime, industry had to adjust to two new realities that had emerged from the Fourth Defense Plan debacle: the need for closer cooperation with the United States and the need to develop greater leverage in that relationship by strengthening autonomous technology at the subsystems level.

4 | The Emerging Paradox: Bilateral Defense Cooperation and the Growth of Technonationalism, 1976–1986

Chapter 3 traced the procurement debate on the T-2/FST-2 and the PXL through to the final decisions of 1976. The fate of these two systems punctuated the end of industry's grand visions under Nakasone. The intellectual groundwork for what would follow had begun under Nakasone's own watch in 1970. In that year a group of self-proclaimed realists led by the JDA's Defense Policy Bureau director, Kubo Takuya, were quietly challenging the premises of Nakasone's planning. Specifically, they targeted the notion that autonomy should be defined only by indigenous capabilities for defense production and deterrence. In fact, Kubo and his allies began to argue, Japan could achieve a more significant level of autonomy by establishing *closer* ties to the United States (much in the way originally intended by Yoshida Shigeru). With Kubo's promotion within the JDA, and Japan's own experience with détente into the mid-1970s, this line of thinking gained currency. Eventually it would form the baseline for the Japanese government's 1976 National Defense Program Outline (NDPO) and the inauguration of a new era of unprecedented bilateral security cooperation between the United States and Japan.

At the same time, however, Japan's ambitions in the area of defense technology did not die with the Fourth Defense Plan. In fact, growing cooperation with the United States throughout the rest of the decade created the political consensus in Japan necessary for a steadily expanding defense establishment—ironically contributing to even larger appetites for defense technological autonomy within industry. Like gunpowder and fire, the incompatible elements of collaboration and autonomy could not coincide long without an explosion. That explosion, of course, was FSX, the subject of the next chapter. But to understand the reasons for the FSX affair—a paradoxical crisis in mutual trust at the height of bilateral cooperation—it is necessary to restart the kokusanka story back in 1970.

From the KB Memo to the NDPO: Building a New Consensus for Defense

At the same time that Nakasone Yasuhiro was galvanizing the various forces behind autonomous defense in 1970, his director of the Defense Policy Bureau, Kubo Takuya, was working quietly on a new defense planning concept that was as modest as Nakasone's plan was ambitious. Kubo formulated his ideas in a memo that he circulated internally in March 1971 under the pseudonym "KB." In the memo, "Thinking About the Development of Defense Forces" (Bōeiryoku Seibi no Kangaekata), Kubo proposed the adoption of a "standard defense force concept" (kibanteki bōeiryoku kōsō), that would base force planning not on possible enemy capabilities in the region but rather on the probable political intentions of Japan's neighbors.[1] Implicit in Kubo's memo was an attack on Nakasone's attempt to broaden Japan's defense industrial base and develop extensive capabilities for unilateral deterrence. Kubo's goal was a defense planning framework that would reduce the scope of defense spending and free the JDA from political rancor.

The KB memo was highly controversial among the senior JSDF officers and JDA officials who read it, particularly given the tone of Nakasone's tenure at JDA. Kubo initially received support for his concept from only a handful of civilian officials in the JDA. That situation changed dramatically, however, with the Nixon shocks and Japan's normalization of relations with China. In his first year as prime minister, Tanaka Kakuei was receiving severe criticism from the Chinese and domestic press and the opposition over the remaining legacy of Nakasone's defense plan. In order to demonstrate the irreversibility of Japan's retreat from the Nakasone concept of large-scale autonomous defense, Prime Minister Tanaka ordered the JDA at a meeting of the NDC in October 1972 to formulate guidelines for limiting Japan's defense capabilities to those necessary for the growing environment of détente of the 1970s. The JDA turned to the KB memo to form the basis for its new doctrine, "Peacetime Defense Force" (Heiwaji no Bōeiryoku), which was announced to the Diet on February 1, 1973, by JDA Director-General Masuhara Keikichi.

The Peacetime Defense Force doctrine set force targets well below those once expected under the Nakasone plan. GSDF personnel goals were set at 180,000, MSDF vessels by tonnage were limited to 250,000 to 280,000, and the ASDF was held to 800 aircraft. There was little or no room for expansion of these levels, and the requirements of the defense industrial base were ignored outright. This brought the doctrine under immediate criticism from industry and the JSDF. Such criticism was expected, however, and would not have blocked the official adoption of the doctrine. What did eventually halt the doctrine, ironically, was the Japan Socialist Party's decision to withdraw initial support after the Party leadership realized that, despite its dovish character, the doctrine implied recognition of the constitutionality of the JSDF. This was something the Socialists were not yet prepared to do. For the time being, the Peacetime Defense Force concept was put in storage.

Kubo bade his time, however, and refined his thinking. In June 1974, in his last month as Director of the Defense Policy Bureau, he circulated a second KB memo. This paper, "Thinking About Our Country's Defense Concept and Defense Force Build-Up" (Wagakuni no Bōeikozo to Bōeiryoku Seibi no Kangaekata), reflected the growing pressure on the JDA to cut defense spending—pressure which resulted from the 1973 oil shock, inflation, and the deepening of détente. The 1974 KB memo also explained in greater detail how Japan's security policy was being defined in terms of relations with the United States. This last aspect of the paper, much more than the concept of "peacetime capabilities," helped to establish the contours of Japan's defense policy priorities for the decade to come.[2]

After outlining the domestic political and economic constraints on defense spending, and chiding previous JDA planners for calculating deterrence only in terms of weaponry, the 1974 KB memo went to the heart of Japan's strategic dilemma of abandonment versus entrapment:

> There is a worry that if Japan has to rely completely on another country's good intentions or power, our ability for independent action will be severely curtailed. On the other hand, if independent military strength is neither possible nor appropriate for Japan, then we must choose alliance with the United States as our first policy. *In that case, balancing and adjusting dependence on the U.S. with the maintenance of Japanese autonomy will become a serious problem.* (emphasis mine)[3]

Kubo's solution to that problem was to accept a degree of military dependence on the United States but recognize that security goes beyond military power. In that broader area of security—what would eventually come to be known as "comprehensive security"—was Japan's room for independent action. According to Kubo, basing defense policy on the U.S.-Japan alliance gave Japan freedom of action by providing Japan's neighbors with a guarantee of "control" over possible Japanese remilitarization and by allowing Japan to play a role "as Asia gropes for a new security system."[4]

For one year Kubo's ideas lay dormant as he moved on to serve as Director of the Defense Facilities Administration. Then, in December 1975 Prime Minister Miki Takeo appointed the dovish but pragmatic politician, Sakata Michita, as JDA director-general. Six months later Kubo was brought back as administrative vice minister. Sakata dusted off the two-year-old "Peacetime Defense Force" document and wrapped in the newer elements of the 1974 KB memo to prepare guidelines for the JDA's new objective—the creation of a long-term National Defense Program Outline (the NDPO).

These guidelines were approved by the NDC in November 1975 and the process of formulating the NDPO commenced the following January. According to the guidelines, the JDA was to proceed with formulation of the NDPO based on five premises:

1. the move toward détente would reduce the importance of force in international relations.
2. the U.S.-Japan security system would be the key to Japan's and the region's defense;
3. Japan would face no immediate military threats;
4. the Peacetime Defense Force doctrine would set the upper limits of front line equipment;
5. due attention would be placed on the improvement of surveillance, logistical support, training, and other "rear area" budget items.[5]

Conspicuously absent from Sakata and Kubo's new definition of security was the development of the defense industrial and technological base. Sakata and Kubo were making a deliberate move away from Nakasone's attempt to build a strong defense constituency around industry. If the Nakasone experience proved anything from their perspective, it was that the constituency for defense spending had to be expanded to include moderates in government and industry, not to mention the Ministry of Finance. Depth of support (industry) had to be sacrificed for breadth of support (the public).

In order to reach the public, Sakata recommissioned the publication of annual Defense White Papers (Nakasone had initiated the first six years earlier) and increased the frequency of National Defense Council meetings. His most significant action on the public relations front, however, was to create a "Forum on Defense" (*Bōei o Kangaeru kai*) that would seek to establish the parameters for a new national consensus on defense policy. The forum consisted of eleven intellectuals from industry, academia, and the media who met six times over a period of three months (April through June). The group had the most open and healthy debate on defense issues Japan had experienced in the postwar period. At the end of three months of deliberations, the forum members continued along the line of thinking initiated by the KB memos, particularly strengthening the emphasis to be paid to "developing mutual trust" in the alliance with the United States.

In its effort to define a new consensus, the Forum on Defense also refocused attention on the traditional industrial and technological issues, which had thus far been ignored by Kubo and Sakata in the preparation of the NDPO. The forum's prescriptions for defense technology took a marked departure from the previous decade of JDA and industry thinking, however, by studiously avoiding kokusanka as the solution to all of Japan's techno-military problems:

> International collaboration has become increasingly important given changes in the advance of science and technology. . . . In the military technology field as well, it is becoming impossible for one country to develop significant weapon systems and maintain dominance on its own.[6]

According to the forum report, Japan could secure its defense technology base by improving its *overall* level of technology: "advanced defense technology could then be developed when necessary." The problem for Japan, according to the report, was that:

> while there was strong interest in defense before the war and there were many defense technology experts, no successor generation [of defense technology experts] has been trained in the postwar period. This problem is difficult to solve, but through various methods, Japan must work to increase the speed of its military technological advances.[7]

Through this language, the forum report sent out several important signals. First, it reassured the defense industry that developing engineers with expertise in defense technology would be an important facet of the JDA's new look under Sakata. But the report also took aim at kokusanka, advocating instead a policy of utilizing Japan's growing commercial technology base to spin-on technology to the military side. Arguments about the importance of military kokusanka for the civilian economy were now being replaced by arguments about the importance of the civilian economy for military production. This broader definition of the defense technology base echoed the comprehensive approach to defense policy of Kubo and Sakata. It also reflected what many began to see as the reality of the growing international diffusion and interdependence in technology.

The Forum on Defense had a central impact on the final draft of the NDPO (due in part to overlap in staffing), which was formally adopted by the NDC and the Cabinet on October 29, 1976.[8] By reasserting the primacy of alliance the NDPO put to rest much of the controversy caused by Nakasone's grab at autonomy. According to the NDPO, defense planning would be "based on the measurement of the continued, effective management of the reliability of the alliance system with the United States." Japan would only develop the capabilities necessary to deter "small scale, limited aggression." The role of R&D and weapons procurement was also addressed by the NDPO within this framework of alliance and limited deterrence:

> appropriate consideration of kokusanka will be continued, including a com-
> bined judgment of the need for acquisition in times of crisis; training and
> education, cost effectiveness, and so forth.[9]

The NDPO thus reduced kokusanka to its lowest priority in the twenty years since the JSDF were formed, a point reinforced by a Cabinet resolution limiting defense spending to 1 percent of GNP, which followed the NDPO's adoption by one week (a concession to the opposition).

Not surprisingly, many in industry, the JSDF, and the LDP were outraged by the language of the final draft of the NDPO.[10] The Miki Cabinet's defense policies seemed to push Japan into the ice age predicted by industry leaders five years before. And yet there was also room for hope. Almost immediately public opinion polls began to show that the NDPO had provided a framework for the development of a national consensus for defense spending. In 1974 the Defense Production Committee, stunned by the loss of the PXL program, had commissioned a quantitative study to analyze the impact of foreign and domestic political forces on procurement decisions. The report's conclusion: without a national consensus for defense spending inside Japan, indigenous projects such as PXL would always be vulnerable to outside pressure.[11] Farsighted observers recognized that the NDPO—bitter medicine though it was—might just establish the political environment for kokusanka that had eluded industry for the previous three decades. That much was encouraging, particularly after the turbulence that JDA and industry had experienced since Nakasone had left the JDA. The key would be adapting the original kokusanka strategy to the new era.

Redefining Kokusanka After the NDPO

Throughout the first half of the 1970s the defense industry felt the previous decade's expanded constituency for kokusanka turn brittle and begin to break apart. The fissure within industry opened most dramatically in 1976, when Doko Toshio, once a vocal champion of kokusanka, withdrew his original support for heavy government spending on the defense industrial base. Industry's interests in trade with the PRC had already dampened Doko's earlier enthusiasm for kokusanka. By the mid-1970s Keidanren was also growing wary of the government's expanding budget deficits and began to fear that corporate tax increases would be used to balance the books. Appointed chairman of a new commission on administrative reform in 1976, Doko moved away from his earlier support for large government R&D projects and instead advocated a reduced government role in the private sector, a move with clear implications for costly programs such as the YS-11.[12]

Keidanren's influence on the LDP and the government as a whole began to decline in this period, due to a combination of the Miki administration's political financing reforms, the Tanaka faction's development of a new, decentralized pattern of fundraising (based on a combination of large corporations and medium and small enterprises in the districts), and the growing diversity of Keidanren's own membership.[13] Reflecting trends in its parent organization, the Defense Production Committee also continued to lose its homogeneity in the mid-1970s. The declining dominance of the systems integrators was evident in changes in TRDI's budget. R&D on propeller and jet aircraft, for example, declined from 61.8 percent of all TRDI work in the Third Defense Plan to 16.9 percent in the Fourth Plan. During the first phase of the NDPO, the amount was only 9.1 percent. In contrast, R&D on electronic systems increased from 10.7 percent in the Third Plan to 27 percent in the Fourth and 34.4 percent in the first phase of the NDPO.[14] The continuing shift in contracts toward electronics companies and away from traditional metal-benders brought not only diversity but also greater competition within the organization's ranks. Particularly noteworthy, according to Defense Production Committee staff, was MELCO's unwillingness to share information with its traditionally close keiretsu ally MHI as both companies competed for production share on the Badge early warning system and the Nike/Hawk surface-to-air missile in the mid-1970s.[15]

At the same time, however, the pluralization of the defense industry in the 1970s did bring new players into the traditional constituency for autonomous development. As the procurement share of major electronic firms such as Tōshiba and Fujitsu increased, so too did their commitment to defense production. Labor also came to see its interests as tied to kokusanka. In 1975 the All-Japan Shipbuilders Union issued a declaration to the government calling for kokusanka of all military equipment. They were followed in 1977 by the All Japan Aerospace Workers Union.[16] Small and medi-

um-sized enterprises also increased their movement into defense contracting as they sought stability after the disruption of the two oil shocks.[17]

The implications of these trends were clear to the JDA and TRDI. Large-
scale autonomous defense projects such as the PXL or AEW were not politically, or even technologically, durable in the NDPO era. Closer defense cooperation with the United States and declining threats abroad made kokusanka across the board difficult to endorse "as a matter of principle," as
Nakasone had advocated. However, defense R&D that utilized and enhanced
the strengths of Japan's commercial technology base would be attractive to
industry and advantageous to the JDA. The NDPO's prescription for "appropriate kokusanka" could therefore be interpreted to mean *appropriately sym-
biotic* with the civilian technology base.

Accordingly, the JDA launched a new R&D system in 1978 based on what it
called "propositional research" (*meidai kenkyū*). Meidai kenkyū would focus
on strengthening Japan's technology "trees" (specific subsystems that drew
on commercial technologies) rather than focusing resources on technology
"forests" (new systems-level projects such as YS-11 or PXL). The JDA considered this new system a bold departure from the "big-ticket item" mentality
of Nakasone and his predecessors. According to the JDA, meidai kenkyū had
four principal features that made it unique to Japan and consistent with the
NDPO's demand for appropriate, "cost-effective" kokusanka:

1. there would be virtually no technology risk;
2. projects would be managed from the top down;
3. full use would be made of commercial technology;
4. R&D would not necessarily lead to full production.[18]

In effect, the JDA was proposing for the first time that industry move to a
regime in which commercial technology would be spun-on for defense
applications, a concept that reflected the growth of dual-use technology, the
government's inability to promise a significant number of large-scale indigenous projects, and the pluralization of the defense industry's membership.
The comprehensive security themes first sounded in the *Forum on Defense
Report of 1975* were finding their way into JDA policy. National strength and
leverage within the alliance need not be determined by defense systems and
defense technologies alone—it would now also be determined by the comprehensive strengths of Japan's overall technology base.

Industry was not entirely opposed to the new meidai kenkyū concept.
They recognized that the emphasis on large-scale projects had taught engineers much about defense technology, but by aiming for too many large scale
aerospace projects at once (PXL, AEW, YS-11, F-1, C-1, etc.) Japan had been imi-

tating the U.S. defense industrial structure instead of playing to its own technological strengths. Without manageable projects, based on indigenous technological strengths and not on licensed U.S. technology, industry would never develop the "know-why" of defense production. The focus on subsystems-level kokusanka was perfectly suited to the growing number of electronics firms engaged in defense production. Finally, the introduction of meidai kenkyū had appeal for defense contractors because it expanded the R&D budget. Following the abandonment of Nakasone's guidelines for kokusanka, R&D spending as a percentage of the JDA budget had dropped from 1.3 percent in 1973 to 0.89 percent in 1976. Meidai kenkyū, in contrast, caused the defense R&D budget to steadily work its way back up from 0.92 percent in 1978 to 1 percent in 1980 and 2.11 percent in 1989—and this at a time when the defense budget as a whole was rapidly expanding following the consensus behind the NDPO.[19]

Industry was not willing, however, to accept the JDA's new attempt to take the "development" out of "research & development." The vital interdependence of the research *and* development stages of defense production had been reinforced for industry during its experience from 1973 to 1979 with the indigenous ASM-1 (air-to-surface missile). The ASM-1 was Japan's first "design-to-cost" weapon, in which a check was made at each stage of development to predict the later effect on cost of production. It was also the first autonomous project to be firmly held to the JSDF's mission specifications and requirements. In its first test, the ASM-1 hit 28 out of 29 targets, prompting JSDF officers to declare it "the greatest air-to-surface missile in the world . . . better than the Harpoon or the Exocet!"[20] What made the ASM-1 a success, from the perspective of systems integrators and subcontractors alike, had been the commitment to produce the weapon and produce it *autonomously*.

The Defense Production Committee attempted to impose these lessons on the JDA's new R&D system in a November 1979 document, "Views on Promoting the Research and Development of Weapons Systems" (Bōeisobi kenkyū kaihatsu no Shinshutsu ni Kansuru Wareware no Kenkai), which stated that:

> Japan's industrial technology level and industrial productivity have attained the top levels globally. If one considers the problems with introducing leading technology, it is now time to use the current base of accumulated technology to advance autonomous research and development. Defense equipment is no exception.[21]

The DPC's resistance to the decoupling of R&D from autonomous production was being echoed at the same time by the JSDF, but for different reasons. Despite ever-closer operational ties to U.S. forces which resulted from the emphasis on alliance of the NDPO, senior JSDF (especially ASDF) staff were beginning to worry about their heavy dependence on the United States for the maintenance and resupply of U.S.-designed aircraft. Many components had to be shipped back to U.S. factories for repair[22] and JSDF officers openly questioned the long-term sustainability of America's military-industrial base as GNP growth in the United States began to slow down.[23] Growing JSDF ties to major defense contractors only reinforced this sort of thinking.

The confluence of JSDF, industry, and JDA philosophies eventually resulted in a compromise that recognized the limits imposed by the NDPO, the importance of spinning-on technology from the commercial side, *and* the continuing importance of kokusanka—both in its positive impact on R&D (the lesson of "design-to-cost") and its role in maintaining leverage and independence vis-à-vis the United States. This synthesis was formulated in a 1979 JDA "New Policy on R&D" (Kenkyū Kaihatsu ni Kansuru Shin Hōshin). The new policy had three stated goals:

> 1. to increase Japan's technology level up to—or possibly beyond—that of the United States and Europe in certain of the most advanced military technologies;
> 2. to use this new higher level of technology as background *to maintain leverage in negotiations with the United States over military technologies* [italics mine];
> 3. to increase the current low-level R&D budget by actually separating research from eventual development.[24]

The 1979 policy statement offered an answer to the central problem presented in Kubo's 1974 memo about the difficulty of maintaining a balance between independence and close relations with the United States, and it did so by returning to the issue that Nakasone had stressed and Kubo had so studiously avoided—the defense technology base. Autonomy in the alliance could be protected, as the new policy statement's second goal made clear, by developing a higher level of technology in order to maintain leverage in negotiations with the United States.

When Prime Minister Ohira Masayoshi established a study group in 1980 under President of the National Defense Academy Inoki Masamichi in order to develop a national consensus for the concept of comprehensive security, the link between defense technology issues and Kubo's original thesis was made even more explicit. The Inoki Commission pointed to the 1979 oil shocks, the Soviet invasion of Afghanistan, and the Vietnamese invasion of Cambodia as proof that economic and energy factors were also integral parts of the nation's security. This "comprehensive" approach was effective politically because it moved Japan's defense debate away from its previous narrow and unpopular military focus. This was a development entirely consistent with Kubo's original intentions. However, the Inoki Commission's attention to economic security inevitably led the group back to defense industrial issues. The appreciation of spin-on and dual-use technologies embodied in the JDA's meidai kenkyū program resonated with the theme of comprehensive security, and in its final report the Inoki Commission recommended substantial increases in defense R&D and procurement. In the decade from the first KB memo to the Inoki Report, the kokusanka debate had come—if not full circle—a good 300 degrees around.[25]

The First Collision: The F-15 and the Opening of a New Regime for Technology Transfers

While the process of building a national consensus for defense policy in the wake of the Fourth Defense Plan returned inexorably to the issue of kokusanka, the renewed priority placed on alliance also grew. In 1978 the United States and Japan signed the Guidelines for Defense Cooperation, opening an era of joint planning and operations and increased scrutiny by each side of exactly what the other would contribute to the alliance—an area of concern following the fall of Saigon in 1975 and Jimmy Carter's 1976 election pledge to withdraw U.S. troops from Korea. The Japanese side originally requested the guidelines in order to guarantee that U.S. forces would in fact fulfill the role described for them in the NDPO. But as the U.S. government considered what *it* wanted from Japan (initial requests for greater command integration were rejected by Tokyo), attention increasingly focused on technology. The U.S. Department of Defense and U.S. industry had identified a number of technologies in which Japan was surpassing the United States and decided that after the free flow of technology to Japan allowed for in the F-4 program, it was time for the Japanese side to foster a flow of technology back to the United States.[26] Tokyo's ability to balance its commitments to bilateral defense cooperation and autonomous defense technology was about to be tested.

In 1980 the Pentagon proposed the establishment of a mechanism for discussing the exchange of defense technology: the U.S.-Japan Systems and Technology Forum (S&TF). The Pentagon had in mind the exchange of technology from Japan to the United States, of course, but the Japanese side came to the first meeting with an entirely different view. Nurtured on three decades of advantageous licensed production and technology flows from U.S. companies, the Japanese government and industry saw the S&TF as an ideal opportunity to push for increases in the level of one-way technology transfers to Japan for the F-15. Specifically, Japan wanted the U.S. side to agree to the release of data packages and production assistance for the F-15's F-100 engine, sidewinder missile, composite materials, and fire control system—all of which the Department of Defense had decided to black box.[27]

In the end, neither side went away with exactly what it expected from the first S&TF, but one signal to the Japanese side was clear: three decades of unquestioned one-way technology transfers were over. The Japanese side's reaction to this prospect was mixed. Advocates of closer bilateral defense ties in the MOFA and the LDP saw defense industrial collaboration as a useful mechanism for establishing mutual trust. The JDA and JSDF saw collaboration as a logical and desirable extension of the principles of the 1978 guidelines, one which drew together the various interests within Japan's defense community. For the defense industry and MITI, joint development would provide an opportunity for close contact with top-rank Western firms. Joint development also had the additional advantage of offering a potential route around the "Three Arms Export Principles" and a form of insurance against the kind of external political pressure that derailed development of the PXL.[28]

At the same time, however, Japan's defense community had serious concerns about the implications of the 1980 Systems and Technology Forum for the autonomy of Japan's defense industrial base. In the end, the U.S. side did not relax its black-boxing of F-15 technology as the Japanese side had requested in the meetings. As a result, kokusanka of the F-15 fell to 70 percent, the lowest level for any aircraft system produced in Japan since the F-86.[29] For the ASDF command, this was a severe shock. It created logistical problems, but more importantly, as one journalist who covered the talks suggests, "it showed the ASDF for the first time that the US was afraid of Japanese technology."[30]

In a 1981 statement to the government, the Defense Production Committee responded to the outcome of the Systems and Technology Forum by attacking the cumbersome mechanism for licensed production and military sales from the U.S. that had caused industry such problems in the F-15 case:

> Given the variety of problems in price, delivery and quality, the [Defense Production Committee] thinks that procurement based on FMS (Foreign Military Sales) should be reexamined.[31]

The same policy statement claimed that increasing U.S. reluctance to transfer technology would "necessitate a significant increase in Japan's budget for autonomous research and development." At its annual meeting in

January 1982, the Defense Production Committee leadership focused specifically on the U.S. Congress, warning that pressure from "protectionist" legislators in the United States would make greater kokusanka unavoidable.[32] Almost on cue, the Pentagon canceled a licensed-production agreement for 103-millimeter artillery several months later because of congressional pressure for an off-the-shelf sale to save American jobs. This was followed by a Congressional General Accounting Office report on the F-15 that called for even *stricter* black-boxing of U.S. defense technology transferred to Japan in the future.[33] The JDA's 1979 new policy on R&D had stated that kokusanka would be an important policy where the goal was to increase leverage vis-à-vis the United States in defense technology negotiations. With the hardening attitudes of the Department of Defense and the Congress, the Japanese defense industry was ready to take the new JDA R&D policy at its word.

Despite industry's misgivings, however, the Systems and Technology Forum successfully established political momentum for technology cooperation and elevated the issue to the level of the Office of the Secretary of Defense in the United States and the Cabinet in Japan. In June 1981, following Prime Minister Suzuki Zenkō's summit meeting with President Reagan and mutual promises to share roles and missions, Secretary of Defense Caspar Weinberger asked Japan if a mechanism could be introduced to transfer certain defense-related technologies to the United States. In response, the Japanese government issued a "Report on Arms Exports to the United States" (Tai Bei Buki Yushutsu ni tsuite) in November of the same year that established that "military technology exports to the United States do not fall under the "Three Arms Export Principles" and are possible based on Article Three of the U.S.-Japan Security Treaty." In March of 1982 Secretary of Defense Weinberger formally requested such transfers during a visit to Tokyo and the new Prime Minister, Nakasone Yasuhiro, instructed his Defense Agency Chief, Omura Joji, and Chief Cabinet Secretary Gotōda Masaharu to respond positively to the request. On November 8, 1983, the two governments exchanged Memoranda of Understanding on Joint Military Technology Transfers.

Once again, the key institution was MITI. Reflecting industry concern, MITI initially objected to the military technology transfer concept because it would lock Japan into a pattern in which the United States would sell Japan weapons but black-box the technology, while Japan would have to give the U.S. technology without being able to sell hardware. MITI's opposition ended in 1983, however, when Yamanaka Sadanori of Prime Minister Nakasone's own faction became Minister. Nevertheless, concern continued at the working level.[34]

MITI's concern was matched by prodefense Diet members in the LDP. The number of politicians participating in the PARC Defense Division meetings and supporting the defense budget had increased dramatically in the years since the NDPO removed much of the divisiveness of the defense debate. The reemergence of East-West tensions after the invasions of Afghanistan and Cambodia also drew conservatives back to defense. In the early 1980s these members became conspicuous enough to be labeled a *zoku*, or policy "tribe" (caucus), by the press. Though generally in favor of close defense cooperation with the United States, many of these politicians also had close ties to the defense industry. From this latter vantage point they criticized the new technology transfer regime as exploitative and based on political priorities other than Japan's needs for self-defense. Particularly outspoken was Mihara Asao, the defense zoku's leader—and usually a friend of the United States.[35]

The Defense Production Committee told a visiting task force from the U.S. Defense Science Board in November 1984 that industry was concerned about a lack of licensing fees and the transfer of Japanese technology to third countries. In the same meeting, members of the DPC asked whether an increase in technology flow from Japan to the U.S. might result in a relaxation of black-boxed technology in systems bought from the United States.[36] For Japanese industry, the question of whether participation in the Joint Military Technology Transfer Agreement would result in a loosening of technology transfers to Japan was—and continues to be—crucial. If anything, the technology transfer agreement as it stood in 1983–1984 suggested a weakening of Japan's own defense industrial base rather than a true bonding with the U.S. through a two-way flow of technology.

Without autonomous capabilities, industry was in no position to demand such reciprocity from the Pentagon. Secretary of Defense Caspar Weinberger's formal call for Japanese participation in the U.S. Strategic Defense Initiative in March 1985 raised the stakes for Japanese industry considerably. Although the government allowed only limited participation in R&D by Japanese firms, the potential spin-offs and spin-ons were considerable. The Japanese side could not approach a closer defense industrial relationship from a position of weakness. Strengthening kokusanka took on a new urgency, and in the area of aircraft, the path to autonomy—or at least equality—was Japan's next generation support fighter: the FSX.

5 | "Return of the Zero Fighter!": The FSX Crisis

When one considers the historical context of the kokusanka debate, it is difficult to imagine how Japan and the United States could have avoided bilateral confrontation over FSX at the end of the 1980s. Japan's relentless pursuit of autonomous defense production already had collided once with its alliance policies in 1970. When PXL and Nakasone's defense plan were sacrificed and the primacy of alliance reasserted through the 1976 NDPO, the 1978 Guidelines for U.S.-Japan Defense Cooperation, and the 1983 Military Technology Transfer Agreement, equilibrium between autonomy and alliance seemed to be reestablished. But the closer defense cooperation initiated in the late 1970s did nothing to solve the causal nexus behind the original kokusanka debate. Even as the United States and Japan opened new areas for defense cooperation, the fuse of autonomy was quietly burning in the decision to pursue indigenous development of the F-1 support fighter and then the FSX. And with FSX the fuse of autonomy hit the powder keg of alliance and exploded dramatically.

But if the FSX was an explosion, it was as illuminating as it was destructive. It revealed that the constituency behind the growing defense budgets of the post-NDPO years was firmly based on the principle of alliance with the

A common entry in Japanese newspaper articles about FSX (e.g., *Nikkei Sangyō Shimbun* [November 11, 1993]).

United States. Within MITI, the LDP, the JDA, and the JSDF—and even the defense industry itself—the pro-kokusanka faction found itself unable to push its objective of autonomy once that objective came into conflict with a broader institutional commitment to smooth alliance relations with the United States.

However, the story does not end there. The FSX issue exploded a second time. When the Reagan administration's unprecedented bilateral agreement for joint development of the FSX came under severe attack from the Congress in the early months of the new Bush administration in 1989, the Japanese government encountered for the first time the kind of technonationalism it had come to expect only from itself. For the first time it now seemed that the United States was rejecting the concept of technological interdependence and openly violating the sanctity of the alliance by mixing trade and security issues.

This emergence of technonationalism across the Pacific had the potential to reenergize the drive for kokusanka. That it has only partially done so is evidence of the durability of the consensus behind the alliance in Japan, but this should provide only small comfort to American policymakers. The FSX crisis demonstrated that the national interests of Japan and the United States can easily diverge when there is no common enemy and the alliance relationship is poorly managed: a lesson not lost on the Japanese defense community.

The Momentum Behind FSX

The FSX story also begins as a nonpolitical one. From the beginning, autonomous development and production were taken for granted by the central core of engineers and program managers associated with the FSX project. The F-1 had been an autonomous project, and there was no question that FSX would be as well. In the view of those working directly on FSX, the emerging themes of joint development and defense industrial collaboration could be dealt with as *kazarimono*—mere decorations—for what would essentially remain an indigenous project. No one in TRDI, MITI, or industry had the foresight to see how the shifting American attitude toward Japanese defense technology would affect their ambitious plan for a *hinomaru* (rising sun) fighter.

MHI executives and TRDI officials first set kokusanka of FSX in motion back in 1967 when they agreed informally that an indigenously designed jet should replace the F-1 (which was then still in the design phase)—and possibly even the F-4EJ. Kokusanka was further solidified in 1975 when the ASDF staff sent a memo asking the JDA to consider an indigenous jet fighter program. Taking their cue from the JDA's movement toward kokusanka, MHI formed a project team by 1979 to utilize the technology of the T-2, F-1, F-104, F-4, and the new F-15 for the FSX.[1] The military mission for the FSX was established ostensibly by Prime Minister Suzuki Zenko's 1981 promise to Ronald Reagan that Japan would defend its territory, airspace, and sea lanes out to 1,000 nautical miles. Then in 1982 MITI's Aircraft and Ordnance Division lent its weight to the project, sending a memorandum to the ASDF staff endorsing autonomous development of FSX "in keeping with the kokusanka established with the F-1."[2] With MITI's endorsement the circle was complete: the defense industry decision makers were solidly behind kokusanka of FSX.

But FSX was not destined to be a mere update of the F-1. Engineers and bureaucrats were thinking in grander terms. By 1984 the JDA recognized that the deployment of new Soviet MIG-29s would render a fighter dedicated to ground support obsolete. The successor to the F-1 had to have the characteristics and capabilities of an air superiority fighter. TRDI had a few projects underway that would help; projects that had grown out of the meidai kenkyū focus on subsystems-level R&D. These included research on composite wing materials, phased array radar, air-to-surface missiles, surface-to-air missiles, and CCV (Control Configured Vehicle) systems. Time was needed to bring these technologies up to the levels that were competitive militarily and commercially on an international scale. Time was found. In 1984 the ASDF determined that the F-1's service life could be extended beyond the 3,500 hours originally expected to 4,050 hours. This meant that the F-1 jets would fly into the late 1990s, leaving just enough time for domestic development of their successors (cynics should note, however, that it is not unusual for air forces to reestimate the life expectancies of their aircraft once they have had an opportunity to fly them for several years).

The expanding military requirements for FSX—something that the ASDF had not been forced to face with previous autonomous programs—also meant that the jet would have to be based, at least in part, on an existing non-Japanese design. The F-1 had been based loosely on the British Jaguar. The FSX design would have to be based even more closely on a foreign airframe. The Japanese aerospace industry was simply too far behind to start up its own learning curve with FSX. Engineers remained confident, however, that even with a small head start from a foreign design, the jet would remain a hinomaru fighter.

The JDA outlined the options for FSX while preparing the five-year defense plan in 1984. According to defense officials, the agency had three options: domestic design, procurement of a foreign aircraft, or conversion of the F-4. TRDI was tasked to assess the prospects for the first of these options, domestic design.

From the beginning, TRDI's assessment was made in close cooperation with industry, which recognized its dependence on foreign design, but was eager to increase the domestic component to the highest degree possible. Leading defense contractors submitted design proposals and helped TRDI engineers with technical assessments. The design proposal for MHI's candidate, the JF-210, bore a striking resemblance to the Northrop/McDonnell Douglas F-18, but according to a study the company prepared for TRDI, the JF-210 would be cheaper than either the F-18 or the F-15. To emphasize the uniqueness of the jet and appeal to JDA officials, MHI engineers added canard wings, another project then underway between the company and TRDI.[3] KHI's design also bore a striking resemblance to the F-18. However, recognizing that the lead on FSX would probably go to rival MHI just as it had with the F-1, KHI engineers pushed for a strong subcontractor position in their own design plan. This meant emphasizing certain areas, such as the cockpit, where KHI had proven new strengths while designing and building the XT-4 trainer (this aircraft will be discussed in detail later).[4]

Armed with these industry proposals, TRDI reported to the JDA on April 2, 1985, that indigenous development of FSX was entirely feasible. Specifically, TRDI recommended eventual production of 250 jets, 100 of which would be F-1 replacements and 150 F-4 replacements. As expected, TRDI intended to leapfrog from a trainer to an air superiority/ground support fighter by basing the design on an existing advanced airframe such as the F-18 and coproducing the engine under license from General Electric or Pratt & Whitney.[5] Shortly after TRDI's decision, the Defense Production Committee made a very public visit to JDA Director-General Katō Koichi to endorse TRDI's decision.[6]

Katō, however, had not yet made a final decision on how to proceed with FSX. Officially, the JDA was still considering all three of its original options, including importing a foreign jet. The F-18, F-16, and the European Tornado were all advanced by JDA officials as possible candidates. Nevertheless, the agency clearly had no intention of settling for either direct off-the-shelf purchases or even for licensed production. One of the foreign jets would serve as a model for a Japanese-designed FSX. Importing was only being forwarded as a carrot for cooperation from the American firms, and the Tornado was only brought up as a stick to suggest that the JDA would go to Europe for the engine if American firms did not cooperate.

The Emergence of U.S. Pressure

By this point, U.S. companies were becoming aware of the Japanese strategy for kokusanka of FSX. Several defense contractors had been approached by the Japanese side to become consultants for a Japanese designed jet—a clear indication that importing was not being taken seriously as an option. The JDA's constantly shifting performance requirements for the jet, and the bluff about cooperating with European corporations, further raised the ire of U.S. companies. Realizing that normal marketing efforts would yield no results against such determination, General Dynamics and McDonnell Douglas petitioned the U.S. Departments of Commerce, State, and Defense to put pressure on the Japanese to buy FSX from a U.S. company.[7]

The Reagan administration was not prepared to start a new trade dispute over the FSX issue, but the Pentagon did have other ways to satisfy U.S. industry by putting quiet pressure on the JDA. In the June 1985 U.S.-Japan defense summit meeting, Secretary of Defense Caspar Weinberger asked Katō directly if Japan had already chosen domestic production of FSX. Katō responded that such a possibility was strong. Weinberger accepted that answer and offered to provide information and a history of American experience with indigenous development.[8] The Japanese side was relieved—FSX had passed its first international political test. JDA officials, the *Asahi Shimbun* pointed out, had not forgotten the case of the PXL. And by comparison to that episode, FSX now seemed immune from foreign pressure. There was reason to believe that the kokusanka line had been preserved.

However, Weinberger's seemingly innocuous offer to "provide information" soon proved to be far more potent than the advocates of kokusanka had initially realized. Within weeks of the Weinberger-Katō meeting, some U.S. officials were using the pretense of "sharing information" to express their opposition to indigenous development of FSX to the JDA—and more ominously from Japanese industry's perspective—to the *Asahi Shimbun*.[9] Sensing that a first-class fight was brewing, the Japanese press began an attempt to force each agency in Tokyo to clarify its position on FSX. A tapestry of panic and chaos spread across the front pages of the major papers in the ensuing weeks. A JDA source, spooked by the sudden U.S. pressure, told the *Nikkei Shimbun* that "the importance of interoperability" had to be remembered and revealed inadvertently that the European option had never been serious.[10] In response, TRDI and industry sources warned the *Yomiuri Shimbun* that turning away from kokusanka of FSX would "close the route towards a 'rising sun' jet forever."[11] Katō would only tell the press that ultimately *he* would make the decision on FSX "based on defense policy, fairness, and effectiveness." It was not at all clear what this meant, but it certainly did not sound like good news for industry. Initial impressions of Weinberger's position had been wrong. The FSX decision was moving up the decision-making ladder too quickly and too loudly.

The momentum against kokusanka expanded most significantly in October 1985, when the Mutual Defense Assistance Office (MDAO) of the U.S. Embassy in Tokyo sent a cable back to Washington advocating a policy of joint development. Once the U.S. side's preference for joint development was official, the Foreign Ministry began elevating *its* pressure against kokusanka. Throughout the months of October and November, the JDA was relying on the Ministry of Foreign Affairs to request information on the F-18, F-15, and Tornado from American and European sources and the Ministry used its liaison function to relay and amplify the anti-kokusanka sentiments of the U.S. side back to the JDA. "The Department of State and Defense's opposition to kokusanka is explicit," a Foreign Ministry source told the *Tokyo Shimbun* on November 5, "and MOFA wants no deepening of the trade friction because of this issue."[12]

By now U.S. and Foreign Ministry officials were openly challenging the ability of the JDA to domestically design and build the FSX. Initially, the advocates and opponents of kokusanka of FSX sparred over the issue of price. The U.S. side, following through on Weinberger's promise to provide "relevant information," released estimates that an indigenous FSX would cost Japan $18 million. The information the Pentagon shared, in other words, was that FSX was too expensive a project for Japan to attempt on its own. TRDI counter-punched. The U.S. estimates were mistaken by as much as 20 percent, they claimed, and possibly more. TRDI's numbers were suspect, of course, based as they were on pre-Louvre Accord exchange rates (making imports appear more expensive), and on the best possible scenario for licensed production of the jet's engine.[13] Nevertheless, the U.S. estimate failed to take into account the cost to Japan of maintaining black-boxed technology. For Japan's internal debate, then, the cost issue was a draw, particularly since JDA had been willing to spend three times the price of imports in the past. The question of importing-versus-autonomous development would be decided by other issues.

"Peacock-like Tails Over Mitsubishi":[14] The T-4 Trainer and TRDI's New Confidence

TRDI's strongest argument for kokusanka eventually came in the area not of price but of technology. At the height of the abstract debate internally and with U.S. officials over Japan's ability to sustain an autonomous jet fighter program, KHI rolled the first XT-4 (trainer jet) prototypes off the production lines of its Gifu assembly plant. The XT-4 was Japan's first computer-assisted "design-to-cost" aircraft. The jet was finished on time, meeting or surpassing all mission specifications, and—as TRDI officials never tired of telling visiting journalists—at one-fifth the cost of the United States' aborted T-46 trainer project. Japan's technological prowess was suddenly visible for all to see.

Equally important in the context of the FSX debate, the XT-4 was a successful example of TRDI bringing all of Japan's individual defense technological strengths at the subsystems level, or "trees," into an integrated system, or "forest." The XT-4 was designed around Ishikawajima Harima's indigenous XF-3 turbofan engine; the first all-Japanese production turbofan, a fact that weakened any leverage that the United States had over the FSX decision based on Japanese reliance on American jet engine technology. Moreover, the XT-4 boasted a significant proportion of composite materials (4.5 percent by weight), which vindicated the ongoing TRDI work on carbon fibers for the FSX.[15]

Yet while the XT-4 had Japanese officials strutting around like peacocks, American observers were far less impressed with the implications of the trainer jet for Japanese autonomy on FSX development. The XT-4 represented the state-of-the-art in intermediate trainer design, but U.S. officials understood well the enormous gap between fighters and trainers—and between Japan's F-3 engine and a front-line fighter jet engine of the type produced by General Electric or Pratt & Whitney. MITI officials' claims that "slapping a ramjet engine on the XF-3 would be no problem" did not have much impact with knowledgeable Americans.[16] The high proportion of U.S. avionics in the XT-4 also weakened the autonomy argument from the perspective of U.S. officials.

The real difference in how U.S. and Japanese observers interpreted the impact of the XT-4 on FSX, however, came from the differences in each side's definition of technological autonomy. No Japanese aircraft or system was truly indigenous in the sense that U.S. experts considered an F-15 or F-16 indigenous. The definition of indigenous design for TRDI and industry came in terms of comparison to the *previous* generation's system in Japan. By this definition, the XT-4 was clearly a fully indigenous program when compared to the T-2. But was it truly "independent" from U.S. defense technology? This question went unanswered by the Japanese side. For the Americans, the answer was clearly "no."

The SH-X: Codevelopment Versus Coproduction

The differences in U.S. and Japanese interpretations of the "autonomy" of the XT-4 and its implications for FSX also reflected the entirely different interpretation each side had made of the emerging defense technology relationship of the 1980s. This difference was most clearly demonstrated in the U.S.-Japanese disagreement over the SH-X antisubmarine helicopter in late 1985 and early 1986.[17]

The SH-X was, according to the JDA and the Maritime Self-Defense Forces, a kokusanka project. In fact, however, the SH-X was little more than the famous U.S. SH-60 Seahawk with a new name. The physical similarities to the SH-60 were difficult for the JDA to deny, of course, but the agency claimed that the inside of the helicopter did indeed contain indigenous technology. U.S. officials soon realized, however, that the "indigenous" technological innards were all being license-produced from the original U.S. subcontractors to the SH-60 program. In short, as one U.S. Embassy official summarized, "the kokusanka of SH-X was pure *tatemae* [pretend]."

Thus, on the eve of the FSX crisis, the two governments debated the definition of the SH-X. Was it a kokusanka project or not? For the Japanese side, the difference was extremely important. *Coproduction* of the SH-60 meant licensed production with a Memorandum of Understanding (MOU) that obliged Japanese industry to report all new technological developments, prevented quick and simple repairs in Japan, and carried an expensive processing charge to the Defense Security Assistance Agency of the Pentagon. On the other hand, *codevelopment*—or recognition of the project as Japanese-led—would allow Japanese industry to depart from the original American system where appropriate, experimenting freely with the spinning-on of indigenous Japanese technology, and, of course, not having to work through the U.S. defense bureaucracy, with its numerous restrictions and surcharges. In short, codevelopment would allow Japan to proceed with the *modus operandi* for bilateral defense technology relations as the Japanese had interpreted them in the late 1970s through meidai kenkyū and comprehensive security: that is, defense technology collaboration—but *with Japan controlling its own technological destiny.*

The U.S. side, in contrast, saw Japan's SH-X as nothing more than an attempt to claim that an American-designed system was not American. At its most benevolent, the pretense of kokusanka of the SH-X was viewed by U.S. policymakers as a foolish appeal to Japanese pride. At the other extreme, however, the SH-X was taken as evidence of Japanese duplicity. The Japanese side expected the easy access to technology of the past based on the imagined technological superiority of the future, and the Americans would not allow it. The U.S. Embassy's Mutual Defense Assistance Office eventually insisted upon, and received, an MOU on the SH-60—an explicit recognition that the SH-X was not a true kokusanka program nor even a codevelopment program.

The implications of the SH-X episode for the kokusanka of FSX were ominous. Nevertheless, TRDI officials remained confident that the new fighter would be developed essentially as a kokusanka project. The FSX had the long history of the F-1 behind it, the T-4 added weight to the case for kokusanka of jet fighters, and the FSX was going to be further removed in design from U.S. jets than the SH-X had been from the SH-60.

U.S. officials, on the other hand, were now determined that the FSX not go through the same ambiguous development that the SH-X had. The SH-X experience taught them that an MOU for FSX would have to be obtained, regardless of Secretary Weinberger's policy of nonpressure. But these officials also recognized that the autonomous development of the F-1 did give the JDA a strong case for kokusanka of FSX. Licensed production along the lines of the SH-60 would not be appropriate in the case of FSX. Instead, MDAO officials spoke of "coproduction plus," a new arrangement that would lead to the kind of equal partnership in defense industrial collaboration that the NATO countries enjoyed with the United States. With such an arrangement, the FSX project would finally add clarity to the defense technology cooperation regime that the United States had attempted to introduce with the first Systems and Technology Forum in 1980.

The Pentagon Proposes Joint Development

The Pentagon took this idea to the Japanese side on January 15, 1986, at the annual U.S.-Japan Security Consultation Committee meeting in Hawaii. During a break in the proceedings, U.S. Assistant Secretary of Defense for

International Security Affairs Richard Armitage unofficially proposed code-velopment of FSX to his Japanese counterparts.[18] The Japanese participants in the meetings no doubt received the proposal with shocked silence. It was left out of all official reports of the meetings and afterward JDA officials continued to insist to the press that the only options for FSX were importing or domestic development, with the latter more likely.[19]

Nevertheless, the intention of the Pentagon was unmistakable. What had once been hints from low-level officials and warnings from the Foreign Ministry had now come at the JDA in the form of a proposal that could not be ignored. As the director of International Security Affairs, Richard Armitage was the strongest protector the U.S.-Japan alliance had in the Pentagon. If he proposed codevelopment, the alternatives that might emerge from other parts of the U.S. government had to be worse from Japan's perspective. Indeed, the JDA was aware by January that the Secretary of Defense's industry advisory board, DPAC, had formed a Japan Committee with the specific intent of lobbying against the FSX project. FSX had taken one more step toward being decided in the highly politicized context of autonomy versus alliance.

For several months after the Hawaii meeting, the JDA was successful in containing and muffling the U.S. proposal for joint development. The idea leaked, however, at the March 12 Budget Committee hearings of the Upper House of Japan's Diet, when a member of the Democratic Socialist Party unleashed the following question on JDA Defense Bureau Director Nishihiro Seiki:

> Is it not true that in addition to the choice of importing and the choice of domestic development, there is also the choice of joint development?

Nishihiro's response, and thus the JDA's indirect response to the Armitage proposal, was to swallow the idea of joint development into the original plan for autonomous development:

> Yes, [there is the choice of joint development] but is that not also a form of domestic development?[20]

The transfer of U.S. technology was essential to the indigenous development of FSX, whether the transfer was labeled as joint development, coproduction, or nothing at all. Nishihiro was drawing a new line in the sand: as long as domestic development remained the guiding principal for FSX, Japan did not have to concede to U.S. demands for MOU's or flowback technology transfers.

And yet the original JDA/TRDI goal of pure kokusanka of FSX was now in jeopardy. Nishihiro's revelation in the Budget Committee hearing demonstrated clearly that Weinberger's promise to provide information was an open door for pressure. For its part, the Pentagon continued to insist that the United States had placed no pressure for joint development and that the decision on FSX was Japan's alone. But the pressure was obvious when JDA sources revealed to the press on March 16 that the decision on FSX would be postponed by one to two years and that the ASDF F-4 Phantoms would be upgraded to provide continuity (*tsunagi*) until the delayed FSX program came on-line.[21] The U.S. idea of codevelopment was further locked into place by Weinberger during his April 3–6 visit to Tokyo, where he designated subordinates in the Pentagon to exchange further information on codevelopment of FSX after he left.[22] An internal JDA account of the meeting claims only that Weinberger reaffirmed that "FSX was Japan's choice" and that Katō proposed cooperation on "information exchange," a repeat of his position in the last defense summit meeting.[23] However, the significance of continued "information exchange" was clear.

For the JDA, MITI, and industry, the key to maintaining kokusanka of FSX was now to contain U.S. involvement (the proposal for joint development) without exposing the Japanese commitment to the original idea of autonomous development. Thus through the spring, summer, and fall of 1986, the JDA changed its tactics—sending technical assessment teams to the United States to examine the F-16 and the F-18 and to Europe to see the Tornado—but retained its strategic goal of kokusanka of FSX.

When a joint MITI-JDA survey team to the United States in June picked up signals that the Pentagon and U.S. industry would push more aggressively for joint development than originally thought, the JDA responded by dispatching a team under TRDI Director-General Tsutsui Ryōzō to conduct a feasibility study. Despite this development, however, officials in JDA and TRDI remained confident that the growing U.S. pressure did not have to compromise the original plan for kokusanka. The jet could remain a Japanese project with total Japanese control of the systems integration and design. The strongest believer in this was probably Tsutsui himself. He had presided over the successful development of the T-4 and the various technological components such as CCV that were expected to make the FSX unique, and he intended to manage the development of the FSX as well.

Tsutsui arrived in the United States in December prepared to argue his case. Educated at the University of Maryland, he was perhaps too direct and honest in revealing his agency's intention of pursuing joint development as only tatemae and indigenous development as the *honne* (true substance). He touted the technological accomplishments of the T-4 and other TRDI-developed systems and technologies to U.S. officials and appeared dismissive of U.S. defense technology. Tsutsui reported to the JDA that the U.S. side understood his position.[24] However, U.S. officials found his attitude "maddening"[25] and saw in Tsutsui's bravado signs of the same JDA planning that had led to the disagreement over the SH-X. In the end, the Tsutsui mission proved to be a major setback for the advocates of kokusanka in Japan. The Pentagon rejected the subtle balancing act that the JDA was attempting. Joint development was not the same as kokusanka, and if Tsutsui and the JDA were describing kokusanka, they would have to accept the political consequences. The U.S. position on joint development of FSX was now immobile.

For the Japanese government, this changed the equation entirely. The hardening of the Pentagon's position in the wake of the Tsutsui trip meant that Weinberger's claims of "nonpressure" were now irrelevant. The Americans, it was clear, could play the game of tatemae and honne as well. And their honne was that autonomous development of FSX would lead to political problems in the alliance. The JDA began making it clear to the press and the U.S. side that joint development of FSX would now be given greater consideration.[26] Tsutsui, under pressure from the new JDA director-general, Kurihara Yūkō, also recommended, in his official trip report to the National Security Council of Japan on December 26, that the JDA proceed with joint development. The NSC concurred by officially dropping *kokunai kaihatsu* (domestic development) as its policy for FSX, and replacing it with *kaihatsu* (development) alone.[27] As part of the same decision, the NSC gave the JDA until the following winter to make a decision on FSX. After a year of diplomatic feints and dodges, the JDA was forced to drop pure kokusanka as an option.

Industry Digs In and the U.S. Senate Takes Aim

By this time Japan's defense industry began to recognize the familiar patterns of erosion in its consensus for kokusanka. The Defense Production Committee had been lobbying extensively for autonomous development but had lost ground in the face of the Pentagon's hardening position and the intense lobbying effort of McDonnell Douglas, maker of the F-18.[28] With the NSC decision to drop domestic development as an option for FSX, the parallels to the earlier loss of the PXL became too strong to ignore. The Defense Production Committee had analyzed the PXL case in its internal 1974 study.

They knew from that experience that a stronger case had to be made for retaining as much of the original commitment to kokusanka as possible.

In order to make that case, Mitsubishi Heavy Industries, Kawasaki Heavy Industries, Fuji Heavy Industries, Ishikawajima Harima, and Mitsubishi Electric formed the FSX Private Sector Joint Research Group (FSX Minkan gōdō kenkyū kai) in January 1987. The group's first public findings on FSX came in a statement to the JDA the next month urging autonomous development. The early report was timed to immediately precede the presentations of General Dynamics and McDonnell Douglas to the JDA.[29] The group argued that superior Japanese cost and quality control and new systems such as CCV developed through TRDI gave Japanese industry a distinct advantage over U.S. companies. And ultimately, the group asserted in its statement, one trillion yen in Japanese taxpayers' money should be spent in a manner that assisted Japanese industry. The industry group acknowledged that U.S. participation in FSX would be important but insisted that it be in the form of technology transfers for the engine and fire control systems rather than in the form of equal joint development.[30] The most important goal was to assure that the prime contractor and designer remain Japanese.

The JDA made no official response to industry's proposal, but unofficially fissures within the agency began to show. The Internal Bureau was clearly leaning toward joint development with the United States, reflecting in part its susceptibility to influence from the Pentagon and the relative importance its officials placed on the alliance. TRDI, in contrast, was much more sympathetic to the industry group proposal. The Institute had worked closely with the five members of the industry group to develop the technologies that both claimed would make an indigenous FSX competitive with any U.S. design. The Air Self-Defense Force staff, which had developed the mission requirements for FSX with an indigenous design in mind, also had a preference for kokusanka along the lines proposed by industry, although its pilots generally preferred getting an American jet so they would not have to wait.[31]

On balance then, the five-member industry group had some reason for confidence that it could partially reverse the tide that had been growing against kokusanka. By the standards of the PXL experience, they had made a strong and persuasive lobbying effort for kokusanka. Inspired, the head of research for the group told the press:

> We will be able to show you an inexpensive FSX that can fly in only four or five years and have technology far past anything the Americans or Soviets have![32]

Unfortunately for Japanese industry, however, the explosiveness of the FSX issue inside the U.S. political system could not even be measured by the standards of PXL and the 1970s.

For the U.S. Congress the FSX decision was symbolically and substantively linked to an ever expanding list of bilateral trade and technology problems with Japan. In 1986 Japan's trade deficit with the United States broke its own record, prompting the Congress to begin work on the Omnibus Trade Bill. The planned purchase of Fairchild, a leading U.S. semiconductor company with substantial defense contract experience, by Fujitsu alerted Americans to the vulnerability of their own defense industrial base to dependence on Japanese technology. Surging Japanese investment as the dollar declined in value suggested that Fairchild would only be the first strategic industry to fall. The list could easily be expanded to include friction over U.S. bidding on construction projects for the Kansai International Airport, cellular telephones, oranges and beef, supercomputers, Japan's failure to honor the semiconductor agreement (which led to $300 million in retaliatory tariffs), and Japanese reluctance to participate in international naval protection for Western shipping in the Persian Gulf.

The cause and effect between these bilateral trade issues and U.S. anger over the FSX decision was brought home for the Japanese Government in March when Senator John Danforth (R-Missouri) sent a semi-public letter to President Reagan arguing strongly against indigenous Japanese development of FSX.[33] Danforth's home state contained the corporate headquarters of both General Dynamics and McDonnell Douglas. U.S. officials had been aware that the Danforth letter was forthcoming since the time of the December 1986 Tsutsui mission; it was one explanation for the Pentagon's growing frustration with Tsutsui's position. Now the Japanese side would get full body contact directly from the U.S. Congress.

The Danforth letter was followed immediately by a series of sharp blows to Japan over related trade and defense issues. On April 13 Weinberger sent a tersely worded letter to JDA Director-General Kurihara Yūkō protesting the export of sensitive technology to the Soviet Union by the Tōshiba Machine Tool Company in violation of COCOM regulations. The Pentagon was angered because the high-technology sixteen-point machine tools would allow the Soviets to dramatically increase the quality and rate of production of super-silent submarine propellers. At the time Kurihara received Weinberger's communication, a Pentagon delegation under Deputy Assistant Secretary Gerald Sullivan was in Tokyo for another information exchange on FSX. More than any other U.S. official in the past, Sullivan pushed hard for joint development of FSX and even stated that the true preference in the Pentagon was for direct purchase off-the-shelf of a U.S. jet.[34] The Sullivan delegation was taken to Japanese research laboratories. They were impressed with certain programs, but left with the conviction that a Japanese-led design for FSX would be a failure. A week after Sullivan's delegation left Japan, Prime Minister Nakasone received a strongly worded letter from Republican Senator Robert Dole and Democratic Senators Robert Byrd and Lloyd Bentsen urging him to not pursue domestic development of the FSX.

Against this high-powered congressional barrage, the group of five Japanese defense contractors fired off an ineffectual volley in return, repeating their assertion to the JDA that their joint research demonstrated irrevocably that a domestically designed FSX would be superior.[35] The members of the joint research group were, in fact, sharing technological information to an unprecedented degree in order to strengthen their case, and Prime Minister Nakasone had guaranteed that the FSX decision would be made on the advice of the technical experts, free of political or trade concerns.[36] The issue was clearly no longer one that could be solved by claiming technological prowess, however. The durability of the alliance was at question and the American side did not believe Japanese technological claims. Moreover, within industry's old ally, MITI, there was growing concern that domestic development of this one jet might have to be sacrificed in order to quell the fires now raging bilaterally over Fujitsū, semiconductors, and now—perhaps most dangerous of all—the Tōshiba incident.

Any doubts that FSX was now a decision bearing fully on the alliance were erased by Prime Minister Nakasone's trip to Washington on April 30 for a summit meeting with President Reagan. The U.S. president did not raise the issue of FSX, but U.S. senators, including Danforth, did. For the first time, the prime minister understood the depth of the political problem. The same politician who had argued for autonomy first and alliance second as JDA director-general almost two decades earlier, now gave his own cabinet's JDA director-general, Kurihara Yūkō, strict instructions that the FSX issue not be allowed to cause damage to the alliance.[37]

For Japanese industry, it was time for a change of tactics. In May the five-member industry research group came out in support of joint development of FSX. "All the Japanese companies had a strong desire for indigenous development," MHI President Iida Ryōtarō told the *Nikkei Shimbun*, "but I myself have a long experience of technology cooperation with U.S. industry, and understand that we simply could not build this alone if we tried to shed the United States."[38] Not only had the FSX debate elevated to the level of alliance

politics, alliance politics had now come around to threaten industry's original technological ambitions. For all the talk of autonomous development,
after all, industry and TRDI had planned from the beginning to leapfrog from
the T-1 to the twenty-first-century generation of fighter support technology
by basing the FSX on an existing U.S. jet and even more so on an existing U.S.
engine. The rising friction over FSX threatened to deprive industry of much
of the technology it required to build FSX as originally planned.

But if industry was willing to make a concession on autonomous development, it was still not willing to abandon the principle of "Japanese-led"
joint development.[39] All previous examples of coproduction had been
worked through the Pentagon with U.S. leadership, under U.S. laws, and
with fees paid to the U.S. government. Iida and others in industry argued
that with this trillion-yen project the Japanese must take the lead. Industry's
proposal resonated within the JDA. In fact, Japanese-led joint development
was emerging as the consensus position in the special joint JASDF/Internal
Bureau committee established by Kurihara in March to consider the various
options for FSX before the NSC imposed deadline expired at the end of the
year.[40] Within the LDP's Defense Division, Japanese-led joint development
also proved to be the most workable compromise among the nationalists,
hawks, and proalliance members who now made up the defense zoku.

On June 28 and 29 Weinberger and Kurihara held a series of meetings on
bilateral defense issues in Tokyo. For the first time Weinberger explicitly proposed either direct import of a U.S. jet or joint development of FSX, based on
the F-15, F-16, or F-18. Kurihara, in response, proposed joint development of
an entirely new FSX. Neither side agreed on how to proceed, except to say that
Kurihara would continue the discussion in Washington in September.[41]

Events in the U.S. Congress now began to accelerate faster than the JDA or
the Pentagon's ability to respond, however. The day after the Kurihara-
Weinberger summit ended, the Senate passed 92 to 5 an amendment to the
trade bill that would have put punitive measures on Tōshiba (the amendment was later withdrawn after heavy lobbying by Tōshiba and its industrial allies in the United States). In July Senators Byrd and Danforth introduced
a "sense of the Senate" resolution into the trade bill calling on Japan to buy
fighters from American companies. This amendment passed 96 to 0. And
throughout the month (and for that matter, ever since) Japanese television
stations repeatedly broadcast the scene of a small group of U.S. congressional representatives bashing Tōshiba radios with sledgehammers.

Against this pressure, the idea of Japanese-led joint development seemed
in as much peril as kokusanka had been the year before. Kurihara, in keep-

ing with his instructions from Nakasone, informed the LDP Defense Division that "greater attention would have to be paid to the U.S. position on FSX."[42] Even MITI had come around solidly in favor of joint development based on an existing U.S. jet, dispatching the director of the Aircraft and Ordinance Division (industry's closest ally within the ministry) to push this position on MHI and the other leading defense contractors. At his October 2 meeting with Weinberger, (rescheduled from September) Kurihara agreed that FSX would be based on joint development of an existing U.S. jet. An elated Senator Danforth broke the news at a press conference, calling the move "a major positive development that could presage a turning point in U.S.-Japan relations."[43]

Now the question was: which jet? JDA sources told the *Mainichi Shimbun* that the U.S. preferred the F-15E.[44] The *Washington Post* reported that the JDA preferred the F-18.[45] The *Wall Street Journal* reported that the F-15 and F-16 were leading contenders.[46] One thing was clear: MHI and the industry joint research group preferred the F-18 and stated so in a report prepared after visiting the United States to examine all of the candidates.[47]

On October 21, in a move that probably surprised the executives at General Dynamics more than anyone else and proved all previous press reports wrong, the JDA announced that the FSX would be based on GD's F-16. The reasons given in internal JDA documents were that the F-16, despite its perceived potential for accidents over the densely populated Japanese islands (it had only one engine and GD had refused to change the design of the plane to add a second), the jet was cheapest and left the most room for adding on the indigenous technologies developed by TRDI and Japanese industry. The F-15, according to the JDA document, was impressive technologically but was too expensive. The F-18 was also rejected as too expensive and dangerous.[48]

There were other reasons that might explain the choice of the F-16 as well. McDonnell Douglas, according to JDA and DOD officials, was inflexible, even arrogant, in its negotiating style. The company had abruptly canceled a meeting in April with the JDA to discuss the F-18, claiming—according to JDA sources—that it was concerned about losing valuable defense secrets.[49] The agency's officials were incensed. Then, perhaps because the F-18 was the known choice of industry, MD insisted on doing any modifications to the airframe itself, at a cost of $1.8 billion.[50] This would have deprived Japanese industry of the experience in systems integration and the opportunity to incorporate special Japanese technologies into the design of FSX. TRDI and industry had already decided to incorporate CCV and phased array radar into the FSX. This meant that the airframe had to have sufficient volume to install and integrate new electronics. The F-16 had more room inside than the F-18, meaning that in both spatial and contractual terms, GD could be more accommodating than McDonnell Douglas. This fact was no doubt reflected in industry's immediate announcement after the selection of the F-16 that GD's jet offered the most room for applying indigenous Japanese technology.[51] In the end, however, as one experienced program manager in the United States who observed FSX noted:

> Because source selection criteria are the most guarded secrets of any weapons systems management organization, ASDF and TRDI are unlikely to ever reveal why the F-16 was chosen.[52]

Crisis Delayed (and Denied): The First MOU

With the selection of the F-16 and the decision to open bilateral negotiations over an MOU to cover joint development, the FSX cleared its first major hurdle. As with the PXL in the previous decade, a compromise had been struck within MITI, the JDA, the LDP, and the ASDF that balanced each institution's broader dependence on smooth alliance relations with the narrower agenda within each institution (in TRDI, the Aircraft and Ordnance Division of MITI, and the hawkish wing of the LDP, for example) for technological autonomy. The compromise on FSX was not achieved without friction and a considerable degree of ill will toward the United States, of course, but even with the abandonment of the original plan for kokusanka, industry could still protect the same general trajectory it had anticipated in terms of technological development.

Industry leaders in Japan were now telling the JDA that joint development was acceptable. According to the chairman of the Society of Japanese Aerospace Companies, "Thinking of the importance of U.S.-Japan Relations and the effective maintenance of the alliance, proceeding with joint development with the United States is most appropriate."[53] Another official noted that, given COCOM and trade friction, industry was lucky to have avoided demands for an off-the-shelf purchase of a U.S. aircraft.[54] U.S. Senator Danforth had also praised the decision to move to joint development, and the protectors of the alliance within the Pentagon and the State Department were congratulating their Japanese colleagues on having moved the FSX issue from a political problem threatening the alliance to a technological problem for engineers.

The point remained, however, that FSX was a political problem precisely because it *was* a technological problem. For decades the political/military caretakers of the alliance in the Pentagon, the State Department, and the U.S. National Security Council and in Japan had kept the bilateral relationship strong by moving trade and technological disputes out of the political arena. This was no longer possible, as both sides would soon learn.

The vague definition of joint development was at the core of the problem. There was no previous model of such cooperation on which to build, and thus each side returned to the experiences they had left behind in the 1970s. For the Pentagon, this meant coproduction, an impression reinforced by the JDA's decision to work on an existing U.S. airframe as had been the case when PXL was dropped for the P-3C. Thus the Defense Security Assistance Agency (DSAA) was given the lead, in part because it fell within the policy side of the Pentagon dominated by Assistant Secretary Armitage, who had pushed joint development in the first place, but also because that agency had responsibility for all licensed production arrangements. DSAA was an agency used to dealing with technological inferiors, however, not creating partnerships for developing new systems.

The impression of the Japanese side, in contrast, was represented by veteran aerospace analyst Sekigawa Eiichi, who claimed that "in the end 80 percent of the FSX will be Japanese."[55] Industry assumed that joint production now bought political protection for pushing ahead with as much kokusanka as possible. Throughout the negotiations with the U.S. side, Japanese officials and engineers stressed that leadership and initiative on the project would be Japanese. As GD President Herbert Rogers told the U.S. Congress, "the Japanese jacked up the radiator cap and drove [their own indigenous] airplane under it."[56] Even as GD and MHI engineers began meeting in December and the new JDA director-general Tawara Kichiro agreed with Secretary of Defense Carlucci in January to move to negotiation on an MOU, the JDA was putting in place all the pieces to make FSX an indigenously led project, including the establishment of an official FSX office within TRDI.[57]

The two sides' different interpretations of joint development emerged as negotiations opened on the MOU from the middle of February to the end of November. Where the Pentagon reportedly insisted on 40 percent U.S. work share at the development stage and 30 percent at the production stage, the JDA responded that such a promise was impossible to make until development actually began.[58] In fact, the Japanese side was quite surprised by the U.S. request. When the United States then insisted that it be allowed to use flowback technology without restrictions (i.e., Japanese technology in the

FSX be treated as only modifications to the basic F-16 design and therefore accessible to the DOD), the JDA was again taken by surprise. Under pressure to show progress by the Tawara-Carlucci defense summit scheduled for June, however, the JDA agreed to the general thrust of the U.S. position. With the beginning of a solution in place, the two sides then entered another difficult six months of negotiation and finally initialed an MOU on November 29, 1988.

The contents of the MOU remained secret at the request of the Japanese government, but various reports suggest that the agreement had the following key points:

1. Six prototypes would be built (2 in the United States);
2. The U.S. side would receive a 35–45 percent share;
3. Engines were put off for later consideration;
4. The U.S. side would have access through the JMTC to new Japanese technology such as gallium arcenide chips, co-cured composite wings (especially attractive to GD, which lagged behind its American competitors in this technology), and phased array radar.[59]

DoD officials believed that they had turned an already strong arrangement for the U.S. military into an even more technologically and financially lucrative agreement. Yet the JDA managed to build into the agreement specific mechanisms to obtain the technological advantages its industry desired, while the mechanisms for transferring technology to U.S. industry remained vague and untested. Rumblings of dissatisfaction emerged in the United States as the Congress roused to weigh back into the FSX dispute.

The Second Explosion

One Japanese journalist who followed the FSX crisis closely has called it "the most unfortunate coincidence of bad luck in the history of postwar U.S.-Japan relations."[60] That the continuing ambiguity over joint development led to a second clash over FSX was a matter of bad policy—not bad luck. But the timing of that clash was arguably the worst it could have been.

In January 1989 the new Bush administration was attempting to push its cabinet appointees through a Democratic Congress infuriated by a particularly mean-spirited presidential election. Those Pentagon officials who had nurtured and protected the U.S.-Japan alliance in the Reagan years—men like the desk officer for Japan in ISA, Jim Auer, and his boss, Richard Armitage—were now gone, and President Bush's choice for a new secretary of defense, Texas Senator John Tower, was debilitated by scandal. In their absence, the Commerce Department and the Congress had increased their influence on international arms agreements with added help from the 1988 Defense Authorization Act, which required the Pentagon to consult with the Department of Commerce on the economic consequences of coproduction agreements such as FSX (the Congress had introduced this amendment in frustration over FSX).[61] The Congress's anti-FSX quiver was further stocked by a disgruntled former official in MDAO who had moved to the staff of Senator Jesse Helms, armed with reams of documents on the FSX negotiations fresh from the U.S. Embassy in Tokyo. This combination of occurrences can only be described as bad luck.

Helms struck first, using the confirmation hearings of Secretary of State-designate James Baker on January 17 to attack the FSX agreement. In the immediate wake of Helms's attack, the *Washington Post* published a widely influential OP/ED piece by former Commerce Department official Clyde Prestowitz that claimed that the FSX agreement would weaken U.S. competitiveness in aerospace manufacturing.[62] With the Pentagon leaderless, senior officials in the Department of Commerce and the office of the U.S. Trade Representative (USTR) increased their calls on President Bush not to submit the FSX agreement to Congress in its then-current form.

On March 20, President Bush announced that he would begin talks with Japan to clarify the FSX agreement. The reaction in Japan was one of shock and anger. Initially, JDA Director-General Tawara and a number of LDP politicians criticized the U.S. position. But the issue was a bleeding wound in the bilateral relationship, something which Nakasone's successor, Takeshita Noboru, could not afford, particularly since he was already mired in political scandal at home (the famous Recruit stock bribery scandal). Takeshita dispatched JDA Administrative Vice Minister Nishihiro to the United States and instructed his political protegé and Assistant Chief Cabinet Secretary, Ozawa Ichiro, to work out a compromise at home.

Takeshita announced his intention to resign over the Recruit scandal on April 24 and used his final days in office to assure that the FSX crisis was resolved before his successor took office. Under this pressure, the JDA had little choice but to accede to the U.S. demands. These were guaranteed 40 percent workshare; Japanese access to the fire control systems but not the commercially valuable flight control software; and a rejection of Japanese insistence on a 50 percent workshare of the engine. The JDA's Equipment Bureau director, in Washington from April 18 to 26, put the finishing touches on the deal before returning to Tokyo, and on April 28 President Bush announced the new MOU in a press conference.[63]

The congressional hurdle still remained, however, and on May 1 President Bush formally submitted the proposed FSX agreement to the Congress for approval. If not rejected within 30 days, the agreement would stand. Senate opponents of the deal pointed to a new General Accounting Office report that alleged that the composite wings and phased array radar technology the U.S. side was supposed to get from Japan in the FSX agreement were inferior to what U.S. industry had already developed.[64] On May 10 West Virginia Senator Robert Byrd introduced a bill that would have severely restricted even the now "clarified" transfer of U.S. technology, particularly relating to the engine, and would have put the FSX project under the partial oversight of the Commerce Department.

When the vote to block the FSX agreement came up on May 16, however, it was defeated 52 to 47. Many senators who supported the agreement were not enthusiastic, following Senator Danforth, who told the *Washington Post* that, while he wanted Japan to buy the F-16 off-the-shelf to help with the trade deficit, "it would be a mistake to pull the rug out from under the Bush administration" after it had tightened the agreement.[65] The Byrd Amendment was vetoed by President Bush later in the summer, and eventually this veto was sustained by a single vote.

In Japan, the political leadership—and especially the defense establishment—were exhausted and bitter. After this second clash over FSX, resentment toward the United States and the alliance ran deep. Japanese industry began launching its own attacks on the terms of joint development, insisting, for example, that the U.S. compensate Japan for the R&D costs of composite materials technology to be transferred to General Dynamics.[66] Eventually, the Japanese government settled this problem by offering to pay such licensing fees to industry itself. On February 21, 1990, Mitsubishi Heavy Industries and General Dynamics finally signed a contract to exchange technical teams and begin joint development of the FSX, after an eighteen-month delay filled with internal and bilateral political conflict. The MHI-GD exchange did not erase the anger, however. As a TRDI official told a Japanese reporter: "Maybe it would have been better if the Congress had done us a favor and just said 'no' to joint development [at the beginning]."[67]

6 | The Limits of Autonomy: The Shifting Defense Constituency in the FSX Debate

The political explosions over FSX illuminated the tensions between the unrelenting pursuit of kokusanka and the increased defense collaboration of the post-NDPO era. Defense spending had grown at 6 percent or more annually throughout the 1980s, but that spending was premised on closer bilateral defense ties to the United States. As a result, even as R&D budgets and indigenization of defense technology expanded, the traditional constituencies for kokusanka grew *more dependent* (rather than more autonomous) on the alliance framework for political legitimization. When fsx emerged as a threat to smooth alliance relations, MITI, the JDA, the JSDF, the LDP defense zoku, and even the defense industry were racked with internal division over the advantages of maintaining the kokusanka line.

FSX ended with a patchy consensus in Japan for joint development and a vague recognition that the future integrity of Japan's defense industrial base demanded some integration with the United States. In the years since FSX, the U.S. and Japanese governments have attempted a series of joint development projects at the subsystems level and the JDA has made a particular effort in its procurement practices to purchase major systems directly from the United States.

However, the FSX explosion did not break the kokusanka line entirely. In fact, for many in Japanese industry and government, the emergence of American technonationalism only deepened the conviction that self-reliance in defense technology should remain a long-term goal. How widespread this view might become is an open question. It will depend on U.S. actions and Japanese attitudes. The latter were profoundly affected by the FSX experience. We examine them in detail in this chapter.

Industry

As has been noted, the defense industry's first position on FSX was that the jet should be developed and produced autonomously—a *hinomaru* aircraft. Initially, at least, the leading contractors were better positioned in political and technological terms than they had been for either the T-2, the F-1, or the PXL. Moreover, autonomous development of the FSX was considered of vital importance to the future of the aerospace industry in general. FSX offered Japanese companies the opportunity to build an entire advanced jet aircraft—until then all of their experience had been with trainer aircraft (even the F-1 "support fighter" was only a slightly modified T-2 trainer). This in turn would be an important step toward developing the ability to build an autonomous candidate to succeed the F-4J and the F-15 in the late 1990s, possibly Japan's first front-line fighter aircraft. And finally, MHI and its subcontractors feared that without autonomous development the aircraft market would enter a slump in the mid-1990s, when the production runs of the F-15 and P3-C were scheduled to end. "If Japan does not get to build on its experiences with the F-1," executives of MHI noted ominously in 1989, "we will fall at least 15 years behind."[1]

After the experiences of the PXL and F-104, however, the defense industry also knew the limits of political support for kokusanka. Institutionally, this was symbolized in the Japan Ordnance Association's (*Nihon Heiki Kogyokai*) reorganization in September 1988 as the Japan Defense Equipment Industry Association (*Bōei Sōbi Kogyōkai*).[2] In contrast to the Ordnance Association's hard commitment to kokusanka, the new Japan Defense Equipment Industry Association took a broader approach to defense production in order to expand both its membership and support for the defense budget. In its founding charter the new association announced its intention to "strengthen the defense industrial base" by supporting research on defense equipment and technology and cooperating with the government on controlling sensi-

TABLE 6.1

Japan's Top Twenty Defense Contractors in 1991

Company	Share of Defense Contracts
Mitsubishi Heavy Industries, Ltd. (ships, military vehicles, aircraft, missiles)	25 percent
Kawasaki Heavy Industries, Ltd. (ships, aircraft)	10
Ishikawajima Harima Heavy Industries, Ltd. (ships, engines)	7.4
Mitsubishi Electric Corporation (electronics, missiles)	6.8
Tōshiba Corporation (electronics, missiles)	4.0
NEC Corporation (electronics)	3.4
Fuji Heavy Industries, Ltd. (aircraft)	2.3
The Japan Steel Works, Ltd. (small arms, ordnance)	1.9
Komatsu, Ltd. (small arms, ordnance, military vehicles)	1.6
Hitachi (electronics, military vehicles)	1.2
Oki Electric Industry Co., Ltd. (electronics)	1.2
Daikin Industries, Ltd. (small arms, ordnance)	1.1
Fujitsu, Ltd. (electronics)	1.1
Nissan Motor Co., Ltd. (aircraft, motor vehicles)	1.0
Cosmo Oil Co., Ltd. (oil)	0.9
Nippon Oil Co., Ltd. (oil)	0.8
Mitsubishi Precision Co., Ltd. (electronics)	0.8
Japan Electronic Computer Co. (electronics)	0.8
Hitachi Zosen Corporation (ships)	0.7
Nippon Koki, Co., Ltd. (small arms, ordnance)	0.7

tive technology transfers abroad (i.e., COCOM). This broader agenda reflected the needs of the changing membership of the original Japan Ordnance
Association: fifteen new corporations—most of them electronics firms—
had joined between 1986 and 1988. The establishment of a broader agenda in
turn attracted five other traditionally nondefense electronic firms to join the
new association in 1989.

As a result, Japan's largest defense industry association entered the FSX
debate with its eyes on much more than kokusanka alone. Firms motivated
by the COCOM issue had a particular interest in avoiding conflict with the
United States (and the fate of the Tōshiba Corporation). In addition, the new
electronics firms had much less of a stake in the indigenous development of
systems than the traditional "heavies" like MHI. Changes in the legal status of
the new industry association were important as well. By reconstituting itself
as a *shadanhojin* (nonprofit public corporation), the Japan Defense Equipment Industry Association was deliberately placing itself under the partial
supervision of the government, with former MITI and JDA officials on its
board for the first time. While this might suggest a closer relationship—and
thus more influence—on the government, the opposite was true. The association's activities and budget were now to be audited by the government
and its agenda on issues such as kokusanka subject to scrutiny and moderation by the government's own policy priorities.[3]

The transformation of the Japan Ordnance Association left only
Keidanren's Defense Production Committee as fully independent spokesman for the defense industry and kokusanka. But most of its members were
also in the new Japan Defense Equipment Industry Association. In addition,
other industry organizations emerged in the 1980s to moderate the traditional autonomous thrust of the defense contractors. One example was the
Asian Council (*Ajia-Hyogikai*), formed in 1979 to promote dialogue on
security issues in Asia among Japanese defense contractors, the government, and—strikingly—American defense contractors and diplomats.[4]
One defense executive noted of these changes in 1988, "it is good to lose the
glaring image associated with the name 'weapons.'"[5] In short, the consensus behind the comprehensive security concept and close defense cooperation with the United States of the early 1980s had broadened the constituency for defense, not only in society at large but within the defense
industry as well.

These changes in the defense industry's political organization led to a
greater flexibility in the FSX debate, but also exposed industry's political
weaknesses. When the JDA began to show signs of complying with U.S. pro-

posals for joint development in 1987, for example, the defense industry's Joint Study Group on FSX abandoned its agenda for autonomous production and, reading the level of political pressure from the U.S., shifted by September 1987 to a position of support for joint development. But industry's hopes that this flexibility would allow them to protect their original goals were dashed. The Joint Study Group's choice of the F-18 turned sour as McDonnell Douglas took increasingly intransigent positions on technology transfer, and the JDA eventually opted for the F-16 instead. Once the F-16 was chosen, industry's goal of "driving an indigenous jet under the hood" was again thwarted, an indication of how limited support for kokusanka had become beyond the immediate circle of MHI, KHI, IHI, FHI, and MELCO.

However, where the broadening of the defense industry's membership base may have diluted the traditional commitment to kokusanka in the first stage of FSX, it also served as a natural amplifier for the resentment against the United States that followed in the immediate wake of the Bush administration's "clarification" of the MOU in 1989. For thirty-five years the Defense Production Committee had released its statements on kokusanka without the general backing of Keidanren as a whole. On May 15, 1989, Keidanren spoke as one. In a statement drafted by the Defense Production Committee and approved for release by Keidanren's top leadership, Japan's powerful business organization called on the government to raise the level of kokusanka; increase spending on defense R&D; spend more on equipment and less on rear area items (i.e., logistics, base support, personnel); and build a large-scale jet engine testing center so that Japanese industry would never have to rely on foreign governments in fighter development programs again.[6] As *Asahi Shimbun* noted, "Japan's core business community has made its first ever endorsement of the domestic development of weapons."[7] From the jaws of political defeat on FSX, then, the defense industry snatched an important victory—though one too late to save kokusanka of FSX itself. The implications of this development will be examined in chapter 7.

The Defense Agency and the ASDF

Events in Washington also had a profound effect on the Defense Agency and the JSDF (in this case, especially the ASDF). Both the civilian and uniformed personnel of Japan's Defense Agency played a far more significant role in the FSX controversy than any of their predecessors had in the procurement debates analyzed earlier in this study. Against the background of the Soviet military build-up in the Far East, the national consensus for a stable Japanese defense build-up (evidenced, for example, by the lack of public reaction to the breaking of the 1 percent limit on defense spending in 1986); and the emphasis on "roles and missions" in defense relations with the United States, the JDA and JSDF staff brought increasing confidence to defense policy making.[8] In personnel matters as well, the JDA showed signs of evolving from its position of dependence on the Ministries of Finance, Foreign Affairs, and International Trade and Industry. The JDA's administrative vice minister at the time of FSX, Nishihiro Seiki, as has been noted, was the first vice minister to emerge from the ranks of the Internal Bureau and not from another ministry.

It was also Nishihiro who appeared in the front pages of the newspapers and on the television screens as Japan's point man for negotiating with the United States at the height of the FSX crisis. In part, Nishihiro's leading role was supported by MITI and MOF, because of their desire to present FSX to the Americans as a pure defense matter and not one of trade, technology, or politics.[9] But Nishihiro also was successful in establishing an autonomous JDA position on FSX, despite the presence of seconded MITI and MOF officials in his agency. This fact was demonstrated clearly in Nishihiro's stern statement to MITI that the JDA would no longer support the ministry's goal of using the defense budget to develop a commercial aircraft industry: "If FSX is vital to the euthanasia of the aerospace industry[,] that is one thing, but [even if FSX is developed autonomously], the next FX front line fighter cannot possibly be an indigenous project." By Nishihiro's admission, the JDA had cooperated in MITI's goal of creating products that would help the commercial aircraft industry, but "after the YS-11 . . . no more."[10]

Japan's uniformed services also developed a more authoritative voice in the 1980s. Particularly noteworthy is the fact that beginning in this period Self-Defense officers began briefing Finance Ministry budget officials directly on items in the defense budget.[11] Diet members also began approaching men in uniform directly, bypassing the civilian bureaucrats. And in personnel matters the first graduates of the postwar National Defense Academy had begun to occupy top billets in the 1980s, bringing with them a newfound esprit de corps (although the civilian bureaucrats continued to hold the ultimate power in deciding military promotions).[12]

Greater institutional integrity in the JDA and a greater sense of military professionalism among uniformed personnel changed the dynamics of the kokusanka debate considerably. Where the political agenda of the civilian bureaucrats of the JDA led them to push for a moderation in kokusanka with FSX, however, senior ASDF officers stuck with indigenous development based on their own military logistical agenda (maintenance efficiency). The ASDF had been willing to make the shift to joint development in 1987 because it would enhance interoperability with U.S. forces and bring technological know-how to Japan. But the ASDF's primary concern in joint development was that Japan have a high enough ratio of kokusanka within the program to eliminate black boxes and dependence on the United States for repairs.[13] This led to a natural alliance between the senior ASDF staff and industry to fight for Japanese retention of the leading role of prime contractor and systems integrator for FSX; an alliance further cemented by the high number of former JSDF generals and admirals in the corporate headquarters of companies like MHI, a personnel link almost completely lacking with the Internal Bureau. TRDI also shared with industry and the ASDF the goal of maintaining Japanese technological leadership on FSX. The Institute's engineers were particularly interested in basing the jet on the F-18, because that airframe would give the most room for integrating indigenous Japanese technologies such as CCV, composite wings, and phased array radar.

Ultimately, however, the defense establishment's position on FSX does not break into a neat pattern of TRDI and ASDF for kokusanka, and the JDA Internal Bureau against it. Crosscurrents confused the issue. The ASDF, for example, disagreed with TRDI and industry over the choice of the F-18. It was, after all, a U.S. Navy jet that ASDF pilots considered inferior to the U.S. Air Force's F-15 and F-16, and the ASDF had close relations with the U.S. Air Force. TRDI, in turn, was not in a position to disregard the political agenda of the Internal Bureau. Tsutsui himself was under the direct command of Nishihiro. As a result, the defense professionals were able to bring a greater element of "military realism" to the FSX debate, but lacked the institutional critical mass to push the decision decisively for or against kokusanka.

In addition, the conflict with the United States over FSX put the JDA and ASDF in a bureaucratic position with which they were almost completely unfamiliar. Throughout the 1980s the JDA and JSDF had developed leverage vis-à-vis MITI, MOFA, and MOF by utilizing information and pressure provided by the Pentagon and the U.S. services. With FSX, the defense bureaucrats were expected to represent Japan in tough negotiations. Other ministries such as MOFA and MITI had to fill the gap. As one MOFA official who played a central role in the FSX negotiations complained:

> The JDA did not have the legal, diplomatic, linguistic or economic policy skills to appreciate what it was doing when negotiating the Memorandum of Understanding with the United States. They were like the mythical figure *songokū* dancing frenetically out on the palm of Buddha's hand.[14]

Moreover, after years of political protection by the U.S. Departments of State and Defense from the acrimony that often surrounds U.S.-Japan trade disputes, the JSDF was ill-prepared for the intensity of the congressional attacks over FSX and the specific demands from DOD for guaranteed work share and technology flow-back provisions in the MOU.

The result was the JDA's capitulation to U.S. demands for tightening the MOU in the final days of the Takeshita administration in April 1989. Unequipped to maintain the integrity of its position internally without U.S. support and lacking a common institutional position on kokusanka, the JDA and ASDF ultimately had little choice but to follow the prime minister's emphasis on maintaining smooth alliance relations.

JDA and ASDF officials would take different lessons away from this experience. For some it was a reminder of the agency's painful lessons from the Fourth Defense Plan: avoid politicization of alliance relations at all costs. For others, however (particularly in the services), FSX reinforced the importance of maintaining indigenous sources of technology whenever possible. The JDA/JSDF consensus formed around the commitment to interoperability and joint development of weapons. But the undercurrents of autonomy continue.

MITI

The most important shift in positions on kokusanka in the FSX controversy took place within the Ministry of International Trade and Industry. As the case study in chapter 3 of the Fourth Defense Plan indicated, MITI's support for kokusanka of PXL changed when autonomous production was determined to be a threat to the ministry's larger agenda for trade and industrial policy. In the case of FSX, as well, the ministry's strong initial support for kokusanka evaporated when the autonomous development of the jet turned into a major trade dispute between the United States and Japan.

In part, MITI's shift in positions reflected an escalation of attention to FSX within the ministry that paralleled the politicization of the jet's development bilaterally. When FSX deteriorated from a technical problem to a trade problem in 1987, it moved from the Aircraft and Ordnance Division to the broader jurisdiction of the Machinery and Information Bureau, the International Trade Policy Bureau, and the Minister's Secretariat. There the political and technological costs and benefits of pursuing autonomous development of FSX were weighed against a variety of other trade and technological issues plaguing the bilateral relationship. Japan was hit in March 1987 with $300 million in retaliatory tariffs for noncompliance with the 1986 Semi-conductor Agreement and was desperately trying to avoid even greater punitive sanctions over the Tōshiba incident. From the perspective of the vice minister of MITI, pursuing indigenous development of FSX in such an environment would cause major damage to the entire bilateral trade relationship for only limited technological gain in one sector of the economy.[15]

Trade politics alone do not explain MITI's behavior in the FSX episode, however. At least as important were changes in MITI's strategy toward the aerospace industry that emerged in the same period. The backdrop for these changes was MITI's recognition of the migration of Japan's industrial base from heavy industries to high-tech industries through the late 1970s and early 1980s.[16] This recognition was reflected institutionally in MITI's establishment of the International Trade Bureau and the reorganization of the Heavy Machinery Bureau as the Information and Machinery Bureau in the 1970s. In the aerospace industry, the recognition was reinforced by MITI's travails in developing commercial aircraft in the 1970s and by dramatic changes in the global aerospace market in the 1980s.

The centerpiece of MITI's efforts to transition from defense-dependent, license-produced aircraft to indigenously designed airliners at that time was the seventy-five-seat YS-11. Industry had begun work on the YS-11 in 1964. By the mid-1970s it was clear that the propeller plane was an engineering success but a total failure in financial and marketing terms.[17] The realization struck at MITI that entering the global aerospace market would take much more than the holy grail of systems integration experience alone. Meanwhile, the traditional strategy of spinning-off military aircraft technology to the commercial sector was also proving frustrating. In October 1984 MHI and the Science and Technology Agency's Aerospace Technology Institute (*Kōkū-uchū gijutsu Kenkyūjo*) began work on transforming the indigenously developed c-1 military transport into a STOL (short take-off landing) aircraft for Japan's smaller airports. The first prototype made its maiden flight in 1988 and was then quietly mothballed for lack of commercial interest.[18]

At the same time that domestic programs such as the c-1 STOL and the YS-11 were failing in Japan's relatively protected marketplace, competition in the global aircraft market was increasing sharply; with it came the risk involved in any aircraft development program. It could not have escaped MITI's attention that even Boeing and McDonnell Douglas were not entirely autonomous aerospace companies any more. By 1987 Japan's share of production for both companies had been increasing steadily for several years. In fact, with the exception of the 1982–1984 recession in world aircraft markets, the growth in Japan's aircraft industry in the 1980s was already being led by the export of commercial aircraft parts ordered by Boeing and McDonnell Douglas.[19]

MITI officials recognized that joint development now offered Japanese industry its best entry into the world aircraft market and that an overemphasis on indigenization of systems integration on national projects was a distraction from the real benefits to be gained from becoming a global player in aerospace production. Accordingly, MITI revised its Aircraft Industry Promotion Act in 1986 to specify that *only* international joint development projects would be eligible for concessional loans from the government. Between PXL and FSX, thinking in MITI had changed profoundly on kokusanka, not only in political terms but in industrial strategic terms as well.

As important as these changes were, however, their full implications did not become apparent to MITI officials until the spring of 1987. Until that point, MITI's Aircraft and Ordnance Division continued to favor the indigenous development of FSX: three decades of industrial policy strategy carry considerable inertia. For the Aircraft and Ordnance Division, indigenous development of military aircraft such as the FSX was complementary to the new policy of international collaboration on the commercial side. It gave Japan, in the words of the JDA's 1979 R&D guidelines, "much more leverage" when collaborating. The politicization of FSX threatened this strategy, however, by demonstrating how difficult it would be for MITI officials to pursue collaboration on one side (commercial) and autonomy on the other (defense). Faced with both pressure from the rest of MITI and a threat to the international collaborative strategy of the 1986 law, the Aircraft and Ordnance Division reversed its position on FSX. The division director personally lobbied senior industry officials to alter their positions on FSX as well, finally convincing the Joint Study Group to reluctantly come out in support of joint development in September 1987.[20]

It is important to note that MITI's cooling to the kokusanka of FSX did not lead the ministry to abandon military production as a central component of the strategy for developing high-tech industries for the twenty-first century. This is clear in an influential report prepared in 1988 by a MITI advisory commission chaired by Kyoto University professor Kōsaka Masataka. The report stressed that high-tech companies must recognize the importance of dual-use technology for both civilian and defense production and urged companies to "participate in the military sector through close contact with top-rank Western firms."[21] As the Kōsaka report demonstrates, the original goals of indigenizing technology did not change with MITI's turn-around on support for joint development of FSX. Rather, MITI recognized that the purely indigenous development of FSX would create political and structural obstacles to this goal. This distinction is important to understanding MITI's policies on international aerospace collaboration since FSX.

The Liberal Democratic Party Politicians

Politicians played an important role in determining the outcome of the FSX debate at several levels. Most conspicuous were the actions of Prime Ministers Nakasone and Takeshita in favor of joint development and the nationalist tirade of renegade Liberal Democrat Ishihara and his followers against it. This pattern of prime ministerial intervention in the name of the alliance and hawkish counterassaults in the name of autonomy should be familiar by now. But FSX also highlighted the emergence of a new element in the LDP defense debate: the defense zoku. This extraparliamentary caucus strengthened in the post-Taiko years and was at once pro-alliance and pro-kokusanka. All three—prime ministers, the hawks, and the defense zoku—merit further analysis.

Let us first examine the actions of the prime ministers. It is striking that the man most responsible for killing kokusanka in 1987 was the same man who had brought kokusanka to its zenith in 1970. But Nakasone Yasuhiro had seen much of the world since his days as JDA director-general. As minister of International Trade and Industry in the Tanaka Cabinet (1972–1974) Nakasone had been responsible for attempting to negotiate an exception for Japan from the Arab boycott that followed the 1973 Yom Kippur War. Struck by the hostile Arab position and the devastating impact of the oil shocks on Japanese industry, Nakasone came to appreciate the value of Japan's strategic relationship with the United States.[22] Nakasone then came to power himself in 1982 following Prime Minister Suzuki Zenkō's mishandling of a summit meeting in Washington with President Reagan. Suzuki had accidentally promised that Japan would defend sea lanes out to 1,000 nautical miles, called the United States an "ally," recanted under pressure for using such "militaristic" language, and finally resigned in disgrace. When Nakasone entered office in November 1982, many Reagan administration officials worried that his previous support of autonomous defense would push the alliance further into chaos. But Nakasone was determined to establish a sharp contrast to Suzuki, and his vehicle to do so was the U.S.-Japan alliance.

In this, Nakasone was not unlike Kishi, who had been seen by many as a dangerous rightist until he took office and placed a high priority on relations with the United States. But where Kishi's stewardship of the LDP during the 1960 Security Treaty revision cost him his job, Nakasone's deepening of the U.S.-Japan defense relationship led to ever higher levels of domestic popularity. For all cabinets, smooth U.S.-Japan relations have been the key to longevity, but Nakasone's cabinet was especially dependent on the bilateral relationship as a source of the *gaiatsu* (external pressure) necessary for his ambitious agenda of administrative reform and expanded defense and foreign aid expenditures. Thus, when Nakasone was confronted with the congressional anger over FSX during his April 1987 visit to Washington, he made clear his priority to Kurihara that FSX not be allowed to damage the alliance—he gave instructions that led Kurihara to formally propose joint development in his defense summit with Weinberger two months later.

Stable U.S.-Japan relations were no less important for Takeshita Noboru, who succeeded Nakasone as prime minister at the end of 1987. Critics of Takeshita claimed that he lacked the international experience and stature to carry on the partnership Nakasone had established with the United States on the world stage. Takeshita's principal rivals for the office of prime minister had been Miyazawa Kiichi and Abe Shintaro, both of whom had extensive foreign policy experience. So sensitive was Takeshita to the charges of being domestic-oriented that he allegedly paid yakuza to intimidate a nationalistic right-wing group into halting its overly effusive and embarrassing praise for his candidacy—a move that would return to haunt him in later years.

By the time FSX reemerged in March 1989, Takeshita was sinking in a sea of public resentment over the Recruit scandal and the new consumption tax, but he was determined that his cabinet not end punctuated by a failed foreign policy. Takeshita delegated his full authority on FSX to Deputy Chief Cabinet Secretary Ozawa Ichirō, a leader in the powerful construction zoku, the cabinet's main troubleshooter, and a relative—by marriage—of Takeshita's. (It is ironic that the two would emerge as rivals four years later.) Ozawa's instructions, like Kurihara's under Nakasone, were to prevent FSX from destroying smooth alliance relations. Based on these instructions, Ozawa called in the vice ministers from MITI, JDA, and MOF and then sat silently and stubbornly for hours while the three sides argued. When it was apparent that each vice minister would offer no further compromise, according to one MOFA observer of the meeting, "Ozawa opened his mouth for the first time and declared that the point in between all three sides would be the new policy."[23] That policy, of course, was to agree to the majority of U.S. demands for clarification of the MOU.

Opinion polls taken of LDP Diet members in March 1989 indicate that among the party's rank and file there was general support for both Nakasone's and Takeshita's handling of FSX.[24] Conspicuous opposition did emerge, however, from Transport Minister Ishihara Shintaro. In his scathing attacks on joint development of FSX in *A Japan That Can Say "No"* and interviews in the *New York Times* and the *Wall Street Journal,* Ishihara conjured up all the most potent images of Japanese national pride and supposed technological superiority. So adversarial was his book that the Defense Advanced Research Projects Agency (DARPA) translated it unofficially for circulation in Washington.

Ishihara's attacks on joint development were reminiscent of the nationalistic appeals in favor of kokusanka by prodefense politicians such as Genda Minoru and Hori Takushirō in past decades. Unlike Genda and Hori, however, Ishihara had no track record on defense policy in the Policy Affairs Research Council of the LDP before FSX—and failed to develop significant influence within the party on defense issues during the debate over the jet. In a meeting of the PARC's Defense Division in February of 1989, for example, Ishihara and ideological soulmate Kamei Shizuka introduced a proposal for the party to develop a position against joint development of FSX, but the motion was killed by the division's chairman, Horinouchi Hisao.[25] Attempts by Ishihara to sabotage joint development in the party's General Affairs Council (the party's next policy deliberative body above the PARC) were also stifled by the council's chairman, Ito Masayoshi.[26]

Ishihara's inability to generate opposition to the FSX deal at the working level of the LDP can be explained in large measure by the influence exerted on the party's defense debate by the defense zoku. This group of politicians emerged on the LDP stage in 1981, following a pattern established by other Diet members in the areas of agriculture, commerce, and construction in the previous decade.[27] In contrast to the prodefense hawks of the past, the defense zoku of the 1980s moved the defense debate closer to the mainstream of thinking in the LDP; hence the isolation of Ishihara. This trend paralleled both the broader movement toward consensus on defense that followed the 1976 NDPO and the consensus-oriented decision-making mechanisms introduced by other zoku in the same period.

Political scientists attribute the ascendancy of the zoku in the 1970s to five factors: the debility of the Diet as a policy-making organ; the high turnover rate of bureaucrats; increasingly strict limitations put on fiscal policy; the growth of policy issues that crossed ministry lines; and the link established by Tanaka between budget formation and vote gathering (pork-barrel politics).[28] The immediate source of the zoku's power is their control over the deliberations within PARC committee, division, and commission meetings. In these meetings laws and budgets are considered and passed or rejected based on unanimous consent. To assure unanimous consent, most zoku establish a small "steering group" (*Seiwa Iinkai*) to determine the agenda and conclusions of the meetings and clear any potential roadblocks with the relevant ministries and interest groups beforehand. Steering groups, in turn, must represent all factions: first, because chairmanships rotate among factions and, second, because a pipeline is required to each of the LDP's competing factions in order to build some degree of consensus and bring pressure to bear on errant members of the PARC committees. For the bureaucrats, the zoku steering groups provide an ally within the party to lobby for budgetary increases and generate political support for the ministry's legislative agenda. As the broker of interest group, bureaucracy, and factional interests, the zoku acts as a strong barrier against intervention from nonexperts within the party.

The defense zoku's emergence was a direct result of the closer relations established with the United States through the NDPO and bilateral defense guidelines of the late 1970s. First, the emphasis on alliance removed the divisive element from the party's defense debate and allowed the creation of a zoku steering group with membership from *all* factions. Before 1980 the party's prodefense politicians were all hawks, typically from the Satō, Kishi, and Funada factions. Moderate and liberal politicians in the Yoshida–Ikeda–Ohira and Miki–Komoto factions were generally aligned against these nationalists in fights over defense planning. As a result of this split, large changes in defense policy, such as the Fourth Defense Plan, often led to factional infighting. Moreover, the limited factional representation of the prodefense hawks led to periodic losses of key defense posts within the PARC. The party's Defense Division (*Kokubō Bukai*), for example, with responsibility for reviewing budgets and procurement plans, was dominated by the hawks (Genda was chair for almost two decades), but leadership of the Investigative Commission on Security (*Anzen Hoshō Chosakai*), with responsibility for longer-range policy deliberation, was evenly divided between hawks and doves throughout its history. In fact, the Investigative Commission was originally established as a way to contain the impact of the hawks within the party.

The second impact of closer alliance relations was on the prestige and influence of the prodefense members themselves. The Reagan administration's pressure for Japan to increase its share of "roles and missions" under the alliance gave politicians a powerful tool to use on the Finance Ministry's Budget Bureau. In the summer and fall of 1981, for example, prodefense Diet members traveled to Washington to promise a significant increase in defense spending and then lobbied the MOF for the same increase that winter, arguing (accurately enough) that failure to meet the original target would betray commitments to an already angry U.S. Congress.[29] Using such tactics, the defense zoku successfully maintained budget increases in the 1980s that averaged 6 percent per year. Defense contractors, JSDF families, and local recipients of "base countermeasure funds" (spending on communities around U.S. and JSDF bases) who depended on these increases were eager to support the political fundraising efforts of zoku members. These constituents were particularly supportive of the mobilized defense zoku in the LDP, because the introduction of the NDPO and the 1 percent of GNP limit on defense spending in 1976 led to annual reviews of defense budgets by the MOF and the JDA. The defense constituencies now needed Diet members ready to act every year on their behalf.

By the time of the FSX crisis in 1987, the defense zoku had attracted a diverse group of politicians to its ranks. Veteran prodefense members noticed that attendance at PARC defense meetings increased from the usual five or six members of the mid-1970s to well over forty politicians.[30] The roster of the Diet members' League for Defense (*Kokubō Giin Renmei*) reached an all-time high of 140 members. And the defense steering group that worked quietly behind the scenes to orchestrate PARC meetings had a dozen members representing all the factions.

Until FSX, the commitment of this new diverse defense zoku to kokusanka was never tested. The paradox of simultaneously supporting indigenization of defense production and promotion of alliance relations never occurred to most members. In 1982 key leaders of the defense zoku created the Dietmembers' League for Promoting Weapons Kokusanka (*Bōei Sōbi Kokusanka Sokushin Giin Renmei*), an attempt to take advantage of younger Diet members' growing interest in defense in order to recreate the 1965 Kokusanka Consultation Committee (dormant since 1972). In the same year, the same leaders created the Diet members' League for Comprehensive Security (*Nichibeiō Sōgō Anzen Hoshō Giin Renmei*), an organization for parliamentary exchange with the United States and Western Europe on security issues. The two groups had significant overlap in membership.

In January 1987, when the U.S. government made the first unofficial proposal for joint development of FSX, several defense zoku members sent a letter to Secretary of Defense Weinberger expressing their strong desire for autonomous development.[31] By the spring, however, the zoku followed industry in agreeing to the idea of Japanese-led joint development. New parliamentary exchanges had given the members of the zoku a close-up view of U.S. congressional anger over the Tōshiba incident, and most agreed with JDA Director-General Kurihara that a narrow definition of kokusanka of FSX was no longer worth the attendant risk to the alliance. Moreover, the zoku leadership was eager to avoid an extensive debate over FSX, knowing that this would accentuate ideological fissures and weaken the steering committee's control over the proceedings of the PARC Defense Division and Investigative Commission on Security.[32]

The Bush administration's demands for clarification of the FSX MOU in January of 1990 almost ruined this delicate balancing act. Members were profoundly angered and vented their frustration in lengthy Defense Division meetings.[33] Initially, proalliance members of the steering committee tried to reassure their colleagues that friends in the U.S. Departments of State and Defense would curb the Commerce Department-inspired review of the original MOU. By that time, however, the key personnel known by the defense zoku were retired, transferred, or on their way out of government. The zoku's key source of leverage internally was in doubt.

In the end the zoku's structural integrity held. Changes in MITI and the defense industry mentioned earlier had weakened the pro-kokusanka members' hand. By 1988, for example, the Diet Members' League for Promotion of Kokusanka was largely dormant. The activities of the Diet Members' League for Comprehensive Security, in contrast, were vibrant and reinforced for members the importance of the alliance. When tested, the alliance proved a stronger unifying theme for the zoku than did kokusanka. As Shiina Motoo, the director of the League for Comprehensive Security, explained in 1990:

> Even if you say that [joint development of FSX] emotionalizes U.S.-Japan defense relations, that would not go beyond one small portion of policymakers. The alliance exists for both countries' national interests, and contributes to the stability of the world.[34]

As the 1990 opinion polls mentioned earlier indicate, Shiina's perspective was mainstream in the LDP by 1989. Nevertheless, the resentment caused by FSX was internalized by many members and raised as many questions as answers about the U.S. commitment to alliance.

Alliance Ascendant?

Within all of the key components of Japan's defense establishment—industry, the JDA, the JSDF, MITI, the LDP—the two stages of the FSX crisis tested the commitment to kokusanka over and against alliance. The fact that the Japanese side abandoned its original commitment to indigenous development of FSX in negotiations with the United States suggests immediately that the commitment to alliance was stronger than the commitment to defense industrial autonomy. The decision-making process and shifting constituencies that led to this conclusion should not be viewed as sudden or temporary but rather as the synthesis of policymakers' past experiments with the two extremes of autonomy and collaboration represented by the Fourth Defense Plan and the NDPO of the previous decade and as the result of their experiences with major weapons systems developed under those plans.

However, to this conclusion must be added two important caveats. First, as a detailed examination of the positions of each actor in the FSX debate has revealed, the definition of technological autonomy had shifted in the decade before FSX. From the creation of the "information" element in the Machinery and Information Bureau in the 1970s to the MITI report on Japan's choices in 1988, a consensus emerged that development of technological know-why depended at least as much on integration and interaction with Western firms as it did on autonomous systems integration. The outcome of FSX hardly represented an abandonment by MITI of the search for a greater role in global high technology. In a sense, it only moved it underground.

The second caveat will resolve itself in the next chapter but must be highlighted here; that is, the resentment generated in all of the major defense constituencies by the American position on FSX. As an examination of MITI, industry, the JDA, JSDF, and the LDP reveals, this resentment translated directly into policy proposals in 1989 and 1990 for strengthening indigenous R&D. The trajectory of these policy proposals in the early 1990s is the clearest indication of the fate of kokusanka and the prospects for Japan's definition of autonomy in the international system in the post–Cold War era; it is the subject of the final chapter in this study.

7 | Defense Production and Alliance in a Post–Cold War World

The FSX controversy left Japan's defense establishment badly shaken. Joint development of FSX had been initiated from above during the Nakasone administration, but in 1988 and 1989 the Takeshita and Uno administrations were too weakened by political scandals to impose any order. In the absence of leadership, contradictory policies proliferated. MITI and MOFA attempted to emphasize joint development, but the resentment and mistrust created in industry and the JSDF by the FSX episode led to redoubled attempts at kokusanka in other areas. Eventually, these grabs for autonomous development were contained to some extent by the shifts in the defense industry coalition explored in the last chapter and by the downward pressure brought on defense spending by the end of the Cold War.

The kokusanka debate was reignited in 1992, however, with the Clinton administration's calls for Japanese participation in theater missile defense and access to Japanese dual-use technology under the Technology-for-Technology Initiative. The Japanese government was now being pressured not only to abandon kokusanka but also to accept a fuller integration of its commercial technological assets into the U.S. defense industrial base. This new threat to autonomy came at a time when neither government was attempting to demonstrate the utility of the political-military dimensions of the alliance absent a Soviet threat. Technonationalism was once again at the center of the alliance agenda that Tokyo saw emerging from Washington. A robust indigenous defense technology base took on renewed importance as an instrument to increase Tokyo's leverage against Washington and empower Japan within the alliance.

The first hints of how Japan might balance the demands of autonomy and alliance in this new environment were contained in two influential reports released by the government in 1994. One was the report of a group established by the JDA Equipment Bureau to study the future of Japan's defense industry after the Cold War: the Defense Industry and Technology Advisory Panel (*Bōei Sangyō Gijutsu Kondankai*). The second report, "The Modality of the Security and Defense Capability of Japan: The Outlook for the Twenty-First Century," was prepared by the Advisory Panel on Defense (*Bōei Kondankai*), created by Prime Minister Hosokawa Morihiro to redraft the 1976 NDPO. Both reports struggled with the implications of the rising political and technological costs of kokusanka, acknowledging the central importance of the alliance to Japanese security but struggling to redefine a strategy for autonomy in an era of shrinking defense budgets. The Defense Industry and Technology Advisory Panel report focused on retaining technological autonomy in the face of U.S. pressure for dual-use technology flows but also emphasized the leverage to be gained in the alliance because of growing U.S. dependence on Japanese dual-use technology. The Advisory Panel on Defense also addressed the utility of autonomous defense production but explored the significance of autonomous capabilities in terms of Japan's new global role, rather than simply as a bilateral issue with the United States.

This chapter begins with an examination of post-FSX aspirations for kokusanka and concludes with an analysis of the reports by the Advisory Panel on Defense Industry and Technology and the Advisory Panel on Defense.

Keeping Alive the Seed of Autonomy in FSX

At the policy level the final word in 1989 was that FSX would be a jointly developed jet based on the F-16, but the devil was still in the details. Despite the U.S. insistence on greater specificity in the redrafted MOU, joint development on the scale of FSX was unprecedented, and many elements of the jet's development were still not settled. For Japanese industry, it was only natural to exploit the lingering areas of ambiguity.

Japanese industry saw its first target of opportunity in the jet's engine. There was little doubt that the engine for the FSX would be based on a U.S.

model, but in the first months after the development MOU on the jet, the specific level of kokusanka for the engine was still unclear.[1] In July 1989 sources in the JDA revealed to the *Nikkei Shimbun* that they had plans to upgrade the capabilities for the autonomously developed jet engine on the ATX (Japan's planned next-generation jet aircraft trainer) so that the engine "would be of the same caliber as the engine for the FSX."[2] ASDF sources indicated that this was necessary to reduce reliance on the U.S. at a time when the Pentagon was restricting Japan's access to technology. Executives from Ishikawajima Harima Industries added that such military kokusanka projects were still important for the development of commercial sectors as well.[3]

Industry lent further momentum to the push for autonomy in engine development in the May 1989 Keidanren policy statement calling on the government to pay for the construction of a new supersonic jet engine testing facility. These new initiatives for autonomy in engine production were powerful symbols of the backlash in Japan against the U.S. side's handling of joint development of the FSX. It was jet engines, after all, that most Japanese executives viewed as the Achilles heel in the original kokusanka plan. Eventually, the momentum for kokusanka of the FSX engine was dealt a setback by the JDA's decision to license produce the F-110-GE 129 engine from General Electric. Hopes that indigenous technology could be utilized even under licensed production were then dashed by the Pentagon's decision that the engine would be built in the United States and exported.[4]

JDA and industry were more successful at keeping kokusanka alive in the FSX project by developing autonomous alternatives for composite materials, phased array radar, CCV (computer configured vehicle), the mission computer, the fire control radar, the electronic warfare suite, the inertial navigation system, and the computer hardware. No sooner was an agreement reached between MHI and GD on joint development than it became clear that GD would have trouble receiving permission from the Department of Defense to transfer these technologies to Japan. As one MHI official noted in April 1990, not entirely without satisfaction, "if the U.S. will not release technologies such as the fire control system, we will have no choice but to develop our own."[5] TRDI attempted to do precisely that. On February 23, 1993, the JDA announced forty-six (out of over two-hundred) subsystems and technologies for FSX that Japanese industry would develop entirely on its own. The JDA claimed that these technologies were not based on licensed production and therefore did not have to be transferred to the United States under the original MOU for joint development.[6] With a production MOU (as opposed to the MOU for codevelopment) still not signed and the jet falling two years behind schedule and over 115 billion yen over budget, industry in Japan attempted to turn chaos into opportunity.[7]

Of course, access to the technology developed by Japan in these areas was one of the advantages the U.S. side had expected to gain from joint production on FSX. The two governments disagreed over the definition of which technology was "derived" and therefore available to the Pentagon gratis and which technology was "nonderived" and therefore available to the U.S. side only with Japanese agreement to cooperate under the provisions of the Joint Military Technology Transfer Agreement of 1983. The JDA yielded to U.S. pressure to include the composite co-cured wings as derived technology and Lockheed Fort Worth (inheritor to GD in the defense mergers of the early 1990s) was paid by Japan to build the wings in the United States. The U.S. had much more difficulty gaining access to the indigenous Japanese technology for avionics.

Japanese industry was responsive to the U.S. side's unanticipated interest in Japan's indigenous technology for phased array radar. Particularly impressive to DOD and U.S. industry was Mitsubishi Electric's highly cost-effective technique for manufacturing the gallium arcenide-based modules for the radar. The production of each of these units cost thousands of dollars each for U.S. industry, compared with hundreds each when produced by MELCO. Phased array radar contains thousands of these modules (like the thousands of optical units in a dragonfly's eye), meaning that learning from Japan's comparative advantage in manufacturing technology could save the DOD billions of dollars on the F-22 next-generation fighter project in the United States. MELCO agreed in 1992 to transfer technology relevant to the manufacturing of the phased array modules, providing one more important example of flowback to U.S. industry from FSX. Online access to MHI's FSX database for Lockheed Fort Worth and the Departments of Defense and Commerce offered the potential for dozens, and perhaps hundreds, of other smaller examples.

In the development stage, then, the FSX program was part kokusanka, part licensed production (of the F-16), and part joint development (including flowback)—a bit of the old and a bit of the new. With the Congress watching closely and the GAO producing regular reports either critical of Japanese technology or of DOD willingness to transfer U.S. technology to Japan, continuing Japanese attempts to "jack up the radiator cap and drive in their own indigenous plane" were mostly foiled. On the other hand, questions about the long-term future of FSX remained. The first flight was scheduled for 1995, with production of 130 jets to begin shortly thereafter, yet by

the summer 1994 there was still no progress toward an MOU on joint production, and the JDA was ready to cut production back to 70 aircraft. The two
sides also continued fighting over U.S. requests for releasability of the co-
cured wing technology to U.S. companies other than Lockheed.[8] Rumors
abounded in Washington that JDA would return to the kokusanka option if
agreement on a coproduction MOU failed. In fact, TRDI continued funding
for subsystem projects related to Japan's FX (next-generation air superiority
fighter), scheduled for development in the year 2008. These technologies
included stealth, infrared radar, "fly-by-light" avionics, and a five-ton-class
engine. JDA and industry officials admitted that the FX R&D projects were
primarily aimed at increasing Japan's leverage in negotiations with the U.S.
over joint development of an F-15 upgrade in the late 1990s, but the thinly
veiled threat of further kokusanka hung over the ongoing production MOU
negotiations for FSX as well.[9]

Other Areas of Kokusanka: Helicopters, Missiles, and Satellites

Despite the bluffs and threats continuing to surround bilateral negotiations
on FSX in 1994, JDA and Japanese industry had no desire to kill the project.
At a time of shrinking procurement budgets, the defense establishment had
invested far too much political and financial capital into the jet. Even the FX
R&D effort was aimed primarily at increasing Japanese leverage in future
upgrades or joint development projects, rather than toward building a purely indigenous jet. Jet fighters were becoming too expensive, too technically
complicated, and too politicized for pure kokusanka—at least for the fore-
seeable future. There were other areas, however, where Japanese industry
might pursue indigenous development with more success.

One system that the aerospace industry was particularly eager to protect
from the joint development fate that had met FSX was the OHX observation
helicopter, which KHI had been designing to replace the U.S.-made OH-6.[10]
KHI managed to retain funding for indigenous design and prototyping of
the OHX in the FY '93 and '94 budgets,[11] and the Pentagon resisted demands
from the Congress that Japan be forced to buy the helicopter off-the-shelf
from the United States. Nevertheless, the U.S. Trade Representatives' Office
and other parts of the U.S. government kept a close eye on the project. The
potential for Japan's domestic commercial helicopter market is considerable,
and the OHX closely paralleled other efforts by KHI to become a dominant
player in the domestic helicopter market by unilaterally modernizing its BK-
117, once a joint project with Messerschmitt Bölkow-Blohm Gmbh.[12]

In addition to the OHX, industry fought to protect the *chu*-SAM, a medium range surface-to-air missile replacement for the Hawk missile, under design by a team led by MHI and Toshiba for incorporation into an anti-missile air defense system (originally called ADI by Japanese defense industry officials), based on the U.S. G-PALS concept (Global Protection Against Limited Strike).[13] The chu-SAM's R&D funding was postponed in 1992 and only kept alive by a thread after that. By 1993 industry recognized that the best hope for keeping chu-SAM alive would be by incorporating it in a jointly developed theater missile defense (TMD) system with the United States. TMD will be examined below.

In the years since the FSX explosion, Japan's defense establishment has also focused on the potential for an indigenously developed military intelligence satellite system. Formal JDA attention to satellites was blocked by a 1969 Diet resolution prohibiting the military use of space. However, the precise meaning of "militarization" has been open to interpretation and has gradually been weakened. Prime Minister Nakasone told the Diet in 1985 that an independent intelligence satellite capability would not necessarily mean the "mil-

TABLE 7.1
Kokusanka Projects in the 1990s (active and proposed)

	Japanese Project	U.S. Alternative
AH-X	antitank helicopter	AH-64, AH-1W
ARM	antiradiation missile	USN/USAF HARM
AHAAM	active homing air-to-air missile	AMRAAM
AT-X	medium jet trainer	T-45
Chu-SAM	mid-range SAM	Corps-SAM
C-X	military transport	C-17
C³I	upgrades	various U.S. programs
FLIRS	forward-looking infrared	U.S.-made FLIRS radar
DVLS	vertical launch system	MK 41
DDX	"mini Aegis"	Aegis
JFDS	flight debrief system	ACMI, REACT
MSDF CDC		U.S. Navy equipment
P-3CX	ASW air platform upgrade	USN P3-C AIP
OHX	observation helicopter	OH-58D, RAH-66
XATM	antitank missile	USA/USMC Javelin
XT-4	advanced trainer	JPATS

Source: The AAIJ (American Aerospace in Japan) Position Paper, June 3, 1994

itarization" of space. That sparked interest at the working levels of industry, JDA, and the JSDF in a system designed for surveillance rather than attack (much as previous indigenous projects in aerospace began from the bottom up in anticipation of an improving political environment for kokusanka).

The Japanese government's July 26, 1994, long-term space plan moved industry one step closer to developing an indigenous satellite system for defense needs. The plan, prepared by the cabinet-level Space Activities Council, called for Japan to double its space budget "for peaceful purposes" between 1995 and 2010.[14] According to senior Japanese officials involved with the plan, this budget could be used for military uses of space that are not "lethal or aggressive."[15] The JDA commissioned its own study to parallel the Space Activities Council. According to the study, which was prepared for the JDA by retired military officers of the independent Defense Research Center, Japanese domestic industry had the potential to develop an indigenous surveillance satellite and launch system (based on the H-II rocket) at the cost of $10 billion.[16] The DRC also floated the idea of a multinationally operated confidence-building surveillance satellite system for Asia, to be developed and operated from Japan. However, the reaction from other Asian capitals and Washington to that concept was universally negative.[17]

The pros and cons of developing an indigenous satellite system sparked the same internal debate that had characterized so many earlier decisions in aerospace. Those in favor of developing an indigenous system cited: U.S. reluctance to share KH-12 surveillance data with Japan; the need to subsidize Japan's uncompetitive H-II launch program; the need for autonomous control of data in any future theater missile defense system; and the need for a bargaining chip to obtain more data and technology in future joint satellite or intelligence sharing programs with the United States. Unlike previous clashes over equipment, the battle lines on satellites did not divide evenly by institution. Advocates of kokusanka appeared throughout the Foreign Ministry, JDA, and JSDF. Opponents of kokusanka of satellites also crossed ministerial lines and included the powerful vice minister of Defense. The opponents cited the high cost (and its attendant threat to crowd out other ongoing projects), the technical superiority of U.S. systems (and thus a preference for negotiating more access to U.S. data), and the political consequences of embarking on a project that could be seen outside Japan as "militarizing space."

Industry's solution for the JDA hesitancy over developing military surveillance satellites was to fold the military surveillance mission into the Space Activities Council's proposed 20.4 billion dollar global Earth observation network. The network would involve launching up to twenty observation satellites for environmental and other peaceful monitoring missions by the year 2010. The dual-use development of satellites would be difficult given the poor working relationship between STA and JDA, but the advocates of kokusanka recognized that even with a crash satellite program it would be years—possibly decades—before Japan developed the infrastructure and analytical expertise to interpret satellite imagery on the ground. Incrementalism was unavoidable and possibly even advantageous.

The Winds of Joint Development

Despite these efforts to keep autonomy alive in FSX and expand it to helicopters, missiles, and satellites, however, more compelling evidence began emerging in the early 1990s that key institutions continued shifting away from kokusanka. In the immediate wake of FSX, this was particularly true for MITI and the JDA, where officials were determined to repair frayed defense and technology relations with the United States. One example of this trend was the fact that Keidanren's proposal for an autonomous jet engine testing facility was taken by MITI and transformed into a feasibility study for a "joint *international* facility," in keeping with the 1986 aerospace legislation.[18] Then in a highly significant move that would cut off one of industry's last remaining links in the development of autonomous jet fighters, the JDA began in March 1990 to examine alternatives to the autonomous development of the ATX indigenous trainer jet program, effectively dooming the domestic program.[19] The government did not intend to cut off support for the defense industry, but the die had been cast with joint development of FSX, and this set the political tone for projects across the board.

An early indication of MITI's conversion to the religion of joint development on the commercial side was a proposal by the Aircraft and Ordnance Division and the Agency for Industrial Science & Technology (*Kogyōgijutsuin*) in early 1990 for an international consortium for the joint development of propulsion technologies for a supersonic hypersonic transport plane (SSHST). The consortium was the government's first foray into aerospace industrial policy after FSX and was the first MITI aerospace development project ever to invite foreign participation. The three Japanese participants, Kawasaki Heavy Industries, Mitsubishi Heavy Industries, and Ishikawajima Harima Industries, initially opposed foreign participation but realized that the 1986 revision of aerospace promotion legislation and MITI's new emphasis on international joint development had ended the kokusanka option for hypersonic transport technology. Likewise, for the U.S. participants in the consortium, Pratt & Whitney and General Electric, the low level of government funding offered by MITI and ambiguity over patent rights and antitrust regulations all presented difficulties. Despite such reservations, however, companies from both the United States and Japan, together with two European companies (SNECMA and Rolls Royce), proceeded with full participation in the consortium, with the eventual goal of developing a Mach 4 prototype.[20] MITI's Aircraft & Ordnance Division built on this experience the following year to develop other consortia for hypersonic transport related R&D and to establish an international joint working group of subcontractors for commercial airline production.[21]

On the military technology side, TRDI also put a new emphasis on joint development in the wake of FSX, but joint development at the subsystems level with a greater reciprocity in risk sharing, funding, and technology flows. Interestingly, TRDI's Director General Tsutsui Ryozo became a champion of this new approach, emphasizing in February 1990:

> I think that in many ways FSX will prove to be a unique case. In the future it will be important for both sides to share the costs and risks of development. And it will be important to have a good two-way flow of technology. FSX is an important first case for joint development, but it is difficult because it is so large and complex. I believe codevelopment of smaller systems or subsystems will be more appropriate in the future.[22]

The Defense Agency argued to industry that support for such codevelopment of subsystems offered the best route around the problems associated with FSX in the future and had substantial support in the United States. To prove this latter point, Defense Agency officials pointed to the 1989 report of the U.S. Defense Science Board's Task Force on Defense Industrial Cooperation in the Pacific Basin, which emphasized expanded defense industry cooperation through joint development of subsystems.[23]

Based on this philosophy, TRDI had in October 1988 proposed collaborative R&D on a range of five technologies, including submarine degaussing to reduce the likelihood of sonar detection, ducted rocket motors for low-flying missiles, and a hybrid millimeter wave-infrared target seeker for guided missiles. The proposals received almost no attention in the U.S. government until March 1990, when TRDI used the occasion of a trip by Senator Jeff Bingaman to Tokyo to refocus attention on the proposal. Bingaman brought the message back to Washington in that and subsequent trips that Japan was willing to cooperate on defense technology and urged the Pentagon to respond.[24]

Secretary of Defense Dick Cheney then brought his own proposal for collaboration on seven "critical" technologies during a trip to Tokyo in April 1990.[25] Cheney's list was developed from the DOD's Critical Technologies list,[26] which focused on broad technology areas rather than specific systems or subsystems. MITI was reluctant to comply with a request for open access to wide swaths of Japan's most sensitive commercial technology but could not afford to reject the proposal out of hand for political reasons. Instead the ministry stalled until the two sides agreed to reduce their combined lists to eleven subsystems and technologies and establish working groups and liaison pipelines to explore the feasibility of each.

With a specific mission and focus, the two sides increased the frequency and intensity of the previously dormant Systems & Technology Forum. These efforts bore fruit in October 1992, when the Japanese side of the Joint Military Technology Commission (JMTC) approved the technology transfer for joint research on the ducted rocket engine[27] and MELCO agreed to a transfer of its active phased array radar technology design for the FSX to Westinghouse and Hughes.[28] The two governments also moved closer to joint development of an "eye-safe" laser.[29] The importance of joint development as part of the thematic glue to the alliance was highlighted in President Bush and Prime Minister Miyazawa's January 1992 Tokyo Declaration (*Tokyo Seigen*), although critics continued to point to the lack of substantive technology transfers in the S&TF format.

As a practical matter, the potential for joint development of systems or subsystems between the United States and Japan is limited, but as a theme in Japanese defense industry planning joint development had an important impact. MITI and JDA efforts to encourage joint development of aerospace and defense systems and subsystems helped to cool the initial post-FSX backlash against cooperation with the United States in industry. The chairman of Mitsubishi Heavy Industries himself commented on the initiation of joint development of FSX in February 1990 that "Japan should no longer try to force kokusanka of projects when the United States has a competitive system or one for joint development."[30] In the same theme, the director of IHI's engine division wrote in an industry journal that: "Whether this new era brings domestic development or international joint development does not matter; what matters is the capability for development itself."[31] This sort of enthusiasm for joint development and open questioning of kokusanka was unprecedented in Japanese industry journals and pointed to a substantial transformation in the way industry strategists viewed defense production.

Industry's eventual conversion to joint development resulted from more than just the government's new internationalism, of course. The vulnerability of purely indigenous projects was becoming evident in the concluding budget years of the 1991–1995 Midterm Defense Plan. In 1992 the JDA proposed outlays of 22.75 trillion yen (in 1990 real yen), but pointing to the collapse of the Soviet Union, the Ministry of Finance cut this total back by 580 billion yen, with threats to trim further in coming years. The list of major acquisitions planned was topped by four AWACS, which could cost over 50 billion yen per plane, with no significant offsets for Japanese industry.[32] Other big-ticket items included 36 MLRS, which would consist primarily of direct imports or knock-down kits; new Patriot missile groups; and Aegis destroyers (largely black-boxed). Meanwhile procurement plans for indigenously designed tanks were cut from 132 to 108 units, ships from 10 to 8, and license production of the F-15 from 42 to 39.[33] The trend of defense budget slow downs continued in 1993 and 1994, so that the JDA's budget request for FY '95, the last year of the Midterm Defense Plan, represented only a 0.9 percent increase from the previous year. Within the JDA's humble $47.3 billion request, procurement shrank by 14.8 percent from the year before.[34]

Industry was devastated by the downsizing of the Midterm Defense Plan. In 1993 MHI projected a 15 percent cut in its 8,000 employees who worked on military-related projects. KHI expected to cut as much as 20 percent of its military-contract workforce. Electronics companies such as Tōshiba began consolidating their defense divisions into other areas of the company.[35] Desperate, industry called on MITI for greater guidance and financial help. MITI refused to commit anything beyond the 10.2 billion yen it had already allotted for international aerospace joint ventures on the commercial side in FY '92. As the head of the Aircraft & Ordnance Division told the *Nikkei Shimbun*: "There is no consensus yet in Japan that the government should make any special considerations for defense contractors."[36]

For Japan's defense establishment, the Midterm Defense Plan taught the inevitability of dependency on the United States for defense technology. The end of the Cold War, the growing importance of collaboration on the commercial side, and the complexity of modern weaponry were trends too powerful to ignore. Other episodes in the early 1990s hammered home this theme, particularly the Gulf War. While some Japanese took heart in the contribution their technology made to the multinational victory over Saddam Hussein, most were impressed with the overwhelming effectiveness of what could only be seen as superior U.S. systems integration and operational doctrine.

The illusion of autonomy in defense technology was also shattered for Japanese industry by the Japan Aircraft Electronics Corporation (*Nippon Kōkū Denshi*) incident. This company was caught in 1991 repairing Iranian guidance systems for air-to-air missiles and was punished not only by the Japanese government but also by the State Department Office of Munitions Control, which temporarily barred the Japanese company from using products built under license from the United States. Given the lack of back-up producers in Japan, and the widespread reliance of prime contractors on even small companies such as Japan Aerospace Electronics, this action effectively shut down much of Japan's defense production for over a month.[37]

Developments on the commercial side also reinforced the Japanese aerospace industry's lost sense of independence. Aircraft components production had grown 220 percent and fuselage subcontracting 268 percent between 1985 and 1989.[38] In 1989 alone export sales rose by 48.1 percent, due to increased deliveries of components for U.S.-built civil airliners. As a result, the share of defense sales for Japan's aerospace industry fell from 80 percent of total sales to 75.6 percent in the same period.[39] MITI's efforts to organize international R&D consortia were therefore entirely consistent with industry's own assessment of Japan's potential areas of competitiveness. As the industry journal *Wing* noted, shrinking defense budgets meant that "the future of whether Japan's aerospace industry will grow or not depends on the international joint venture projects on the commercial side."[40]

For industry, joint development therefore took on a new significance. In a dramatic departure from earlier thinking, 36 percent of Keidanren Defense Production Committee members responded in a 1993 MIT-Japan Program survey that they favored the expansion of joint development of defense-related subsystems with U.S. industry.[41] Rather than distracting resources from indigenous projects, joint development was now seen as a useful way to keep domestic projects alive. Industry had come full circle. Defense cooperation with the U.S. had launched Japan's indigenous defense industry in 1953. Forty years later defense cooperation with the United States was once again industry's best hope to nurture defense production.

Theater Missile Defense

If industry was warming to the idea of joint development on the military side, though, it clearly had no intention of repeating the pattern set with FSX. The 1993 MIT-Japan Program survey demonstrated a strong lingering distaste for the negotiations surrounding the controversial jet. As the survey results indicated, industry preferred U.S.-Japan joint development of *subsystems*, with control at the systems level in the JDA's hands. FSX had failed to meet that model. The next large system to face the test would be Theater Missile Defense.

Theater Missile Defense is the mission of the Pentagon's Ballistic Missile Defense Office (BMDO), the successor to President Reagan's Strategic Defense Initiative Office (SDIO). In contrast to SDI, however, TMD enjoys fairly widespread, bipartisan political support in the United States. The system would provide upper- and lower-tier defense against ballistic missile attacks, based on a combination of Aegis cruisers at sea, AWACS in the air, and surface-to-air missiles such as Patriot and THAAD (theater high-altitude air defense) on land.

Japanese interest in TMD developed at two levels. For industry, it represented the next step in complexity from Japan's own chu-SAM–based Air Defense Initiative (ADI). With chu-SAM funding delayed and political support for ADI uncertain, participation in the U.S.-pushed TMD program was an attractive alternative—or life support system—for Japan's own missile development program. Industry had already developed a working relationship with the probable major U.S. contractors for TMD through the 1989–1993 DOD-funded Western Pacific Defense Architecture Study (WEST-PAC).[42] For the JDA and the government, TMD also offered the best defense against the North Korean Nodong ballistic missile, which was test launched in the direction of the Japanese home islands in late 1992. In terms of mission and technology, TMD was not to be ignored.

However, like the oni (demons) in Japanese fairy tales, TMD brought Japan as many risks as magical riches. When Secretary of Defense Les Aspin was in Tokyo in October 1993 and asked Japan to participate in TMD, the JDA and industry detected that they had only three options: joint development (involving transfer of some Japanese technology to the U.S. side), buying TMD off-the-shelf, or engaging in gradual technology exchanges.[43] Japanese industry was not yet confident enough in its missile defense technology to enter negotiations on joint development, and an off-the-shelf procurement would have meant the death of chu-SAM. Moreover, TMD's estimated 10 billion dollar price tag for Japan would have crowded out the current procurement plans of each of the services, prompting one wag in the JDA to compare the missile system to "having [the sumo wrestler] Akebono climb into my little household bathtub."

Japanese movement on TMD was further complicated by the entry of the Socialist Party into the government in 1994. Prime Minister Murayama

Tomiichi was forced to accept the constitutionality of the SDF and the alliance in order to smooth the transition of the Socialists into a coalition government with the Liberal Democratic Party and Socialist-Sakigake (Harbinger Party) in June 1994, but his party intensified its opposition to TMD as the price for these concessions.[44] Finally, Japanese commentators in and out of the government continued to question the technical feasibility of "hitting a bullet with a bullet," further reinforcing Japanese caution on missile defense systems.[45]

In order to prepare the technical and political responses to U.S. proposals for participation in TMD, Japanese industry established a working group of eight companies in August 1994 under the Japan Association of Defense Industries (JADI).[46] The JADI group was quietly backed by the Procurement Bureau of the JDA and was similar in function to the interindustry study group established to rebut U.S. pressure for joint development of FSX in 1986. While BMDO was eager for an early Japanese commitment to participation in TMD, there was also a recognition in Washington of the political sensitivities surrounding the issue of missile defense. BMDO thus held to a simple request for Japanese participation in a joint study of Japan's theater missile defense needs rather than a more complex architecture or procurement study. The JDA agreed to participate in September 1994.[47] Meanwhile, the JADI study group continued building its case for as much kokusanka of TMD as possible.

The JADI group focused on four scenarios for joint TMD collaboration that the Pentagon's BMDO had proposed in June 1994. The BMDO scenarios were:

1. a Japanese forward-deployed navy upper-tier, ground lower-tier system at a cost of $4.5 billion (based on upgrades of existing Japanese plans to deploy four Aegis destroyers, four AWACS, and twenty-four land-based Patriot fire units);

2. a Japanese deployed-in-bastion navy upper-tier, ground lower-tier system at a cost of $16.3 billion (based on upgrades of existing deployment plans plus two new Aegis and new surveillance radar for support);

3. a Japanese ground upper-tier, lower-tier system centered on six THAAD sites at a cost of $8.8 billion;

4. a Japanese combined upper-tier ground lower-tier system combining five THAAD sites and existing Patriots and Aegis at a cost of $8.9 billion.[48]

BMDO presented the four scenarios as informal thought pieces rather than official proposals, but the menu provided some enticing fare for Japanese industry.

Under the BMDO proposals the Aegis upper-tier missile system and the IRST cueing for the missiles were to be jointly developed by the U.S. and Japan; the THAAD and surveillance radar were to be jointly produced. Implicit in the schedule for BMDO's scenarios was the hint that Japanese delays would lead to lost opportunities for codevelopment. On the other hand, the price tag for participation in TMD was enormous. Committing to TMD deployment would create the risk that Japanese defense budgets might be drained to purchase a huge off-the-shelf system from the United States.

In short, TMD presented Japanese industry with a new kind of challenge. The system was far too large and complex for a credible indigenous alternative, but the mission and the potential technological advantages were significant. On the other hand, so was the risk, and there was no precedent for Japan signing onto a system that the U.S. military had not yet tested and deployed. Achieving cooperation on TMD would require a new level of trust between the defense industry communities in both countries, but the task of rebuilding that trust after FSX was being complicated by renewed DOD pressure for access to Japanese commercial technology.

The Technology-for-Technology, or Perry, Initiative

The Clinton administration's first proposals for collaboration on TMD in spring 1993 (in anticipation of Aspin's fall visit) were accompanied by a parallel proposal for expanding reciprocity in technology transfer, which was quickly dubbed "the Perry Initiative." The Perry Initiative's aim was to achieve the sort of transfer of Japanese nonderived, dual-use technology to the U.S. defense industrial base that William Perry had originally envisaged as an official of the Carter administration's Defense Department. In the view of Clinton administration DOD officials, the original Perry scheme had been distorted by the Reagan and Bush administrations into a hollow political symbol, which won U.S. industry little or no access to Japan's commercially based dual-use technologies. The goal of some Department of Defense technology strategists in 1993 was to use large projects such as TMD to entice the Japanese government into providing access to areas that had thus far been beyond the reach of the JMTC and S&TF structures.

For officials in Japanese government and industry, much of the logic of the Perry Initiative was difficult to deny. Declining defense spending in both countries legitimized the concept of drawing on a common defense technology base. The growing importance of spin-on technologies, particularly in the areas of flat panel displays, semiconductors, and new composite materials, meant that Japan could make an important contribution to alliance burden-sharing. Japan's commercially based technological strengths also gave industry a card to play in negotiations over joint development of defense subsystems in the future.

But from the Japanese perspective there was also a disturbingly adversarial tone to the Perry Initiative. The concept of government-mandated "reciprocity" implicit in the Pentagon's proposal paralleled the Clinton administration's insistence on "objective criteria" in trade negotiations with Japan. Moreover, by coupling TMD joint development with the Perry Initiative, DOD officials were implicitly threatening to make future licensing of U.S. defense technology contingent upon Japanese transfers of dual-use technology to the United States. In effect, the Clinton administration appeared to be holding the defense of the Japanese homelands against nuclear attack as a hostage to be traded for Japan's most critical dual-use technology. From the standpoint of autonomy, the Perry Initiative touched on the most sensitive nerves, reinforcing insecurities about technological dependence on the U.S. and effectively strengthening all of the original arguments for kokusanka.[49]

In the spring and summer of 1993, however, kokusanka of TMD was simply not an option. Given industry and government's growing political, budgetary, and technological dependence on a combination of joint development and coproduction, outright rejection of the Perry Initiative was not an option either. With little room for maneuverability, Japan's defense community was under siege. The appropriate response to such a situation was suggested by the architecture of Japanese castles, which are designed to channel the attacks of superior forces, divide them, and contain them in mazelike cul-de-sacs where they can be dispatched by lesser numbers of troops. The Japanese government applied this same tactical solution to the Perry Initiative.

The first stage was to divide the Perry Initiative from TMD. The JDA was not opposed to the concept of reciprocal technology transfer, but the logic of the post-FSX joint development schemes was that small, subsystems collaboration was far more likely to succeed than large, political systems-level projects such as FSX. The JDA argued that, if anything, TMD was even larger and more politically complex than FSX. DoD officials agreed; attaching the Perry Initiative to TMD would make the difficult political job of winning support for ballistic missile defense within Japan even more difficult.

Moreover, movement on the Perry Initiative might be delayed by the slow build-up to collaboration on TMD. The Defense Department officially separated the Perry Initiative from TMD in October 1993, when Aspin declared that TMD was only a matter to be decided in the context of defending the Japanese islands.[50] At about the same time, the Pentagon quietly changed the name of the Perry Initiative to the Technology-for-Technology Initiative.

After separating TMD from the newly dubbed TfT, the Japanese government's next instinct was to contain the proposal in cul-de-sacs where it could be addressed on terms more advantageous to the JDA. The logical place was the S&TF, where the JDA could respond to the Technology-for-Technology proposal by offering collaboration on new defense subsystems, such as upgrades for the F-15 and the Patriot missile.

The JDA's instinctive move away from commercially based technology and onto the familiar territory of defense technology was not simply a tactic to defang the TfT. Defense and Foreign Affairs officials in Japan remained cognizant of the political and technological advantages to be gained from increased collaboration with the U.S. The problem was that the TfT asked the Japanese government—and especially the JDA—to do something they were unable to do: deliver commercial technology from unwilling firms. As presented to the Japanese side, TfT would have U.S. firms license defense technology to Japanese companies in exchange for their dual-use technology. However, the technology the Pentagon listed (flat panel displays, etc.) was held by those Japanese companies *least* interested in obtaining U.S. defense technology and *least* dependent on the JDA, or even MITI, for business and guidance. These were firms such as Kyōcera and Sharp—companies that rose to success *in spite* of MITI's industrial policy, and certainly without the assistance of the JDA. Those Japanese companies most dependent on U.S. licensing of technology (MHI, KHI, etc.) in turn, had the *smallest* amount of commercially based dual-use technology to offer the Pentagon. Finally, those companies that had some attractive commercial technology and also did business with JDA (MELCO, NEC, Hitachi, etc.) were difficult for the JDA to influence because their defense divisions were small (1–3 percent of total business on average) and getting smaller. The CEO of one of these firms threatened to withdraw from defense production altogether if forced to turn over dual-use technology without appropriate compensation.

Without incentives for Japanese industry, the JDA faced an almost impossible task—responding to the DOD on the terms expected by Deutch. The obvious alternative was increased U.S. pressure, possibly even blackmail via U.S. defense technology. This prospect troubled JDA, MOFA, and industry. It also troubled U.S. industry. Of the twenty-five major defense exporters to Japan surveyed by the MIT-Japan Program in 1993, not one listed "access to Japanese technology" as an important incentive for doing business with Japan. All companies listed "expanding sales."[51] For the Japanese side, U.S. industry's ambivalence toward the TfT was a mixed blessing. It weakened the DOD's implicit threat to withhold licensed production of U.S. systems (because that threatened U.S. sales), but it also meant that the Japanese government had no concrete U.S. industry proposals to work with if defense technology collaboration was to be rescued at all.

Thus, while the castle defense had worked for the JDA and industry at a tactical level by dispersing the immediate threat of TfT to theater missile defense and Japanese commercial technologies, the larger strategic problem remained: Japan's shrinking defense procurement budgets and the growing complexity of modern weapons systems necessitated greater collaboration with the United States. Through the S&TF avenue the Japanese side offered various counterproposals to the DOD that highlighted Japanese industry's potential to contribute dual-use technology to joint development of *military* subsystems. However, to a large extent the DOD was still focused on commercial technologies, and many of the subsystems proposed by the JDA were already being surpassed by faster development schedules in the United States.

The Defense Industry and Technology Advisory Panel

As the DOD and JDA talked past each other regarding TfT, the JDA Procurement Bureau was engaged in its own intense debate with industry and the rest of the Japanese government over the future of Japan's defense industrial base and the appropriate level of interaction with the defense industry of the United States. FSX, the high yen, and the sudden decline of procurement spending had deflated the kokusanka movement as no previous shocks to the Japanese system had since 1945. With TMD the Japanese government was being asked to place the initiative and planning for a huge portion of its defense industrial base in the hands of the Pentagon. With TfT Japanese industry was being asked to provide its most sensitive commercial technologies to U.S. firms, or risk the loss of U.S. support for Japan's indigenous defense industries. The question had to be asked: how much was Japan's indigenous defense industrial base now worth? For the JDA and defense contractors the answer was obvious: *everything!* But the arguments had to be made anew for the rest of the policy community as well as industry.

The director of the JDA Equipment Bureau established two advisory panels in March 1993 to do the work. The first, the Advisory Panel on Defense Equipment Procurement (*Bōei Sōbihin Chōtatsu Kondankai*), had thirteen members from industry and was chaired by the director of the Japan Association of Defense Industries. The group's report was completed by December of the same year and represented little more than a rehashing of previous industry demands to the government: centralize R&D within the government, streamline the procurement system, reform the contracting rules, and remove obstacles to diffusion of technology between the civilian and defense sectors. The overall conclusion was predictable but unsupported and unpersuasive: Japan's defense industrial base was crucial to the nation and should be maintained and eventually expanded.[52]

The Equipment Bureau's second group, the Advisory Panel on Defense Industry and Technology (*Bōei Sangyō Gijutsu Kondankai*) was far more rigorous and influential in its attempt to define the future role of kokusanka. The group, chaired by Tōkai University professor Karatsu Hajime, delivered its report to the JDA in March 1994. The shadow of TFT and TMD were subtly present throughout the Karatsu report. It began by noting how the Gulf War demonstrated that "the possession of advanced technologies is itself an effective deterrent against threats," reinforcing on every page the importance of diffusing technologies between the civilian and defense sectors (the report commented with alarm on the fact that economic recession in Japan has threatened spin-ons to the defense industrial base). Japan's civilian technologies are assets of national security, the report reminded its readers, and must be nurtured:

> Japan's indigenous defense technology is based on the application of advanced civilian technology, a unique element that is now being highly evaluated even in the United States and drawing attention from around the world to the importance of technologies that have dual-use applications. . . .

> We should reappreciate [our civilian technologies] and use them to develop new advanced defense technologies, increasing deterrence and our national security.[53]

Following this line of logic, the Karatsu group asserted that Japan's civilian dual-use technologies are assets of national security—not only in their deterrent effect against potential foes but also in their impact on negotiations with the United States for access to *its* defense technology. To take maximum advantage of technological assets in this way, however, requires a comprehensive view of technology that incorporates both the civilian and the military dimensions. Japan's civilian technologies are only national security assets when there is a robust indigenous defense development program that "expands the possibility for domestic procurement, thus *increasing* [Japan's] negotiating power when systems are introduced from abroad."[54]

Interestingly, the Karatsu report explicitly based this argument on the 1970 JDA Basic Policy on Equipment Production and Development. As noted in chapter 3, this policy pronouncement represented the Japanese government's strongest statement *ever* in support of kokusanka (declaring that indigenous development and procurement should be taken "as a matter of course"). The 1970 Basic Policy was the creation of Nakasone Yasuhiro and was superceded by the 1976 NDPO and a series of other policy decisions. It had not appeared in JDA documents for over two decades. But for Karatsu and the JDA's Advisory Panel, Nakasone's 1970 Basic Policy was a necessary buttress for Japan's defense industry policy in the face of U.S. pressure on TFT and TMD. Originally conceived as a blueprint to expand the autonomous Japanese defense technology base, Nakasone's vision was now being used to protect Japan's indigenous technologies and increase leverage over the United States in an era of shrinking defense production and complex technological interdependence.

The Karatsu report brought new life to kokusanka as leverage in dealing with the United States on TMD and TFT, pointing implicitly and explicitly to the fact that an indigenous *defense* technology base protected Japan's indigenous *commercial* technology base and increased its value in negotiations with the United States. The report even listed in detail the dual use technology areas on which the JDA should focus its efforts.[55] However, while the Karatasu group successfully used the pressure of TFT and TMD to resurrect kokusanka, it failed to address the underlying technological and political trends that were chipping away at Japanese defense technological autonomy in the first place. Military systems were becoming too expensive and complex to develop independently. The report acknowledged, therefore, that Japan should advance the improvement or upgrade of systems jointly with the United States, including greater exchanges of personnel into both countries' laboratories (and by implication the unprecedented entry of U.S. military researchers into Japanese company laboratories).

But was indigenous defense technology aimed only at increasing leverage with the United States, or was the goal still expanding indigenous capabilities at the systems level as expressed in the 1970 Basic Policy? The advisory group avoided a direct answer, noting only that: "regarding the advancement of specific R&D plans, the decision on autonomous development versus U.S.-

Japan joint development versus other options, must be made on a case-by-case basis."[56] "A case-by-case basis" suggested a far less resolute commitment to kokusanka than Nakasone's original plan to favor indigenous production "as a matter of course." The Karatsu Panel could not get around the fact that while kokusanka remained a useful tactic, it had become an implausible strategy. The broader national security strategy that the tactic of kokusanka would serve was suggested by the report of the prime ministerial advisory panel that had been meeting parallel to the Karatsu group.

The Advisory Panel on Defense: Setting a Course for Defense Planning in the Twenty-First Century

On July 18, 1993, Prime Minister Miyazawa lost a no-confidence resolution in the Diet and was forced to resign. The prime minister had failed to deliver promised political reform, and thirty-six angry rebels in his own party labeled themselves reformers and left party ranks to help bring him down. Less than one month later, against all expectations, this group of rebels established their own party (the Renewal Party, or *Shinseitō*) and formed a coalition government with their erstwhile enemies, the Socialists, together with six smaller parties. The new coalition partners chose as their first prime minister Hosokawa Morihiro, once a member of the LDP Tanaka Faction, later a prefectural governor, and now leader of the grass roots reformist Japan New Party. After almost four decades of uninterrupted rule, the LDP was out of power.

The eight parties in the new coalition government brought with them all of the rivalries they had formerly held as LDP factions, subfactions, and opposition parties. But the very existence of the coalition was clear evidence that the traditional ideological poles on defense issues were no longer relevant. With each passing month in power the Socialists swallowed more and more of the old LDP line on international issues. For the future, those members of the Renewal Party who had been active on defense issues while in the LDP anticipated expanding the definition of Japan's role in international security policy. Ozawa Ichiro, the secretary general of the Renewal Party, had chaired an LDP special commission on security issues in 1992 that advocated a greater Japanese role in UN peacekeeping and other multilateral security missions.[57] Ozawa and his fellow travelers wanted the coalition government to address this agenda after political and tax reform measures were passed and any remaining Socialists could be co-opted into a new party that would be poised to rival the LDP's long-term rule.

However, Hosokawa recognized that defense issues were still highly divisive and could be exploited by enemies of the fragile coalition. Ozawa, who controlled much coalition policy, agreed. For the time being, the prime minister would commission a special advisory panel to deliberate on revising the 1976 NDPO to serve Japan in a post–Cold War world. Hosokawa chose Asahi Beer chairman Higuchi Hirotarō to chair the panel and asked him to draft a security policy vision for the next century. The panel of nine industrialists, scholars, and former government officials met twenty times between February and July 1994 and delivered its completed report to the prime minister on August 12, 1994.[58]

Sitting in Hosokawa's place was Murayama Tomiichi, a Socialist who had come into power as the titular head of an unlikely new LDP-Socialist alliance that had driven out Hosokawa's. Hosokawa and his allies in the Renewal Party had fallen victim to scandals of their own, and it was not clear what role the Higuchi Panel's report would have under the new antireformist LDP-Socialist coalition. At one level, nothing had changed: the new coalition, like the coalition before it, had promised to follow the basic contours of the traditional LDP policies on defense and foreign affairs. But then foreign policy was the farthest thing from the minds of most politicians in Japan in 1993 and 1994. The end of the Cold War framework and new electoral reform had already shattered the old political system and the rough outlines of new parties and new coalitions were beginning to emerge. In this fluid setting, Japanese politicians were focused on winning elections and maintaining power—not on determining long-term security policy. The Higuchi Panel report was accepted with thanks by Murayama and then shelved.

While the Higuchi Panel report may have been set aside by the tumultuous political events of 1994, however, the concepts it contained were not. Politics were in chaos, but business and the bureaucracy were still relatively stable. The panel's experts represented all the key actors in these two legs of the iron triangle: MITI, JDA, MOF, MOFA, and industry (defense and nondefense). In the process of preparing their report, they developed a consensus view that would inevitably serve as the baseline for revision of the NDPO and defense policy planning in the next century. The report's recommendations read not as a single thesis on Japan's security but rather as list of Japan's strategic options. Ever-present was the issue of autonomy. The Higuchi report presented a menu for guarding against entrapment on the one hand and hedging against abandonment on the other. And in the report's eclectic vision, defense production played a critical role.

In its précis the Higuchi Panel report recommended that Japan formulate a new comprehensive security strategy for the post–Cold War era resting on three pillars: multilateral cooperation, alliance with the United States, and maintenance of a modern and efficient military. The importance of the alliance was evident throughout the report, with specific recommendations for improving interoperability, including: combined operational planning; a NATO-style acquisition and cross-servicing agreement; joint R&D on weapons; continued support for U.S. forces in Japan; and "positive efforts toward introducing a missile defense system in collaboration with the United States."[59] In its specificity and commitment to alliance interoperability the Higuchi report moved well beyond the 1975 prime ministerial commission on defense on which it was modeled. Indeed, the Higuchi report stated clearly that the alliance would take on even greater importance in the future.

However, the report also emphasized the growing economic conflict between the United States and Japan and questioned whether Washington would continue to demonstrate leadership in Asia in the multilateral world that was likely to emerge in the next century. In fact, the first draft of the report placed the possibility of U.S. withdrawal from Asia at the center of its argument for altering Japan's security policy in the future. That draft was changed under JDA and MOFA influence, but the flavor of U.S.-declinism lingered in the final report's conclusions.

Prominent among those conclusions was the thesis that Japan should play a greater role in multilateral security arrangements, since U.S. leadership will "depend to a certain extent on actions of nations in a position to cooperate with the United States."[60] In effect, U.S. leadership in a multilateral world would depend on the ability of nations like Japan to increase their autonomous defense capabilities. The report was specific on what these capabilities should be: "a well-organized c^3i system...including the use of reconnaissance satellites; the acquisition of midair refueling and long-range transport aircraft; and the maintenance of autonomy and independence in equipment procurement and defense related technology."[61]

The report's trinary nature was clever but vague. The world expected Japan to play a greater role in multilateral institutions, and the report linked that politically correct aspiration to the need for greater autonomous capabilities. Those capabilities also served as a hedge against U.S. withdrawal (abandonment), of course, and as a hedge against having technology and budgetary resources swallowed within U.S. demands for TMD and TFT (entrapment). The report noted, for example, that Japan should collaborate with the United States on ballistic missile defense but also stressed that

"Japan *itself* should hold the capability of dealing with and defending against ballistic missiles" (emphasis mine).[62]

The question of capabilities versus development was at the core of the report's vagueness. The report emphasized the importance of indigenous satellite capabilities, for example, but did not mention indigenous *development* per se. Industry's preference was for kokusanka, of course, but key members of the panel blocked the inclusion of "indigenous development" in the draft to keep open the possibility that surveillance data could be downloaded from U.S. satellites. Similarly, the report recommended developing the capability for long-range aircraft for peacekeeping operations. Many within JDA and MOFA preferred that this capability be provided by the U.S. Air Force as an example of alliance interoperability or through the introduction of U.S.-made c-5s or c-17s. Others preferred the development of an indigenous c-x transport plane based on the c-1.

The report also urged that Japan conduct joint research and development of weapons with the United States but added that this should be done "with other countries" as well.[63] For some members of the panel, the inclusion of "other countries" was necessary to open avenues for multinational teaming on theater missile defense and to help build in economies of scale for Japan's choking second- and third-tier defense contractors. However, other members of the panel, with the backing of industry, saw defense collaboration "with other countries" as a useful tool for weakening or eliminating Japan's "Three Arms Export Principles." In fact, early proposals for the Higuchi report included explicit calls for elimination of the arms export ban.

The effectiveness of the "European card" (the "other countries" referred to in the report) was well understood by industry and government in Japan. A highly publicized international strategic alliance between the Mitsubishi Group and Daimler Benz in April 1990 had sent shock waves through the U.S. aerospace community in Tokyo.[64] Throughout the FSX controversy, French aerospace companies also offered their fighters as inexpensive alternatives for joint development.[65] U.S. industry debated the significance of these developments (as opposed to the symbolism) throughout 1989 and 1990,[66] but when British Aerospace sold both the ASDF and the Maritime Safety Agency a package of BAe-125 aircraft for search-and-rescue and flight-check in the spring of 1990, there was no longer any question that the U.S. aerospace industry risked losing its exclusive relationship with JDA. The BAe-125 purchase represented the first sale of fixed-winged aircraft from a non-U.S. foreign supplier in the history of the Japanese military.[67]

Arms exports and the European card were explicit nowhere in the Higuchi report. Nor was the *development* of an indigenous satellite system or long-range aircraft. If anything, the report's specifics were mostly related to the alliance. As the report asserted repeatedly, the alliance had been confirmed as the most important element in Japan's security mix. However, the report also suggested clearly that the U.S. commitment to the alliance could change. Implicit throughout its pages, therefore, was a blueprint to make possible a reemergence of kokusanka should the United States fail to demonstrate leadership in the new multilateral security world envisaged by the report's authors.

The report's lack of an explicit endorsement of kokusanka did not just reflect divisions within the panel regarding the relative weight to be given to alliance, multilateralism, and autonomy. It also reflected the panel's unanimous recognition that earlier strategies of kokusanka were beyond the bounds of political and technological feasibility in a post–Cold War world. The report paid considerable attention to the weaknesses of Japan's domestic defense industry, noting that despite past efforts at indigenization, a major part of the JDA's equipment "is either imported from the United States or manufactured domestically under license from U.S. defense contractors."[68] Far from trumpeting the dual-use accomplishments of private industry, the report commented with alarm that many Japanese firms might exit defense production altogether, given the declining budgets for procurement. For that reason, according to the Higuchi Panel, "it is vitally important to maintain autonomy and independence in equipment procurement and defense-related technology, partly with a view to facilitating technological exchanges with the United States."

The Higuchi Panel's report reached many of the same conclusions regarding kokusanka as the 1975 advisory panel created to pave the way for NDPO and the 1980 commission on comprehensive security. All three advisory groups struggled with the opportunity costs of pursuing indigenous weapons development and concluded that while weapons autonomy should not be allowed to jeopardize the alliance, it would be a vital element both for preserving Japan's leverage and freedom of action within the alliance and as a hedge against U.S. withdrawal or fatigue. When viewed in consecutive order, it also is clear that the 1975, 1980, and 1994 reports gradually moved Japan away from the narrow military definitions of autonomy of the early 1970s and toward broader definitions in which kokusanka is only one element in the mix that allows Japan to address its comprehensive security needs. This broadening of Japan's security option shifted kokusanka of mil-

itary weapons systems away from center stage, but also reinforced the importance of maintaining an independent defense technology base to empower
Japan within the alliance and hedge against withdrawal.

The difference in the international system between the 1994 Higuchi
report and its predecessors is also important. The 1975 and 1980 reports were
written at a time when the Cold War lent a linear simplicity to the U.S.-Japan
security relationship. From the perspective of the United States, each
Japanese decision to expand defense capabilities or burden-sharing brought
Japan further into the Western Alliance. New roles and missions for the JSDF
were legitimized by U.S. strategies to contain the Soviet Union. For Japan's
internationalists and defense hawks alike, U.S. pressure was critical for developing domestic support for an expanded security role. It was in that context
that the 1975 and 1980 reports were written.

In 1994, however, the linear simplicity of the Cold War was missing.
Japan's new multilateral aspirations could also legitimize the development of
autonomous capabilities, for, as the Higuchi Panel noted, the ability of the
U.S. to lead in a multilateral world depends on the actions and capabilities
of nations such as Japan. The elevation of multilateralism to near-equal status with the alliance in the Higuchi Panel report was risky from the perspective of the JSDF: multilateralism could justify disarmament just as easily as
rearmament. However, the shift in emphasis did move Japan's security off of
the two-dimensional axis of the Cold War and into a fluid three-dimensional realm where Japanese defense planners would have the flexibility to adapt
to whatever circumstances might be created by the unpredictability of U.S.
leadership in a nonbipolar world. The three-dimensional approach to
Japanese security also gave defense planners flexibility to adapt to the fluid
state of Japanese domestic politics.

The Higuchi report reflected changes at the working level of the alliance
relationship after the Cold War as much as it anticipated new directions. As
the report suggested, the greatest variable in Japan's future security would be
the United States. Since the Gulf War, the United States had demonstrated a
growing preoccupation with economic affairs, and this broke apart the
interagency coordination on the defense relationship within Washington
that had developed in the 1980s. The Department of State and the National
Security Council came to play a minor role in managing the alliance. Even
within DOD, initiatives toward Japan were increasingly pursued as discon-
nected parts during the first two years of the Clinton administration. Force
structure decisions of critical importance to Japanese security and the credibility of the U.S. forward presence in Asia were dictated by budget priorities

rather than policy. Japanese policymakers, once accustomed to working with the DOD to develop strategies for quick domestic acceptance of new Japanese commitments to the alliance, were now being bombarded with uncoordinated demands on TFT, TMD, and host-nation support. Once managing alliance relations would have been an opportunity for Japanese officials or politicians to contribute directly to their nation's new international agenda. By 1993, managing the alliance was more akin to trade negotiations, where bureaucrats' instincts in Japan were to resist and delay, not to build.

By the time of the Higuchi Panel report, the changes in U.S. posture toward the management of the alliance had begun to erode the proalliance network that had developed on the Japanese side in the 1980s. The LDP defense zoku, once a crucial actor in building interfactional support in the political world for new alliance initiatives, was scattered with the fall and resurrection of the LDP. Within the Foreign Ministry, the critical mass of strategic thinking began flowing from the North American Affairs Bureau's Security Division toward the newly created Policy Planning Bureau, which was formed out of the United Nations Bureau and carried over much of its emphasis on multilateralism. Voices in the Japanese system calling for interoperability and strengthening of U.S.-Japan roles and missions were drowned in the cacophony of other voices urging balanced force structure or new capabilities for peacekeeping.

These shifting patterns at the working level of Japanese alliance management took place against the backdrop of profound changes in Japan's political world. The LDP–Socialist–Sakigake coalition represented only a transition to new political parties that would emerge in the years ahead. The leadership of the Murayama coalition (from both the LDP and JSP side) viewed security issues as an unnecessary irritant in coalition relations, something to be managed with as little exposure to daylight as possible. Under the surface, however, the new generation of leaders in the LDP held a variety of views on security, ranging from the multilateralist bent of Foreign Minister Kono Yohei to the unilateralist hawkish perspectives of Ishihara Shintaro and Hashimoto Ryutaro. The opposition parties—Shineitō (Renewal), Komeitō (Clean Government), Nihon Shintō (Japan New Party), and the Minshutō (Democratic Socialist Party)—formed a common front in September 1994 under the banner of the new "Reform" Party (Shinshinto). They too kept discussion of defense issues under the surface but quietly debated a variety of perspectives.

The gradual evolution of two major parties (plus the Communist Party) anticipated structural changes that would result from new electoral rules passed by the Diet in January 1994. The new electoral rules would move Japan's lower house constituencies from 511 multiseat districts to a mix of 300 single and 200 multiseat districts (the latter in regional blocks). The pressure of the 300 new single-seat districts was expected to force a starker debate on issues. In this context, security policy could reemerge as a determinant in the formation of new parties, just as it was in the formation of the LDP back in 1955. In the early 1990s the U.S. government could take comfort from the fact that the Socialists' acceptance of the constitutionality of the JSDF and the alliance removed the possibility that any major new party would be created on an anti–U.S.-Japan alliance platform. On the other hand, U.S. neglect of the alliance opened the possibility that ambitious conservative politicians might call for more independent Japanese security roles in their political platforms or advocate a shift in Japanese budget priorities away from host nation support and joint development of weapons such as TMD and toward indigenous projects.

None of these developments in themselves pointed to an automatic expansion of autonomous Japanese defense capabilities, the collapse of Japan's consensus for alliance, or a resurgence of kokusanka. Kokusanka, as originally conceived in the 1950s, eluded Japan for technological and political reasons. The failure to achieve autonomy in defense production reinforced the commitment of Japan's political elite to the principle that the alliance must remain at the core of Japan's strategic planning. There should be no doubt that the alliance remains Japan's first choice in the 1990s. The question implicit in the Higuchi report was whether the alliance should be Japan's *only* choice for guaranteeing security in an unpredictable world. As both the Karatsu and Higuchi reports implied, all three of Japan's choices— Japan's ability to contribute to security in a multilateral context; Japan's empowerment as a full technological and political partner within the alliance; and Japan's ability to provide for self-defense should the alliance wither—necessitate some degree of kokusanka. Each option requires the maintenance and nurturing of a robust indigenous defense technology base. The degree to which that technological and industrial objective comes to dominate Japanese security planning in the future will ultimately depend on the United States.

Conclusion

Kokusanka of aircraft may be finished for as long as I am at MITI, but no one can say what will happen in the future.
-An official of MITI's Aircraft and Ordnance division, as quoted in *Defense News* (April 2, 1990)

For Japan's defense establishment the years 1952 to 1992 tested the Meiji leaders' premise that greater autonomy in defense production leads to greater national sovereignty. Initially, the pursuit of military technological autonomy and technoeconomic development did not seem contradictory to many of Japan's postwar policymakers and industrialists. In the early years of the alliance with the United States, Japan's vulnerability in the international system was linked to relative technological backwardness, just as it had been in the early Meiji period. And the United States seemed willing to provide technology transfer, financial support, and political cover for Japan to develop an indigenous defense industry.

However, as Japan's defense establishment attempted to develop and expand autonomous defense production in the Second and Third—and, most important, Fourth—Defense Plans, the implications of autonomous defense production for the alliance became more apparent. With the Fourth Defense Plan, the Defense Agency under Nakasone read the *relative* U.S. withdrawal from Asia and Japan's *relative* increase in indigenous defense technology as creating an opportunity for establishing greater military, political, and industrial autonomy. What the technonationalists discovered in short order was that Japan still depended on the U.S. not only for technology and deterrence but for domestic political support of kokusanka as well. The Nixon shocks swept the ground out from under Nakasone's JDA not only by removing the external threat but also by shifting the U.S. role in Japan's internal defense industrial debate from support for production to pressure for purchases of U.S. equipment.

The political-military bonding of the U.S. and Japan in the late 1970s and early 1980s reasserted the primacy of alliance in Japanese defense policy making and also provided political cover for the resuscitation of kokusanka. The JDA, industry, and MITI moved away from pushing large national projects across the board and focused instead on developing systems that would nurture indigenous technological strengths. U.S. policymakers' recognition of these strengths led to initiatives in the early 1980s for defense technology collaboration. As far as Japanese industry was concerned, however, these agreements, like the political-military agreements before them, existed primarily to stabilize the alliance so that the pursuit of kokusanka could proceed unhindered. Again, the shock came—this time with FSX—that the pursuit of technological autonomy could not be separated from political issues, which in turn affected Japan's broader economic position.

How could it be that the pursuit of kokusanka would be frustrated in this way, even as Japan's defense expenditures and share of critical technologies steadily increased and the relative political-economic hegemony of the United States in Asia decreased? Two trends evident in the postwar history of Japan's search for autonomous defense production provide answers to that question.

First, while it is undeniable that Japan's technological competitiveness has been increasing throughout the postwar period, the prospects for technological autonomy in defense production have been *decreasing* at an even faster pace. As Raymond Vernon notes, there has always been a tension for military planners between the goals of autonomy and the superiority of military technology. This tension has been:

> measurably increased by the intertwining of national economies in the past few decades, which has been accompanied by the increasing differentiation of products and processes. These have led to an increasing proliferation of niches and specializations in the productive world, and an increasing traffic across national borders of differentiated goods and services.[1]

And therefore:

> any nation that is determined to rely upon its own products, its own technologies, and its own enterprises to fulfill its defense needs will pay a far higher premium for such a policy than in years passed, costs that will be expressed

not only in terms of money but also in a sacrifice in the quality of its military equipment.[2]

This growing diffusion of technology has in turn exacerbated MITI's attempts to develop an indigenous commercial aircraft industry. MITI was one of the most important forces behind kokusanka, but as systems-level development of commercial aircraft became increasingly difficult to attain, the ministry had no choice but to pursue collaboration with Western firms at the components level: a strategy that would be jeopardized by the highly political indigenization of military aircraft such as FSX.

Second, the political costs associated with kokusanka have also grown. Japan's exploration of a larger political role in Asia has led to a renewed appreciation of the link between close security ties to the United States and freedom of Japanese action in the region. The demise of the "arsenal of Asia" concept of the early 1950s sent the first signal that normalization of Japanese economic activity in the region depended on Japanese defense *not* straying outside of the alliance framework. Tanaka's abandonment of the Fourth Defense Plan and call for "Peacetime Defense Capabilities" also reflected the trade-off that had to be made on the defense industrialization side in order to normalize relations with China—a decision that ultimately had the support of many original advocates of kokusanka, such as Keidanren's chairman, Doko Toshio. Nakasone's own journey from championing kokusanka in 1970 to imposing joint development of FSX on his own government in 1987 reflects the evolution of Japanese strategic thinking about the importance of the alliance. In spite of Ishihara's charges that Nakasone abandoned Japanese sovereignty in the FSX episode, the prime minister's goal was clearly to carve a larger strategic role for Japan in regional and global affairs.

Within Japan, consensus behind growing defense expenditures and expanded roles and missions for the Self-Defense Forces has also been premised on close alliance ties of the sort that technonationalist confrontation with the United States might disrupt. As John Dower reminds us, the consolidation of the conservatives and the formation of the U.S.-Japan security relationship were closely linked in the early 1950s. With time, alliance relations became the centerpiece for the growth of the defense zoku and also for the LDP to reach out to moderate prodefense members of the Democratic Socialist Party and the Komeito.[3] Even with the split of the LDP in June 1993, the ideological core remained where it was at the height of the defense zoku's membership. The consensus around alliance has caused both the far right and the far left to wither or move toward the center. The closer bilateral defense relationship that resulted was not just the natural byproduct of a common external threat. In fact, the United States and Japan took their most significant steps toward defense cooperation (the guidelines, for example) at a time of détente. The alliance served many more Japanese interests in domestic politics and international affairs that went beyond simply deterring Soviet forces.

These two trends have meant that even as the momentum for kokusanka carried forward in terms of Japan's relative technological and political power, the opportunity costs increased to each member of the original coalition behind kokusanka. In the case of FSX, for example, TRDI, MITI's Aircraft and Ordnance Division, the ASDF, the LDP defense zoku, and Keidanren's Defense Production Committee all proceeded from 1967 to 1985 with full consensus and confidence at the working level that the jet would be developed autonomously. When the issue of kokusanka became politicized in a bilateral setting in 1986, however, these sections, divisions, and institutes had their policies altered or overturned as their parent organizations moved to protect their broader constituencies and institutional objectives. MITI had to keep bilateral cooperation alive in commercial aerospace and was still trying to put out the fires cause by the Tōshiba incident and the nagging trade surplus with the United States. The JDA and JSDF had to maintain U.S. political support for increasing the defense budget over Finance Ministry and opposition party resistance. Industries did not want to jeopardize their expanding exports of subcomponents to Boeing or their growing technology collaboration with top Western firms. The LDP defense zoku did not want fighting within the ranks.

It must not be forgotten that from the beginning, the coalition for kokusanka represented a plurality of interests. Technonationalism may have been a common emotional or ideological impulse for the engineers, politicians, and officials who pushed for indigenization, but there was no monolithic national strategy for autonomy. As the Japanese adage goes: "There is a section but no bureau, a bureau but no ministry, and a ministry but no government" (*ka g'atte kyoku ga nai, kyoku g'atte shō ga nai, shō g'atte seifu ga nai*). The different priorities brought to the search for autonomous defense production created a natural fault line for the kokusanka coalition to split as political and technological opportunity costs mounted.

Recalculating Autonomy

The search for postwar autonomy in defense production ended with the discovery that Japan had achieved autonomy neither in technology nor military capabilities—nor even in domestic decision-making processes. Tokyo faces a dilemma of entrapment versus abandonment in the 1990s, just as it did in the 1950s. However, the failure of kokusanka to win Japan control of its destiny in an uncertain world and an unpredictable alliance has not meant a complete repudiation of autonomy. Instead it has led to a recalculation of the meaning of autonomy.

What Japanese policymakers learned through the struggle for kokusanka was that the value of an indigenous defense technology base in a complex interdependent relationship is in making that interdependence as *mutual* as possible. As the 1994 Karatsu and Higuchi panel reports suggested, kokusanka continues in importance for the leverage it gives Japan in its security relationship with the United States. This notion was well expressed by a former TRDI official who wrote in a 1990 industry journal that the U.S.-Japan security relationship should be based on the recognition of each side being "indispensable to the other" in defense technology terms.[4] The potential for growing reliance on Japanese technology in advanced U.S. weaponry has been well documented in two separate studies prepared for the DOD's Defense Advanced Research Projects Agency (DARPA) by the Analytical Systems Corporation (TASC) and the Institute for Defense Analysis (IDA).[5] As the Karatsu Panel report asserted, the value of Japan's dual-use technology base is elevated in relations with the United States when Japan has a robust autonomous weapons development program. It is for that reason that kokusanka can still play an important role in increasing Japan's value to the United States and empowering Japan within the alliance.

The value of kokusanka as a hedge against abandonment extends to economic relations as well. As one MITI official commented in March 1989, joint development projects in aerospace are necessary to fight U.S. protectionism and technonationalism by "deepening the mutual dependency of U.S. and Japanese industrial and technological capabilities."[6] Just as defense technology interdependence empowers Japan as a security partner, it also increases Japan's clout in the growing number of international consortia that are resulting from the increased risks, costs, and diffusion of technology associated with high-tech projects (particularly in aerospace). Thus, while Japan's aerospace industry is a failure on the terms it originally set for itself (there are no indigenous Japanese successors to the YS-11 and the F-1), the strategy of kokusanka will have proven successful if Japanese industry is able to use its indigenous capabilities to become an equity partner in consortia to design hypersonic aircraft for the next century.

For all of these reasons it is likely that Japanese industry and government will guard jealously those technological assets they hold in areas such as electronics, new materials, and robotics. MITI is putting administrative muscle into restricting technology flows out of Japan in the 1990s the way it worked to foster technology flows into Japan in the previous three decades. The ministry placed unilateral restrictions on the transfer of chemical and dual-use military technologies in the fall of 1992 and assured that Japan remained one of the more aggressive advocates of a restrictive regime to follow cocom with the announcement of an Asian Export Control Initiative in early 1995.[7] The Foreign Ministry paralleled MITI's initiatives with the issuance of new guidelines for foreign aid in the summer of 1992 that would restrict aid and technology transfers to countries engaging in excessive defense production. MOFA also proposed monitoring of international arms flows to and from aid recipients in Asia.[8] These initiatives flow naturally from the comprehensive security concept and represent an effort to harness national technological assets to Japan's new role in global security. It is also worth noting, however, that MITI's tightening of technology export restrictions has hindered DOD efforts to gain access to critical dual-use technologies, providing further insulation for indigenous capabilities.

In short, technology is no less important an asset of national security for Japan, despite the lessons learned from the pursuit of autonomous defense production. Moreover, it should not be concluded from the demise of the original strategies for kokusanka that an inalterable consensus has emerged in Japan on the role of defense technology and production in the nation's security and economic development. As the Higuchi report suggested, alliance with the United States is of paramount importance, but Japan will continue to have strategic choices for the future. The goal of indigenization of technology will continue to dominate Japan's approach to joint development projects such as TMD. Ultimately, the calculation of the opportunity costs involved with kokusanka will hinge on actions taken by the United States.

The Other Side of the Coin: The American Dilemma

If Japan has faced a dilemma between entrapment and abandonment, so too has the United States. On the one hand, continuing to transfer defense technology to Japan feeds competitive indigenous Japanese capabilities; on the other hand, restricting technology feeds political support for indigenous alternatives to U.S. equipment. While the history of kokusanka demonstrates an evolution in Japanese understanding of this dynamic, however, there is some question as to American policymakers' understanding of the problem.

Part of our own inability to deal with the implications of the kokusanka dilemma stems from the fact that the Pentagon has historically been able to interrupt indigenous Japanese programs with impunity. From the PXL to aircraft carriers, the SH-X, and the Japanese-designed FSX: the graveyard of indigenous Japanese systems killed by U.S. pressure is vast. Sometimes U.S. policymakers have had a rational political, economic, or military reason for ending the kokusanka of a system. The sh-60 and fsx are two good examples. At other times, U.S. pressure against kokusanka has been the unintended result of broader policies such as the Nixon shocks, or the result of simple bribery that had little to do with U.S. national interests (the two Lockheed scandals, for example).

The consequences of a heavy U.S. hand in Japanese defense industrial policy have often escaped the attention of American analysts. When autonomous development of a system such as fsx is derailed because the U.S. government treats Japan as an adversary and denies Japanese industry technology, the push for kokusanka is often reinforced. When the U.S.'s military commitment to the region is also in question, kokusanka is even further entrenched for the long term. Eventually, U.S. pressure may cut short whatever grasp for military or technological autonomy results. But each clash of this sort also erodes the long-term credibility of the United States. As we have seen, when Japan's kokusanka battles pit military-industrial autonomy against the alliance, the alliance usually prevails. The problem will come when the U.S. commitment to the alliance lacks the credibility to make this comparison matter to Japanese policymakers any more. At that point, both U.S. strategic *and* economic interests will suffer.

The answer, of course, is not for the U.S. government to encourage the flow of defense-related technology to Japan as the Pentagon did in the 1950s and 1960s. Such policies feed the appetite for autonomy as effectively as policies that restrict technology do. U.S. policy cannot match all of these diverse political, military, and technological priorities behind the defense industrial debate in Japan—but it can match enough to contain technonationalism and turn Japanese technological strength to the mutual benefit of both countries. Specifically, this requires:

1. *Developing a balanced assessment of Japanese technological strengths.* Japan should no longer be treated as a junior partner in defense-related technology. The U.S. defense establishment must shake its NIH (not-invented-here) mentality and dismissive attitude toward non-U.S. technology. At the same time, Japanese technology should not be overestimated. Technological assessments must be *comparative* to U.S. capabilities or alternatives. The United States has yet to develop the expertise that will allow accurate assessments that avoid these two extremes.

2. *Recognizing the legitimate self-defense needs of Japanese forces.* Access to repairs, intelligence, subcomponent replacements, and system

upgrades are not trivial matters to Japan's Self-Defense Forces, and by ignoring these elements of national security in the past, the United States has strengthened the JSDF's incentives for developing autonomous capabilities.

3. *Aggressively participating in joint-development efforts, with a recognition that the Japanese participants will attempt to obtain as much technology as they can from the project and that the U.S. side should do the same.* The U.S. must also recognize in such projects that domestic constraints in Japan, such as the "Three Arms Export Principles," may obstruct attempts to move from joint development to joint production. Such regulations should be clarified to help technology transfer but not eliminated in a way that encourages exports to third countries. Similarly, while there is recognition in Japan that technology transfers have been overwhelmingly in favor of Japan for the past four decades, this *alone* is rarely viewed as sufficient reason by Japanese officials or industrialists to justify Japanese technology transfers back to the United States. U.S. participants must bring something to the table. Nevertheless, the value of collaborative projects should not be measured only in the quantitative terms of U.S. jobs saved or data packages transferred. There is also inherent long-term benefit for U.S. companies and labs to be gained from integrating into Japan's R&D structure.

4. *Maintaining a positive commitment to forward deployment of U.S. troops and the U.S.-Japan alliance system.* When bilateral defense technology issues come to be discussed purely in terms of economics and technology, the United States will lose its most important supporters in the Diet, the Ministry of Foreign Affairs, and the JDA. The U.S. government must engage these officials in a proactive way to identify bilateral, regional, and global security goals. Similarly, important force structure decisions in Asia must be made by the Pentagon with careful consideration of the impact on Japanese (and other regional powers) own plans for autonomous defense capabilities.

5. *Recognizing and utilizing clout selectively.* The United States' influence on Japan is not on the increase. After a certain point, relentless pressure to obtain defense technology or sell U.S. systems increases the attractiveness of European partners to Japan. French, British, and German firms have been expanding their forays into the Japanese defense and aerospace markets since FSX, and strike quickly in the wake of any U.S.-Japan friction over defense technology. To this end, the U.S. side must establish better internal policy coordination. The

acquisition and policy components of the Office of the Secretary of Defense, the DOD labs, and industry must all contribute to a carefully calculated decision on what the United States expects out of technology and defense relations with Japan. The future of U.S. credibility and clout depends on such coordination.

In short, the United States must follow the Japanese comprehensive security model in approaching alliance relations with Japan. The technological, operational, and political dimensions of our bilateral security relationship must be viewed as interconnected parts of a whole.

Japan's postwar experience with defense production demonstrates that technology need not be a divisive element in alliances—even after the demise of a common enemy focuses the two nations' attention on mutual competitiveness. The possibilities for bilateral technological collaboration are vast after the Cold War. In light of the economic losses of both countries' defense industrial bases, there is great potential benefit from joint development and defense technology transfer. The global threats from proliferation of weapons of mass destruction also call for a harnessing of combined U.S. and Japanese technological strength. Other possibilities exist in the areas of energy resources and the environment. In short, the history of kokusanka demonstrates not only the fact that the United States and Japan cooperate in spite of technology—but also that technology issues will increasingly force us to cooperate in order to guarantee our mutual security.

Epilogue

As this book went to print in the summer of 1995 Keidanren issued yet another statement on defense production, this time in anticipation of a revised National Defense Program Outline. The May 11 "Call for a Defense Program for a New World Order" did not mention kokusanka once, noting only that declining defense budgets must be offset with steps to "maintain and enhance the defense production and technology base" and "make it possible to undertake joint R&D and production with the United States, with which Japan has close ties in security matters."[1]

Almost five decades earlier Keidanren also marked the initiation of the postwar U.S.–Japan security relationship with calls for close defense industrial cooperation. In the early 1950s Japanese industry needed U.S. technological assistance. In the 1990s Japanese industry will need a cooperative relationship with U.S. firms to help offset the stranglehold of Japan's shrinking defense market and the arms export ban. Despite forty-five years of kokusanka, Japanese defense producers have been unable to break their dependence on the United States.

Should the United States gloat over this situation? Absolutely not, because the undeniable reality is that forty-five years into the U.S.-Japan security relationship we are now more dependent on Japan as well. The U.S.

military presence in Japan provides a base for U.S. economic influence in East Asia and serves as the strategic hub for our regional and global power projection. Japanese dual-use technology continues to grow in importance to our own defense industrial base.[2] Japan's support is often indispensable to our own agenda for global leadership (and not always forthcoming).

The graveyard of abandoned kokusanka projects in the postwar era is testimony to the resilience of the U.S.-Japan alliance within Japan's political system and the limits of autonomy, whether technological or political/military. The United States and Japan have built an alliance that helped to win the Cold War and to lay the security foundations for what could be decades of dynamic economic growth in the region. It may be that East Asia develops cooperative security mechanisms that can replace the system of bilateral alliances now in place. Until such a time comes, however, the United States and Japan will have to take steps to redefine the alliance so that it has the flexibility to deal with the ambiguous and diverse security environment of the future. During the Cold War we built modes of alliance cooperation based largely on who we stood against. Now we must develop interoperability based on who we intend to stand with.

In 1994 Nobel Literature Prize Laureate Oye Kensaburo stunned his Norwegian audience by declaring himself "a marginal man in a marginal society." The logic of kokusanka—hedging against entrapment or abandonment by the United States—was often the logic of a marginal country. But Japan is no longer marginal to the security of East Asia and the stability of the world. For the U.S.-Japan alliance to mature beyond the era of kokusanka, both countries must decide what their roles and missions will be in maintaining peace and stability in the region and the globe. Ultimately the question of who builds what should be determined by the more fundamental question of how the two countries plan to share the task at hand.

Notes

Introduction

1. The theme of entrapment-versus-abandonment was developed by Glenn Snyder in "The Security Dilemma in Alliance Politics," *World Politics* 32 (July 1984): 461–95.

1. The Allure of Autonomy: Defense Production and Alliance, Defense Production and the Economy

1. E. H. Norman, *Japan's Emergence as a Modern State* (New York: Institute of Pacific Relations, 1940), 133.
2. Meiron and Susie Harries, *Soldiers of the Sun: The Rise and Fall of the Imperial Japanese Army* (New York: Random House), 127.
3. David Asher, "Convergence and Its Costs: The International Politics of Japanese Macroeconomic Liberalization, 1918–1932" (unpublished manuscript, London School of Economics, January 1991).
4. William J. Lockwood, *The Economic Development of Japan* (Princeton: Princeton University Press, 1954), 42.
5. Chalmers Johnson, *MITI and the Japanese Economic Miracle: The Growth of Industrial Policy, 1925–1975* (Stanford: Stanford University Press), 175–77.
6. See, for example, James Fallows, *Looking at the Sun: The Rise of the New East Asian Economic System* (New York: Pantheon, 1993); Laura D'Andrea Tyson et al., *Politics and Productivity: How Japan's Development Strategy Works* (New York:

Harpers, 1989); John Zysman et al., *The Highest Stakes: Economic Foundations of the Next Security System* (New York: Oxford, 1992); Richard J. Samuels, *Rich Nation/Strong Army: National Security and the Technological Transformation of Japan* (Ithaca: Cornell University Press, 1994).

7. Richard J. Samuels, "Reinventing Security: Japan Since Meiji," *Daedalus* (Fall 1991): 48.
8. Samuels, *Rich Nation/Strong Army*, 34.
9. Robert Reich, "The Rise of Technonationalism," *Atlantic Monthly* (April 1987).
10. Samuels also points out that the term "technonationalism can connote 'techno-protectionism' in Japan and must therefore be used with care and precision." See Samuels, *Rich Nation/Strong Army*, x.
11. Ishihara Shintaro, *"No" to Ieru Nihon* (A Japan that can say "no") (Tokyo: Kōbunsha, 1989), p. 19.
12. Ibid., 85.
13. *The Asian Wall Street Journal* (November 7, 1989).
14. Yoshihara Koichiro, *Nihon no Heiki Sangyō* (Japan's arms industry) (Tokyo: Shakai Shisuosha, 1988), 85.
15. Keidanren Bōei Seisan Iinkai (The Keidanren Defense Production Committee), "Bōeisobi Kenkyū kaihatsu no shinshutsu ni kan shite Wareware no Kenkai" (Our view on the promotion of R&D for defense equipment) (November 22, 1979).
16. Samuels, *Rich Nation/Strong Army*, 5–8.
17. Joseph Schumpeter, *Capitalism, Socialism, and Democracy* (New York: Harper, 1942). Scholars at the Berkeley Roundtable on the International Economy has applied Schumpeterian theory to Japan to claim that there is a unique Japanese "Technoeconomic Paradigm"—a construct that hits on the forces behind the kokusanka debate but may present them as far too monolithic. See also Tyson et al., *Politics and Productivity*.
18. R. E. Johnson, "Transfers of United States Aerospace Technology to Japan," in Raymond Vernon, *The Technology Factor in International Trade* (New York: Columbia University Press, 1970).
19. One U.S. official involved in the F-104 program told R. E. Johnson: "We were paid to put them in business and we gave them everything we had" (ibid., 317).
20. Interview with Tsutsui Ryozo, TRDI Director, by the author in *Defense News* (January 19, 1990).
21. Interview with JDA official in Tokyo (April 18, 1990).
22. For example, a 1969 survey prepared by the Keidanren Defense Production Committee found that in the prior year defense contractors paid for 37 percent of R&D costs for parts development, compared to the JDA Technology Research and Development Institute's 63 percent; 72 percent of subsystems R&D costs to TRDI's 27 percent; and 49 percent of systems level R&D, compared to TRDI's 49 percent (note: the total is not 100 percent because other minor costs are not included). See Senga Tetsuya, "Bōeichō buki kenkyū kaihatsu no jitsuno chosa" (Survey of Defense Agency R&D), *1970 Jietai Sōbi Nenkan* (Defense equipment yearbook) (Tokyo: Asagumo Shimbunsha Press, 1970). The report noted that companies often must recover losses later in the production stage. There are no

similar studies available for recent years, but interviews with JDA and industry officials suggest that the ratio of TRDI to company R&D funding has not changed significantly.

23. Keidanren Defense Production Committee, *Bōeiseibi Shokutoku no Sentaku: Keidanren no Poréshee Assessmento Shian* (Choices in rules for acquiring defense equipment: A Keidanren policy assessment) (November 1974).

24. Ibid.

25. "Issues and Trends in Industrial/Scientific Technology: Towards Techno-Globalism" (MITI, June 1992), 25.

26. Hugh Patrick and Henry Rosovsky, *Asia's New Giant: How the Japanese Economy Works* (Washington, D.C.: The Brookings Institution, 1976), 419.

27. *Jietai Sōbi Nenkan*, 1965–1992 issues.

28. Keidanren Defense Production Committee, "Defense Production in Japan" (January 1993), 2–3.

29. Patrick and Rosovsky, *Asia's New Giant*, 44–45.

30. *1971 Jietai Sōbi Nenkan*, 389.

31. Keidanren Defense Production Committee, *Bōeiseibi Shokutoku no Sentaku*.

32. Nagai Yonosuke, *Heiwa no Daisho* (Compensation for peace) (Tokyo: Chūōkōronsha, 1967).

33. Ibid., 160.

34. Ibid., 160.

35. Interview with Defense Production Committee director at Keidanren headquarters (March 28, 1990).

36. Quoted in "The United States and Japan in 1991: Discord or Dialogue?" (Washington, D.C.: The Johns Hopkins School of Advanced International Studies/Edwin O. Reischauer Center for East Asian Studies, 1991), 98.

37. Ibid., 97.

38. John Dower, *Empire and Aftermath: Yoshida Shigeru and the Japanese Experience, 1878–1954* (Cambridge: Harvard East Asian Monographs, 1979), 369.

39. See Kōsaka Masataka, *Shushō Yoshida Shigeru* (Yoshida Shigeru, Prime Minister) (Tokyo: Chūōkōronsha, 1968).

40. *Bōeicho, Jietai* (Japan Defense Agency/Japan Self-Defense Forces: History and organization) (Tokyo: Bōeikenyūka, 1988), 74–94.

41. Tomiyama Kazuō, *Nihon no Bōeisangyo* (Japan's defense industries) (Tokyo: Tōyōkeizai, 1979), 109.

42. *Bōeicho, Jietai*, 125.

43. *Defense of Japan 1989* (Japan Defense Agency), 148.

44. *Wagakuni ni okeru Bōeiryoku Seibi no Keika* (Trends in Japan's defense equipment build-up), 121. This internal study was prepared by the JDA as a blunt assessment of the agency's history of defense planning.

45. Vernon, *The Technology Factors in International Trade*, 354.

46. U.S. Department of Defense, *DoD Regulations for Foreign Military Sales* (DoD 5105. 3383-M): chapter 7, "Preparation and Processing of FMS Cases," pp. 700/1–704/7, and chapter 14, "Special Programs and Activities," pp. 1400/1–1401/27.

47. Interview with a member of the U.S. Aerospace Industry Association of Japan in Tokyo (May 10, 1990).

2. "On Sea, on Land, and Then On to Space!": The Growth of the Defense Industry's Political and Technological Base, 1950–1969

1. Until 1963 these were Shin MHI, Mitsubishi Nihon Kōgyō, and Mitsubishi Zōsen Shipbuilding.
2. *Umi ni Riku ni soshte Uchū e: Mitsubishi Jūkōgyō no Shashi* (On sea, on land, and then on to space: The company history of Mitsubishi Heavy Industries) (Tokyo: MHI, 1991), 87.
3. James Auer, *The Postwar Rearmament of Japanese Maritime Forces, 1945–1971* (New York: Praeger, 1973), 87.
4. The corporate links from the prewar to postwar periods were strong. Nakajima was broken up, but five of the resulting companies reformed as Fuji Heavy Industries in 1953. Another part of Nakajima fused with Nissan in 1961. In 1989 a vice president of Nissan took over as president of Fuji Heavy Industries, prompting rumors of a full reorganization of the Nakajima Corporation.
5. Reinhard Drifte, *Arms Production in Japan: The Military Applications of Civilian Technology* (London: Westview, 1986), 10.
6. John Dower, *Empire and Aftermath: Yoshida Shigeru and the Japanese Experience, 1878–1954* (Cambridge: Harvard East Asian Monographs, 1979), 432.
7. Ibid., 387.
8. *Bōei Seisan Iinkai Jūnenshi* (The ten-year history of the Defense Production Committee) (Tokyo: Keidanren, 1964), 14.
9. Keidanren, "Heiwa Jōyaku ni tai Suru Kihon Yōbō" (Basic request on the peace treaty), in *Bōei Seisan Iinkai Jūnenshi*, 16.
10. *Nihon Heiki Kogyokai Sanjunenshi* (Thirty-year history of the Japan Ordnance Association) (Tokyo: Nihon Heiki Kōgyōkai, 1983), 3.
11. Keidanren, "MSA Ukeire ni kan Suru Ippanteki Yoboken" (General request on the acceptance of the Mutual Security Agreement), in *Bōei Seisan Iinkai Jūnenshi*, 13.
12. *1967 Jietai Sōbi Nenkan*, 374.
13. Ōtake Hideo, "Nihon ni okeru Gunsan kansuru fukugōtai Keisei no Bunseki" (Analysis of the formation of Japan's military-industrial complex), in Ōtake Hideo, ed., *Nihon Seijino Sōten* (The Japanese political debate) (Tokyo: Sannichi Shōbō, 1990), 38.
14. *Yomiuri Shimbun* (December 12, 1952).
15. *Nikkei Shimbun* (August 2, 1953).
16. *Bōeicho, Jietai*, 59.
17. Ibid., 56.
18. Auer, *Postwar Rearmament*, 96.
19. Miyazawa Kiichi, *Tokyo-Washington no Shidan* (Tokyo-Washington secret diary) (Tokyo: Jitsugyo, 1957).
20. Dower, *Empire and Aftermath*, 447.
21. *Bōei Seisan Iinkai Jūnenshi*, 71.
22. *Bōei Seisan Iinkai Jūnenshi*, 106.
23. *1967 Jietai Sōbi Nenkan*, 374.
24. *Wagakuni ni okeru Bōeiryoku Seibi no Keika* (Trends in Japan's defense equipment build-up), 5.

25. Ibid., 6.

26. *Bōei Seisan Iinkai Junenshi*, 200.

27. *Bōeicho, Jietai*, 269.

28. *Wagakuni ni okeru Bōeiryoku Seibi no Keika*, 9.

29. *Bōei handobukku* (Defense handbook) (Tokyo: Asagumo Shimbunsha Press, 1992), 15.

30. *Wagakuni ni okeru Bōeiryoku Seibi no Keika*, 8–9.

31. Yoshihara Koichiro, *Nihon no Heiki Sangyō* (Japan's arms industry) (Tokyo: Shakai Shisuosha, 1988), 91.

32. Anthony Sampson, *The Arms Bazaar: From Lebanon to Lockheed* (New York: Viking, 1977), 225.

33. Tomiyama Kazuō, *Nihon no Bōeisangyo* (Japan's defense industries) (Tokyo: Tōyōkeizai, 1979), 116–18. See also "Sengo Sangyoshi e no Teigen" (Statement on postwar industry), an interview with the Keidanren Defense Production Committee director in *Economisto* (June 28, 1976).

34. *1968 Jietai Sōbi Nenkan*, 387.

35. Higher cost estimates during the year put pressure on the JDA to increase the level of components imported. The LDP promised the Diet that the jets would only cost 2 million dollars each and did not want to break that promise given the high level of controversy surrounding the jet and the new treaty. Industry argued successfully that such a move would hinder repairs and drive up costs anyway (*Bōei Seisan Iinkai Jūnenshi*, 282).

36. *1968 Jietai Sōbi Nenkan*, 389.

37. *Bōei Handobukku*, 32.

38. *Bōeicho, Jietai*, 269–72. From 1952 to 1954 this institute had been the NSA Technology Research Institute and from 1954 to 1958 the JDA Technology Research Institute. The addition of "Development" to the Institute's title signified its new role.

39. *Bōei Handobukku*, 31–32.

40. *1967 Jietai Sōbi Nenkan*, 380.

41. *Nihon Keizai Shimbun* (May 23, 1960). See also Yoshihara, *Nihon no Heiki Sangyō*, 108. The committee was built on the back of the Defense Production Study Group, an organization set up in 1958 to link the Defense Production Committee, the Japan Ordnance Association, and two smaller industry associations.

42. *Asahi Shimbun* (July 4, 1963). See also Yoshihara, *Nihon no Heiki Sangyō*, 95–100.

43. *Wagakuni ni okeru Bōeiryoku Seibi no Keika*, 40.

44. Ibid., 48.

45. *1967 Jietai Sōbi Nenkan*, 368.

46. *Nihon Keizai Shimbun* (October 30, 1969).

47. *Nihon Keizai Shimbun* (September 15, 1969).

48. The association presented its report in a meeting with the JDA in August 1967 (*1968 Jietai Sōbi Nenkan*, 390). The Japan Aircraft Industry Association later changed its name to the Society of Japanese Aerospace Companies (SJAC).

49. Report of the *Nihon Heiki Kōgyōkai* (Japan Ordnance Association) in the *1968 Jietai Sōbi Nenkan*, 388.

50. Japan Ordnance Association, "Dorubōei ni taisuru Yōbo" (Request regarding dollar defense), *Nihon Heiki Kōgyōkai* (December 25, 1967).

3. "Self-Defense to the Fore, Alliance to the Rear!": The Nixon Doctrine, the Fourth Defense Plan, and the Political Zenith of Kokusanka, 1970–1976

1. *1968 Jietai Sōbi Nenkan*, 387.
2. See *A U.S. Foreign Policy for the 1970s*, President Nixon's official statement on what would be known as the "Nixon Doctrine."
3. *Asahi Shimbun* (March 19, 1970).
4. *1989 Defense of Japan*, 82.
5. Op. cit.
6. *1978 Jietai Sōbi Nenkan*, 367; *1970 Jeitai Sōbi Nenkan*, 487.
7. *1970 Jietai Sōbi Nenkan*, 421.
8. "Sengo Sangyōshi e no Shōgen" (Statement on postwar industrial history), *Economisto* (September 6, 1977), 78.
9. Ōtake Hideo does a thorough analysis of the range of business inputs into the defense debate of the 1970s in *Nihon no Bōei to Kokunai Seiji* (Japan's defense and domestic politics) (Tokyo: Sannichi Shobō, 1986).
10. *Asahi Shimbun* (November 11, 1970), 106.
11. "Sōbi no Seisan oyobi Kaihatsu ni kan Suru Kihon Hōshin" (Basic policy on equipment production and development) (July 18, 1970). Listed in the *1971 Jietai Sōbi Nenkan*. The basic policy was a *tsutatsu* (policy decision) at the bureau level and was never subjected to Diet review or interministerial debate. The LDP Policy Affairs Research Council Defense Division—a sympathetic audience—did review the policy.
12. Senga went on to note that Nakasone's commitment to Japan's defense industrial base was recognized because he had also been a strong promoter of rocket development as Science and Technology Agency director-general ("Sengo Sangyōshi e no Shōgen," *Economisto* [September 6, 1979]).
13. "Jiki Bōeiryoku Sōbi Mondai ni Kansuru Wareware no Iken" (Our opinion on the next defense program equipment issue), Keidanren (August 1970). Also, *Wagakuni ni okeru Bōeiryoku Seibi no Keika* (Trends in Japan's defense equipment build-up), 119.
14. *Wagakuni ni okeru Bōeiryoku Seibi no Keika*, 60.
15. *Ibid.*, 103.
16. *Asahi Shimbun* (October 22, 1970).
17. *1972 Jietai Sōbi Nenkan*, 417.
18. *Asahi Shimbun* (October 8, 1971).
19. *Asahi Shimbun* (February 9, 1972).
20. *Asahi Shimbun* (October 8, 1971).
21. *Asahi Shimbun* (February 8, 1972).
22. Kent Calder, "Kanryo vs. Shomin: Contrasting Dynamics of Conservative Leadership in Post-War Japan," in Terry MacDougall, ed., *Political Leadership in Contemporary Japan* (University of Michigan Papers in Japan Studies no. 1, 1982), 14.
23. John Emerson and Leanord Humphries, *Will Japan Rearm? A Study in Attitudes*

(AEI Hoover Policy Studies no. 9, December 1973), 70.

24. "Sengo Sangyōshi e no Shōgen," *Economisto* (September 13, 1977).

25. Development of an early warning aircraft (AEW) had also been a priority in the Nakasone Plan, but the AEW development schedule was still premature compared to the FST/T-2 and PXL programs. Consequently, AEW was soon dropped as a priority by industry and the JDA given the new political pressures on the defense budget.

26. *Asahi Shimbun* (October 9, 1972).

27. "Sengo Sangyōshi e no Shōgen," *Economisto* (September 13, 1977).

28. *Asahi Shimbun* (October 8, 1972).

29. *Asahi Shimbun* (October 9, 1972).

30. John Creighton Campbell, *Contemporary Japanese Budget Politics* (Berkeley: University of California Press, 1977).

31. *Asahi Shimbun* (evening edition, October 9, 1972).

32. *Asahi Shimbun* (October 10, 1972).

33. *Asahi Shimbun* (October 9, 1972).

34. *Heiki Sangyo no Genjo*, 68.

35. "Sengo Sangyōshi e no Shōgen," *Economisto* (July 26, 1977).

36. The Aircraft Industry Association (*Nihon Kōkūkikōgyōkai*) complained in 1972 that "a faction in the JDA believes it is acceptable to have a significantly reduced aircraft manufacturing capability in peacetime" (*1973 Jietai Sōbi Nenkan*, 486).

37. "Kokusanka o Meguru Shomondai" (Various problems of autonomous production) in the *1972 Jietai Sōbi Nenkan*, 425.

38. "Sengo Sangyōshi e no Shōgen," *Economisto* (July 26, 1977).

39. Recounted by Senga in *Economisto* (September 13, 1977) and in Yoshihara Koichiro, "Sangyō Shidōkata ga Motarasu Mono Rokuheedo Jiken" (The Lockheed incident: Caused by the style of industry leadership), *Economisto* (March 9, 1976).

40. "Kokusanka o Meguru Shōmondai," in the *1972 Jietai Sōbi Nenkan*, 425.

41. *Nihon Keizai Shimbun* (January 27, 1973).

42. *Wagakuni ni okeru Bōeiryoku Seibi no Keika*, 103–4.

43. Anthony Sampson, *The Arms Bazaar: From Lebanon to Lockheed* (New York: Viking, 1977), 259.

44. Keidanren Defense Production Committee, "Bōei Sōbi Shokutoku hoho no Sentaku" (The choices for acquiring defense equipment—Keidanren "Policy Assessment") (November 1974).

45. *Wagakuni ni okeru Bōeiryoku Seibi no Keika*, 103.

46. Keidanren Defense Production Committee, "Wagakuni Bōei Sangyo no Genjo Bunseki to Kongo no Taio" (An analysis of Japan's contemporary defense industry and future policy) (August 1977).

47. Report of the *Nihon Kōkū Uchū Kōgyōkai* (Japan Aerospace Industry Association) in the *1976 Jietai Sōbi Nenkan*, 456.

48. *1975 Jietai Sōbi Nenkan*, 450.

49. *Tōkyo Shimbun* (October 10, 1987).

4. The Emerging Paradox: Bilateral Defense Cooperation and the Growth of Technonationalism, 1976–1986

1. Katahara Eiichi, *The Politics of Japanese Defense Policy* (Ph.D. dissertation, Griffith University, 1990), 135.
2. Kubo Takuya, "Wagakuni no Bōei Kōzō to Bōeiryoku Seibi no Kangaekata: KB Kojin Rombun" (Thoughts about our defense structure and defense capabilities: A private KB memo) (Japan Defense Agency, June 1974).
3. Ibid., 12.
4. Ibid., 7.
5. Katahara, *The Politics of Japanese Defense Policy*, 151.
6. Bōei o Kangaeru kai Jimukyoku hen (The Forum on Defense), ed., *Wagakuni no Bōei o Kangaeru* (Thinking about our nation's defense) (September 1976), 37.
7. Ibid., 37.
8. Interview with PARC Defense Division Staff Director at LDP Headquarters (May 6, 1988).
9. Wagakuni ni okeru Bōeiryoku Seibi no Keika (Trends in Japan's defense equipment build-up), 94.
10. Ōtake Hideo, *Nihon no Bōei to Kokunai Seiji* (Japan's defense and domestic politics) (Tokyo: Sannichi Shobō, 1986), 139.
11. This was the 1975 Keidanren Defense Production Committee Policy Assessment on Acquiring Defense Equipment referred to in chapter 3.
12. Interview with Keidanren official in Washington, D.C. (October 25, 1991).
13. Industry's own special pipe into government, the Kokusanka Consultation Committee, had been out of action since 1971, when a panicky JDA director-general promised to disband the group in response to intense questioning about its activities by opposition party members in the Diet's Lower House Budget Committee. Recounted by Senga in "Sengo Sangyoshi e no Teigen," *Economisto* (July 26, 1977).
14. *Wagakuni ni okeru Bōeiryoku Seibi no Keika*, 96.
15. Interview with Keidanren official in Washington, D.C. (October 25, 1991).
16. *Asahi Shimbun* (March 20, 1978).
17. *1979 Jietai Sōbi Nenkan*, 467.
18. *Wagakuni ni okeru Bōeiryoku Seibi no Keika*, 195.
19. Keidanren Defense Production Committee, "Defense Production in Japan" (January 1993), 7.
20. *Wagakuni ni okeru Bōeiryoku Seibi no Keika*, 40.
21. Keidanren Defense Production Committee, "Bōei Sōbi Kenkyū Kaihatsu no Shinshutsu ni Kansuru Wareware no Kenkai" (Our views on the promotion of defense systems R&D) (November 22, 1979).
22. Interview with ASDF officers in Tokyo (July 10, 1989).
23. This attitude was apparent in all interviews conducted with ASDF officers for this book.
24. *1979 Jietai Sōbi Nenkan*. Separating R&D funding from a commitment to production is a recurring theme for the JDA in times of tight budgeting.

25. "The Comprehensive National Security Study Group Report" (July 2, 1980). See also Mike Mochizuki, "Japan's Search for Strategy," *International Security* (Winter 1983/1984), 159.

26. Yoshihara Koichiro, *Nihon no Heiki Sangyō* (Japan's arms industry) (Tokyo: Shakai Shisuosha, 1988), 34.

27. Ibid., 34.

28. "Nihon no Heiki Sangyō wa Doko e Iku? Chumoku Sareru Nichibei Kyodo Kaihatsu no Ugoki" (Where will Japan's weapons industry go? The focus on trends in U.S.-Japan joint development), *Economisto* (November 20, 1980).

29. The kokusanka level for the F-104 had been 85 percent. For the F-4 it had been 90 percent.

30. Interview with Chuma Kiyofuku, defense editorial writer for the *Asahi Shimbun* in Tokyo (July 1989).

31. Keidanren Defense Production Committee, "56 Chugyo ni Taisuru Kenkai" (Views on the 1981 midterm Defense Procurement Plan) (April 9, 1982). These attacks on FMS continued in Keidanren publications through 1986.

32. *Asahi Shimbun* (June 2, 1982).

33. General Accounting Office, "U.S. Military Co-Production Programs Assist Japan in Developing Its Civil Aircraft Industry" C-ID-8204 (March 4, 1982), unclassified version.

34. Gotoda Masaharu, *Naikaku Kanbōchōkan* (Chief Cabinet Secretary) (Tokyo: Kōdansha, 1989), 30–35.

35. Interview with staff of then JDA Director-General Omura Joji (March 15, 1990). The concerns of prodefense LDP Diet members are also reflected in Mihara Asaö et al., *Nihon no Bōei: Kore de Yoika?* (Japan's defense: Will this do?) (Tokyo: Jiūsha, 1985), 42–47. This book is a rapporteur's report from a roundtable discussion by LDP and DSP members.

36. Keidanren Defense Production Committee, "Nichibei Buki Gijitsu Kyōryoku Mondai ni tsuite" (On problems in U.S.-Japan weapons technology cooperation), a report in the *1984 Jietai Sōbi Nenkan*, 491.

5. "Return of the Zero Fighter!": The FSX Crisis

1. Yoshihara Koichiro, *Nihon no Heiki Sangyō* (Japan's arms industry) (Tokyo: Shakai Shisuosha, 1988), 183, and Ōtsuki Shinhi and Honda Masaru, *Nichibei FSX Sensō* (The U.S.-Japan FSX war) (Tokyo: Rosonsha, 1991), 5–7.

2. Ōtsuki and Honda, *Nichibei FSX Sensō*, 28.

3. Mitsubishi Heavy Industries, "Jikisentoki (An) ni Tsuite" (Regarding the proposal for the next [proposed] jet fighter) (1985), 1–27.

4. Kawasaki Heavy Industries, "Shōrai Sentōki no Sisutemu Sutadi" (System study for the future fighter jet) (February 1985), 1–13.

5. *Asahi Shimbun* (April 2, 1985).

6. *Asahi Shimbun* (evening edition, April 4, 1984).

7. Testimony of General Dynamics CEO Herbert F. Rogers before the House Foreign Affairs Committee "U.S.-Japan Security Cooperation Hearing," 231–32. Quoted in Gregg Noble, "America, Japan, and the FSX Jet Fighter Plane: Structural

Asymmetries in Bilateral Negotiations," a paper prepared for the 1990 Meeting of the Association for Asian Studies, Chicago, April 5–8, 1990.

8. Ibid.

9. *Asahi Shimbun* (June 23, 1985).

10. *Nikkei Shimbun* (July 9, 1985).

11. *Yomiuri Shimbun* (July 11, 1985).

12. *Tōkyo Shimbun* (November 5, 1985).

13. *Nikkei Shimbun* (December 26, 1985).

14. This description was given to Richard Samuels by a U.S. defense official. Quoted in Samuels, "Defense Production and Industrial Development: The Case of Japanese Aircraft," in Laura D'Andrea Tyson et al., *Politics and Productivity: How Japan's Development Strategy Works* (New York: Harpers, 1989), 301.

15. Peter Middleton and Janice Lowe, "XT-4: Potent with Potential," *Flight International* (2/9 January, 1988): 17–21.

16. Interview with JDA official seconded from MITI, Aircraft and Ordnance Division, in Tokyo (April 18, 1990).

17. Gregg Rubinstein recognized the importance of the SH-60 case when he was deputy director of MDAO and explained it to the author in an interview in Washington, D.C. (September 15, 1992).

18. Ibid.

19. *Tōkyo Shimbun* (January 26, 1986).

20. *Mainichi Shimbun* (March 13, 1986).

21. *Yomiuri Shimbun* (March 17, 1986).

22. JDA sources told the *Yomiuri Shimbun* afterward that they viewed this as an official proposal from Weinberger for joint development (*Yomiuri Shimbun* [April 27, 1986]).

23. JDA, "FSX ni kan Suru Seibi no Kento Kekka ni tsuite" (Regarding the results of the FSX equipment study) (October 21, 1987), 10. This was the JDA's internal memorandum explaining the choice of the F-16 with attached summaries of the various bilateral meetings. See also the account by Ōtsuki and Honda, *Nichibei FSX Senso*, 80.

24. R. Tsutsui, "December Mission," *Bōei Gijitsu* vol. 15, no. 2 (February 1995).

25. Interview with former MDAO official in Washington, D.C. (September 15, 1993).

26. *Mainichi Shimbun* (December 23, 1986).

27. Ōtsuki and Honda, *Nichibei FSX Senso*, 361.

28. Ibid., 361.

29. Tawara Soichiro, "FSX o Zanpai" (The crushing defeat of FSX), *Shukan Bunshun* (November 6, 1989), 63.

30. *Nikkei Shimbun* (February 15, 1987).

31. Ibid.

32. *Asahi Shimbun* (March 11, 1987).

33. *Mainichi Shimbun* (evening edition, March 18, 1987).

34. *Asahi Shimbun* (April 19, 1987). See also Ōtsuki and Honda, *Nichibei FSX Senso*, 89.

35. *Nikkei Aerospace* (May 7, 1990).

36. *Mainichi Shimbun* (April 8, 1987).

37. Ōtsuki and Honda, *Nichibei* FSX *Sensō*, 106–8. See also interview with Tsutsui Ryozo by the author in *Defense News* (February 19, 1990).

38. *Nikkei Shimbun* (May 17, 1987).

39. *Nikkei Shimbun* (May 16, 1987).

40. *Nikkei Shimbun* (June 16, 1987).

41. Ōtsuki and Honda, *Nichibei* FSX *Sensō*, 362, and *Nikkei Aerospace* (May 7, 1990).

42. *Nikkei Shimbun* (July 10, 1987).

43. *Washington Post* (October 3, 1987).

44. *Mainichi Shimbun* (September 3, 1987).

45. *Washington Post* (September 27, 1987).

46. *Wall Street Journal* (October 5, 1987).

47. *Sankei Shimbun* (September 2, 1987).

48. JDA, "FSX ni kan Suru Sōbi no Kentōkekka," 7–9.

49. *Mainichi Shimbun* (April 11, 1987).

50. *Washington Post* (September 27, 1987) and *Wall Street Journal* (October 5, 1987).

51. *Mainichi Shimbun* (October 22, 1987).

52. Ōtsuki and Honda, *Nichibei* FSX *Sensō*, 212.

53. Norio Endo, former program manager for the F-14 and a leader in the U.S. aerospace business community in Japan.

54. *Tōkyo Shimbun* (October 22, 1987).

55. *Wall Street Journal* (October 22, 1987).

56. Quoted in Noble, "America, Japan, and the FSX Fighter Plane," 11.

57. *Nikkei Aerospace* (May 7, 1990), 16.

58. Ibid.

59. *Aviation Week & Space Technology* (June 13, 1988), 25, and *Asahi Shimbun* (April 7, 1989).

60. Ina Hisayoshi, national security correspondent for the *Nikkei Shimbun*.

61. Section 84 of the National Defense Authorization Act for FY 1989 requires the DOD to "regularly solicit and consider comments and recommendations from the Secretary of Commerce with respect to the commercial implications of such military memorandum of understanding or related agreements and the potential effects of such memorandum of understanding or related agreements on the international competitive position of the United States industry" (from *Legislation on Foreign Relations of the United States through 1989* [March 1990], 913).

62. *Washington Post* (January 29, 1989).

63. *Nikkei Aerospace* (May 7, 1990).

64. U.S. General Accounting Office. U.S.-Japan FS-X Codevelopment Program. Testimony of Frank Conahan. May 16, 1989.

65. *Washington Post* (May 17, 1989).

66. *Wall Street Journal* (November 29, 1989).

67. Tawara, "FSX o Zanpai," 64.

6. The Limits of Autonomy: The Shifting Defense Constituency in the FSX Debate

1. *Nikkei Sangyō Shimbun* (October 22, 1989).

2. *Yomiuri Shimbun* (September 26, 1988).

3. Keidanren's influence vis-à-vis the government comes precisely because the organization does not have membership from MITI or other government agencies.

4. The Asian Council, "The Asian Council's Activities Record" (March 1993), lists an average of ten exchanges with U.S. or European defense executives or experts per year.

5. *Yomiuri Shimbun* (September 26, 1988).

6. Keidanren, " Jiki Bōeiryoku Sōbi Keikaku ni Taisuru Yōbō" (Demands for the next Defense Equipment Plan) (May 15, 1989).

7. "Beikoku no Atsuryoku e no Hanpatsu" (Reaction against American pressure), *AERA* (May 30, 1989), 17.

8. See for example, Hirose Katsuya, *Gunjin to Kanryō: Bunmin Tōsei no Genkai* (Bureaucrats and soldiers: The limits of civilian control) (Tokyo: Iwanami Shoten, 1989), 217. Hirose argues that civilian control over JSDF activities is declining because the Internal Bureau and MOFA officials do not have all of the information they need to understand the weapons systems and tactical doctrine they oversee.

9. Interview with MOFA National Security Division official in Tokyo (March 7, 1990).

10. Ōtsuki Shinji and Honda Masaru, *Nichibei FSX Sensō* (The U.S.-Japan FSX war) (Tokyo: Rosonsha, 1991), 106–7.

11. *Asahi Shimbun* (March 2, 1986).

12. Kuboniwa Keiichiro, "Civilian Control of the Military Shaken by Uniformed Leaders," *Japan Economic Journal* (May 31, 1986).

13. RIPS, *Asian Survey 1989* (Tokyo: Research Institute for Peace and Security), 29.

14. Interview with MOFA official in Tokyo (March 7, 1990).

15. Ōtsuki and Honda, *Nichibei FSX Sensō*, 118. Also confirmed in interviews with Aircraft and Ordnance Division officials.

16. Dan Okimoto, *Between MITI and the Market: Japanese Industrial Policy for High Technology* (Stanford: Stanford University Press, 1989), 55–60.

17. The exact figure was 36 billion yen. The lessons of the financial failure of the YS-11 are vividly described by Tojo Teruo of MHI in a nine-part interview in the *Nikkei Sangyō Shimbun* in early 1990.

18. *1984 Jietai Sōbi Nenkan*, 496.

19. MITI, *Tsusan Kōhō* (Industry-trade report) (February 1986).

20. *Nikkei Aerospace* (May 7, 1990).

21. Tsūshō Sangyō Shō Daijin Kanbo (MITI Ministerial Secretariat), ed., *Nihon no Sentaku* (Japan's choices) (June 1988), 116.

22. Nakasone also is said to have "learned from his experience as JDA director-general" (Ōtsuki and Honda, *Nichibei FSX Sensō*, 112).

23. Interview with MOFA official in Tokyo (March 7, 1990).

24. *AERA* (March 7, 1989).

25. Ōtsuki and Honda, *Nichibei FSX Sensō*, 215. Kamei, as leader of the Study Group on Fundamental National Problems (Kokka Kihon Mondai Kenyūkai), was often critical of Japan's reliance on the United States.

26. Interview with LDP PARC staffer for the Defense Division at LDP headquarters in Tokyo (April 12, 1990).

27. See, for example, *Jiminto Seichōkai* (The LDP Policy Affairs Research Council) (Tokyo: Nihonkeizai Shimbunsha, 1983).

28. Ibid. See also Michael Green, "Bōeizoku: Defense Policy Making in Japan's Liberal Democratic Party" (MIT-Japan Program Working Paper, April 1992).
29. Described in "1982 Bōei Yosan no Hensei Katei" (The formulation of the 1982 defense budget), a series in *Asahi Shimbun* that ran from February 16 to March 26, 1982.
30. Mihara Asao, quoted by Takemura Ken in *Gekkan Jiyū Minshu* (The monthly Liberal Democrat [the LDP's party journal]) (October 1985), 60.
31. James Auer, "FSX wa koshite Ketchaku Shta" (This is how FSX was resolved), *Chuo Koron* (June 1990), 162.
32. Interview with LDP PARC staff (April 12, 1989).
33. Several of which were witnessed by the author (I was then working for a defense zoku member).
34. Ōtsuki and Honda, *Nichibei* FSX *Sensō*, 217.

7. Defense Production and Alliance in a Post–Cold War World

1. The main candidates were Pratt & Whitney's PW 229 and GE's F-110/129.
2. *Nikkei Sangyō Shimbun* (July 18, 1989).
3. IHI began work on adapting the T-4 jet trainers and the indigenously developed F-3 engine for civilian use in the YSX 75-seat commercial airliner project planned by MITI (*Nikkei Sangyō Shimbun* [July 18, 1989]).
4. Hata Takeshi, "Will FSX Take Off?" *Tokyo Air World* (January 1993). English translation, 30.
5. Interview with MHI spokesman in Tokyo (March 25, 1990).
6. *Nikkei Shimbun* (February 23, 1993).
7. "FSX Fighter Program Hits Turbulence in Cost, Politics," *Insight* (December 17, 1990). Mitsubishi engineers were concerned that they might not be able to develop the software. Their participation in SDI research had revealed just how far behind Japan was in defense-related software (*Nikkei Shimbun* [March 30, 1989]).
8. *Nikkei Shimbun* (February 14, 1995).
9. *Nikkei Shimbun* (September 3, 1994).
10. *Asahi Shimbun* (June 15, 1990). The helicopter had been under design by KHI and TRDI since 1986 (*Asahi Shimbun* [July 21, 1989]).
11. *Bōei Gijutsu* (Defense Technology Journal) (September 1992), 45–56.
12. *Nikkei Sangyō* (November 11, 1993).
13. This missile project began officially with R&D on the seeker in the 1990 TRDI budget (*Nikkei Shimbun* [April 20, 1990]; also *Nikkei Shimbun* [August 9, 1992]).
14. Michael Mecham and Eiichiro Sekigawa, "Japan to Consider Doubling Space Budget," *Aviation Week & Space Technology* (August 8, 1994).
15. *Defense News* (August 1, 1994).
16. *Mainichi Shimbun* (August 16, 1994).
17. *Defense News* (August 29, 1994) and *Mainichi Shimbun* (evening edition, August 16, 1994).
18. *Kōkū Shimbunsha Wuingu* (Aerospace newsweekly wing) (January 17, 1990).
19. *Defense News* (April 23, 1990).
20. *Defense News* (February 19, 1990).
21. MITI's budget for aerospace development in 1990 was 222 million yen: 68 million for research on the supersonic transport; 18 million for a feasibility study of

an international codevelopment system for avionics; 18 million for the feasibility study on the large-scale international engine testing facility; and 118 million for work on the ysx. MITI and industry hoped to produce the ysx in partnership with either Deutsch Aerospace, CATIC of the PRC, or Aerospatiale, CASA, and Aeritalia. However, the prospects did not look good for either partnership (*Japan Aviation Directory, 1991* [Tokyo: Kōkū Shimbunsha Wuingu, 1991], 19).

22. Interview with author in *Defense News* (February 19, 1990).

23. TRDI's Tsutsui, for example, brought this report to the attention of industry representatives in interviews and speeches. One example is in *Kōkū Shimbunsha Wuingu* (March 28, 1990).

24. Bingaman trip report and letter to Undersecretary for Acquisition John Betti (February 9, 1990).

25. *Asian Wall Street Journal* (February 26, 1990).

26. The Department of Defense, *Critical Technologies Plan* (March 15, 1990). The Pentagon listed Japan as "significantly ahead in some niches of technology": semiconductor materials and microelectronic circuits; machine intelligence and robotics; photonics; superconductivity; and biotechnology materials and processes (11). The last area was not pursued because of extreme Japanese sensitivities about experimentation with biological warfare during the Second World War.

27. *Nikkei Shimbun* (October 29, 1992).

28. *Nikkei Shimbun* (October 6, 1992).

29. Op. cit.

30. *Kōkū Shimbunsha Wuingu* (February 17, 1990). Similar comments were made in an interview in *Keizaikai* by MHI Chairman Iida Yotaro (October 27, 1992).

31. *Kōkū Shimbunsha Wuingu* (January 23, 1991).

32. "Defense Agency Reopens Talks on Purchase of AWACS Planes," *Nikkei Weekly* (October 5, 1992).

33. Although much of this was set aside for FSX, 69.4 billion yen out of 129.1 billion yen in FY1992, for example. *Bōei Gijutsu* (September 1992), 45–56.

34. Sekigawa Eiichiro, "Japan Hikes Space Budget, but Defense Tapers Off," *Aviation Week & Space Technology* (September 19, 1994).

35. "Broad Budget Cuts in Defense Seen as a Sign of Rudderless Policy," *Nikkei Weekly* (January 25, 1993).

36. Ibid.

37. Sanctions were put on the Nippon Kōkū Denshi (Japan Aircraft Electronics Company) in September 1991 after the company was caught repairing and returning (i.e., exporting) missile components to Iran. After a 2 billion yen settlement on March 11, 1992, the sanctions ended, but the impact on aerospace and defense production was "beyond estimation," according to the JDA (*Nikkei Sangyō Shimbun* [March 12, 1992]).

38. Sanemori Kikuta, *Kōkūki Buhin* (Aircraft Components) (Tokyo: Nikkei Shimbunsha, 1990), 105.

39. *Japan Aviation Directory* 1990–1991, 17.

40. *Kōkū Shimbunsha Wuingu* (February 13, 1991).

41. Michael Green, "Japanese Industry Views of Bilateral Defense Industrial Collaboration: Results of the MIT-Japan Program Survey" (MIT-Japan Program Working Paper, March 1994).

42. Paul Beaver, "The Threat from the North," *Jane's Defence Weekly* (May 21, 1994).

43. *Yomiuri Shimbun* (November 3, 1993) and *Mainichi Shimbun* (October 7, 1993) in representative articles noted that Aspin gave Japan three choices: joint development, purchase a U.S. system, or cooperate through incremental technology exchanges (in fact, the latter was implicitly contained within the first two). The *Mainichi*, citing JDA officials, concluded that TMD represented a DOD attempt to draw on Japan's strengths to save the U.S. defense industrial base.

44. Shinjidai no Anzen Hosho Seisaku Seitei Iinkai (Committee for establishing security policies for a new era), "Heiwa e no Chōsen" (The challenge toward peace) (August 8, 1994). Page 8 of this Socialist Party policy document calls for nonparticipation in TMD. The policy paper was released at the Socialists' 1994 Party Congress but was not officially approved.

45. Ina Hisayoshi, "Doubts Over Cost Effectiveness Shouldn't Shoot Down Missile Defense Proposal," *Nikkei Weekly* (October 14, 1994).

46. *Nikkei Shimbun* (September 1, 1994).

47. *Mainichi Shimbun* (September 10, 1994).

48. Paul Beaver, "Japan Weighs Up Missile Defence Options," *Jane's Defence Weekly* (August 13, 1994).

49. *Asahi Shimbun,* in its October 29, 1993, editorial on the "Perry Initiative" and TMD, questioned the U.S. motivations and urged caution. At least one Japanese monthly news journal, *Sentaku,* claimed that TFT was actually a part of the trade-oriented Framework Talks (*Sentaku* [September 1994]).

50. Barbara Opall, "One on One: Kenneth Flamm, Principal Deputy U.S. Secretary of Defense," *Defense News* (January 24, 1994).

51. Matthew Rubiner, "U.S. Industry and Government Views on U.S.-Japan Defense Technology Collaboration," (MIT-Japan Program Working Paper, April 1994).

52. JDA, "Bōei Sōbihin Chōtatsu Kondankai Hokōkū Sho" (Report of the Advisory Group on Defense Equipment Procurement) (December 1993).

53. JDA, "Bōei Sangyō Gijutsu Kondankai Hokōkū Sho" (Report of the Advisory Panel on Defense Industry and Technology) (March 18, 1994).

54. Ibid., 2.

55. The report focused on: aircraft (stealth technology, cockpit technology, engine ceramics, aerodynamic analysis, STOL, unmanned aircraft, etc.); missiles (passive sensors, composite seekers, data integration, etc.); ordnance; vehicles; shipbuilding (stealth, new design, composite materials); ASW (sound sensing and homing technology, sonar information processing technology, torpedo engine technology, robotics, etc.); early warning (AEW, satellite surveillance, etc.); c^3i (data processing, fast processing, systems integration, etc.); electronic warfare; training; logistical support (CALS, virtual reality, etc.); base area countermeasures (ibid., 19–20).

56. Ibid., 15.

57. LDP, "Kōkūsai Shakai ni okeru Nihon no Yakuwari: Anzen Hosho Mondai ni kan Suru Teigen" (Japan's role in the international community: Proposals on security issues) (February 3, 1993).

58. The Advisory Group on Defense Issues, "The Modality of the Security and Defense Capability of Japan: Outlook for the 21st Century" (August 12, 1994— official English translation). Analysis in this section is also based on a series of

"on background" interviews conducted with three of the panel's members in Tokyo between September 13 and 16, 1994.

59. Ibid., 24.
60. Ibid., 3.
61. Ibid., 20.
62. Ibid., 24.
63. Ibid., 27.
64. *Nikkei Sangyō Shimbun* (March 7, 1990). Clearly Mitsubishi was nervous about jeopardizing relations with Boeing and downplayed the relationship as much as Daimler trumpeted it. The longer-term goal of the two companies was cooperation in space. "A German-Japanese Flirtation Sure to Produce U.S. Jitters," *Insight* (April 16, 1990).
65. MHI received offers to build the FSX based on the Rafael fighter, *Nikkei Sangyō Shimbun* (July 10, 1989).
66. The U.S. Aerospace Industry Association in Japan prepared a draft white paper warning Washington about the European invasion but eventually decided not to send it after division within the ranks.
67. *Kōkū Shimbunsha Wuingu* (February 25, 1990).
68. "The Modality of the Security and Defense," 27.

Conclusion

1. Raymond Vernon and Ethan Kapstein, "National Needs, Global Resources," *Daedalus* (Fall 1991): 5.
2. Ibid., 19.
3. The U.S.–Japan–Europe Diet Members' League for Comprehensive Security (Nichibeiō Sōgō Anzen Hoshō Giin Renmei), for example, brought the opposition members of the DSP and Komeito into international interparliamentary conferences together with members of the LDP.
4. *Bōei Gijutsu* (April 1992).
5. Institute for Defense Analysis, "Dependence of U.S. Defense Systems on Foreign Technologies" (IDA paper P–2326–1/90); and the Analytic Science Corporation, "Foreign Vulnerability of Critical Industries" (March 1, 1990).
6. *Nikkei Shimbun* (March 30, 1989).
7. MITI added sixty-five new items to its technology export control list (*Nikkei Shimbun* [October 2, 1992]). In addition, a MITI advisory panel urged in the spring of 1993 that Japan should take the lead in introducing tighter export controls in a post-COCOM regime (Nakamae Hiroshi, "Tighter Rein Urged for Arms Technology," *The Nikkei Weekly* [March 29, 1993]).
8. *Nikkei Shimbun* (October 1, 1992).

Epilogue

1. Keidanren, "A Call For a Defense Program For a New World Order," May 11, 1995 (Provisional Translation). See also, "Slow Seppuku: All Defence Industries Live by Political Whim. Japan's May Die by It," *The Economist*, June 10, 1995.
2. See for example Joe Nye, "The Case for Deep Engagement," *Foreign Affairs*, Vol. 74, No. 4, July/August 1995.

Bibliography

Books, Documents, and Journal Articles in Japanese

Asagumo Shimbunsha. *Jietai Sōbi Nenkan* (Self-Defense Forces equipment yearbook), 1962–1993. [These yearbooks contain the major policy statements of the Keidanren Defense Production Committee, the Society of Japanese Aerospace Companies, and other defense and aerospace industry associations for given years.]

——. *Bōei Handbook* (Defense handbook). Tokyo: Asagumoshimbunsha, 1992.

Asahi Shimbunsha Wangan Kiki Shuzaihan, ed., *Wangan Sensō to Nihon* (The Gulf War and Japan). Tokyo: Asahi Shimbunsha, 1991.

Auer, James. "FSX Wa ko Ketchaku Shta" (This is how FSX was resolved). *Chūō Kōron*, June 1990.

"Beikoku no Atsuryoku e no Hanpatsu" (Reactions against American pressure) *AERA*, May 39, 1989.

Bōeichō Sōbikyoku. "Bōei Sangyō Gijitsu Kondankai Hōkokusho" (Report of the Advisory Group on Defense Industry and Technology), March 1994.

——. "Bōei Sōbihin Chōtatsu Kondankai Hōkokusho" (Report of the Advisory Panel on Defense Equipment Procurement), December 1993.

Bōei Kenkyūkai, ed. *Bōeichō/Jietai* (Japan Defense Agency/Japan Self-Defense Forces: History and organization). Tokyo: Bōei Kenkyukai, 1988.

Bōei Nipponsha. *Jieitai Nenkan* (Self-Defense Forces yearbook), 1965–1992.

Bōei o Kangaeru Jimukyoku. *Wagakuni no Bōei o Kangaeru* (Thinking about defense), September 1976.

Chūma Kyōfuku. *Saigunbi no Seijigaku* (The political science of rearmament). Tokyo: Chishikisha, 1985.

Etō Shinkichi and Yamamoto Shinobu. *Sōgō Anpō to Mirai no Sentaku* (Comprehensive security and future options). Tokyo: Kōdansha, 1991.

Gotoda Masuhara. *Naikaku Kanbōchokan* (Chief Cabinet Secretary). Tokyo: Iwanami Shoten, 1989.

Hirose Katsuya. *Gunjin to Kanryō: Bunmin Tōsei no Genkai* (Bureaucrats and soldiers: The limits of civilian control). Tokyo: Kōdansha, 1989.

Hōgaku Seminar, ed. *Korekara no Nichibei Anpo* (The future of U.S.-Japan security). Tokyo: Nihonhyōronsha, 1987.

Inoguchi Takashi. *Zoku Giin no Kenkyū* (A study of Diet members caucuses). Tokyo: Nihonkeizai Shimbunsha, 1987.

Ishihara Shintaro. *"No" to Ieru Nihon* (A Japan that can say "no"). Tokyo: Kōbunsha, 1989.

Japan Defense Agency. *Defense of Japan* (1989 through 1993 editions). Tokyo: Japan Times.

—. "FSX ni Kansuru Seibi no Kentō Kekka ni Tsuite" (Regarding the results of the FSX Equipment Study), October 21, 1987.

—. *Wagakuni ni okeru Bōeiryoku Seibi no Keika* (Trends in Japan's defense equipment build-up), 1982.

Jiuminshuto (LDP). "Kokusaishakai ni okeru Nihon no Yakuwari: Anzenhoshō Mondai ni Kansuru Teigen" (Japan's role in the international community: Proposals on security issues), February 3, 1993.

Kanemaru Shin. *90 Nendai no Anzen Hoshö* (National security for the 90s). Tokyo: Nihon Senryaku Kenkyūsentā, 1980.

Kawasaki Jukogyo (Kawasaki Heavy Industries). "Shōrai Sentoki no Shisutemu Study" (System study for the future fighter jet), 1986.

—. *Kyujunen no Ayumi: Kawasaki Jūkōgyōshōshi* (The ninety years walk: A short history of Kawasaki Heavy Industries). Tokyo: KHI, 1986.

Keidanren Bōei Seisan Iinkai (Keidanren Defense Production Committee). "Bōei Sōbikenkyukaihatsu Shinshitsu ni kan Shite Wareware no Kenkai" (Our view on the promotion of R&D for defense), November 22, 1979.

—. "Bōei Seibi Shokutoku Hōhō no Sentaku: Keidanren no Porishee Assessumento Shian" (Choices in rules for acquiring defense equipment: A Keidanren policy assessment), November 1974.

—. "Defense Production in Japan," November, 1994.

—. *Bōei Seisan Iinkai Junenshi* (The ten-year history of the Defense Production Committee). Tokyo: Keidanren, 1964.

Kikuta Sanemori. *Kōkūki Buhin* (Aircraft components). Tokyo: Nikkeishimbunsha, 1990.

Kinoshita Hirō. *Amerika Wa Nihon ni Nani o Motometeiru ka? Haitekku Anzen Hoshō* (What is America asking of Japan? High-tech national security). Tokyo: Nikkankōgyōshimbunsha, 1991.

Kōkū Shimbunsha Wuingu. *Japan Aviation Directory, 1990–1991*. Tokyo: Kōkūshimbunsha Wuingu, 1991.

Kōsaka Masataka. *Shushō Yoshida Shigeru* (Yoshida Shigeru, Prime Minister). Tokyo: Chūōkōronsha, 1968.

Kubo Takuya. "Wagakuni no Bōei kōzō to Bōeiryokuseibi no Kangaekatta: kb Kojin Ronbun" (Thoughts about our defense structure and defense preparedness: private kb memo), June 1974.

Mihara Asaō et al. *Nihon no Bōei: Kore de Yoi ka?* (Japan's defense: Will this do?). Tokyo: Jiūsha, 1985.

MITI. "Issues and Trends in Industrial/Scientific Technology: Towards Technoglobalism," June 1992.

Mitsubishi Jūkōgyo (mhi). *Umi ni Rikku ni Sōshte Uchū e: Mitsubishi Jūkōgyō Shashi, 1964–1989* (On sea, on land, and then on to space: The corporate history of Mitsubishi Heavy Industries, 1964–1969). Tokyo: mhi, 1989.

—. "Jiki Sentoki (An) ni Tsuite" (Regarding the proposal for the next jet fighter), 1985.

Miyazawa Kiichi. *Tōkyo Washington no Shidan* (Tokyo-Washington Secret Diary). Tokyo: Jitsugyō, 1956.

Murō Tadashi. *Bōeichō-Jimintō-Kōkū Giwaku* (jda-ldp aircraft scandal). Tokyo: Sannichi Shoten, 1979.

Nagai Yōnosuke. *Heiwa no Daishō* (Compensation for peace). Tokyo: Chūōkōronsha, 1967.

Nihon Heiki Kōgyōkai. *Nihon Heiki Kōgyōkai Sanjunenshi* (Thirty-year history of the Japan Ordnance Association). Tokyo, 1983.

—. "Doru Bōei ni Taisuru Yōbō" (Request regarding dollar defense), December 25, 1967.

Nihon Hosō Shuppankyokai, ed. *Gunshuku ga Sekai Keizai o Kaeru* (Disarmament will change the world). Tokyo: nhk, 1989.

Nihonkeizaishimbunsha, ed. *Jimintō Seichōkai* (The ldp Policy Affairs Research Council). Tokyo: Nihonkeizaishimbunsha, 1983.

"Nihon no Heiki Sangyō Wa Dokō e Iku: Chūmoku Sareru Nichibei Kyōdō Kaihatsu no Ugoki" (Where will Japan's arms industry go? The focus on trends in U.S.-Japan joint development). *Economisto*, November 20, 1990.

Okazaki Hisahiko, Nishimura Shigeki, and Satō Seisaburo. *Nichibei Dōmei to Nihon no Senryaku* (The U.S.-Japan alliance and Japanese strategy). Tokyo: php, 1991.

Ōtake Hideo. "Nihon ni Okeru Gunsankanfukugōtai Keisei no Bunseki" (An analysis of the formation of Japan's military industrial complex). In Ōtake Hideo, ed., *Nihon Seiji no Soten* (The Japanese political debate). Tokyo: Sannichi Shōbō, 1984.

—. *Nihon no Bōei to Kokunai Seiji* (Japan's defense and domestic politics). Tokyo: Sannichi Shoten, 1986.

Otsuki Shinji and Honda Masuharu. *Nichibei fsx Sensō* (The U.S.-Japan fsx war). Tokyo: Rōsonsha, 1991.

Ōzawa Ichiro. *Nihon Kaizō Keikaku* (Blueprint for a new Japan). Tokyo: Kōdansha, 1993.

Satō Seisaburo and Matsuzaki Tetsuhisa. *Jimintō Seiken* (The ldp government). Tokyo: Chūōkōronsha, 1986.

"Sengo Sangyōshi e no Shōgen" (Statement on postwar industrial history). *Economisto*, September 6, 1977.

Shinjidai no Anzen Hoshō Seisaku Seitei Iinkai (The Program for Establishing Security Policies for a New Era). "Heiwa e no Chōsen" (The challenge toward peace), Japan Social Democratic Party, August 8, 1994.

Takemura Ken. "Jimintō 'Bukai' no Kenkyū: Kokubō Bukai" (A study of the "divisions" of the ldp: The Defense Division). *Gekkan Jiūminshu*, January 1986.

Takemura Masayoshi. *Chisakutomo Kirari to Hikaru Kuni Nihon* (Japan: A small but shining country). Tokyo: Kōbunsha, 1994.

Tawara Sōichiro. "FSX o Zanpai" (The crushing defeat of FSX). *Shukan Bunshun,* November 6, 1989.

Tejima Ryūichi. *Nippon FSX o Ute: Nichibei Reisen e no Dokasen, Shinzero Keikaku* (Shooting Japan's FSX: The plan for a new zero, a fuse for the U.S.-Japan Cold War). Tokyo: Shinchosha, 1991.

Tomiyama Kazuō. *Nihon no Bōei Sangyō* (Japan's Defense Industry). Tokyo: Tōyōkeizai, 1979.

Tsushōsangyōsho Daijin Kanbo (MITI). *Nihon no Sentaku* (Japan's choices), June 1988.

Tsushōsangyōsho (MITI). *Sangyōgijitsu no DoD to Mondai* (Trends and problems in industrial technology). Tokyo: MITI, 1990.

Yamashita Masamitsu, Takai Susumu, and Iwata Shichiro. *TMD: Senniki Dandō Missairu Bōie* (TMD: Theater missile defense). Tokyo: TBS Brittanica, 1994.

Yoshihara Koichirō. *Nihon no Heiki Sangyō* (Japan's arms industry). Tokyo: Shakaishisuosha, 1988.

——. "Sangyō Shidōgata ga Motarasu Mono Rokuheedo Jiken" (The Lockheed incident and the style of industrial leadership). *Economisto,* March 9, 1976.

Japanese Language Periodicals

NEWSPAPERS

Asagumo Shimbun
Asahi Shimbun
Bōei Tsushin
Economisto
Kokushimbunsha Wuingu
Mainichi Shimbun
Nikkan Kōgyō Shimbun
Nikkei Aerospace
Nikkei Business
Nikkei Sangyō Shimbun
Nikkei Shimbun
Tōkyo Shimbun
Yomiuri Shimbun
Zaikai

MAGAZINES

AERA
The Asian Council Brief
Foresight
Gaikō Forum
Gekkan Jiūminsu

Gekkan Bōei Antenna
Gekkan Bōei Gijitsu
Keidanren Geppō
Nihon Koku Uchū Kōgyōkai
Nikkei Business
Securitarian

Books, Documents, and Journal Articles in English

Alexander, Arthur. "Of Tanks and Toyotas: An Assessment of Japan's Defense Industry." RAND Note N-3542-AF. Santa Monica, Cal., 1993.

Arms Control and Disarmament Agency (U.S). *World Military Expenditures and Arms Transfers, 1990*. Washington, D.C.: Government Printing Office, 1991.

Army Materiel Command. *Assessment of Research and Development Opportunities in Defense-Related Technologies, September 1989.*

Asher, David. "Convergence and Its Costs: The International Politics of Japanese Macroeconomic Liberalization, 1918–1932." Unpublished manuscript, London School of Economics, 1991.

Auer, James. *The Postwar Rearmament of Japanese Maritime Forces, 1945–1971*. New York: Praeger, 1973.

——. "The U.S.-Japan FSX Agreement: Cooperation or Competition in High Technology." *Business in the Contemporary World* (Summer 1990).

Berger, Thomas. "From Sword to Chrysanthemum: Japan's Culture of Anti-militarism." *International Security* 17, no. 4 (Spring 1993): 119–50.

Calder, Kent. *Crisis and Compensation: Public Policy and Political Stability in Japan*. Princeton: Princeton University Press, 1988.

Campbell, John. *Contemporary Japanese Budget Politics*. Berkeley: University of California Press, 1977.

Catrina, Christian. *Arms Transfers and Dependence*. New York: Taylor and Francis, 1988.

Chapman, J. W. M., Reinhardt Drifte, and Ian Gow. *Japan's Search for Comprehensive Security: Defence, Diplomacy, Dependence*. London: Francis Pinter, 1983.

Chinworth, Michael. "Financing Japan's Defense Build-Up." MIT-Japan Program Working Paper, December 1989.

——. "Industry and Government in Japanese Defense Procurement: The Case of the Patriot Missile System." MIT-Japan Program Working Paper, April 1989.

——. *Inside Japan's Defense: Technology, Economics, and Strategy*. Washington, D.C.: Brasseys, 1992.

Congress of the United States. *Legislation on Foreign Relations of the United States Through 1989*. March 1990.

Cronin, Patrick and Michael Green. *Redefining the U.S.-Japan Alliance: Tokyo's National Defense Program*. McNair Paper 31. Institute for National Security Studies, National Defense University, November 1994.

Curtis, Gerald et al., eds. *Japan's Foreign Policy After the Cold War: Coping with Change*. Armonde, N.Y.: M. E. Sharpe, 1993.

Department of Commerce (U.S.). *FSX Radar Technology Symposium*. (Information Packet). June 22, 1992.

Department of Defense (U.S.). *Critical Technologies Plan.* March 15, 1990.

—. *Report of the Defense Science Board Task Force on Defense Industrial Cooperation with Pacific Rim Countries.* (Office of the Undersecretary of Defense for Acquisition). August 1989.

—. *Findings of the U.S. Department of Defense Technology Assessment Team on Japanese Manufacturing Technology, Final Report.* June 1989.

—. "Preparation and Processing of FMS Cases," DOD Regulations 5105.38-M.

Dower, John. *Empire and Aftermath: Yoshida Shigeru and the Japanese Experience.* Cambridge, Mass.: Harvard East Asian Studies Monographs, 1979.

Drifte, Reinhardt. *Arms Production in Japan: The Military Applications of Civilian Technology.* London: Westview, 1986.

Emmerson, John, and Leonard Humphries. *Will Japan Rearm? A Study in Attitudes.* AEI Hoover Studies no. 9, December 1973.

Fallows, James. "Containing Japan." *The Atlantic Monthly,* May 1989, 40–54.

Friedman, George and Meredith LeBard. *The Coming War with Japan.* New York: St. Martin's, 1991.

Gaddis, John Lewis. "International Relations Theory and the End of the Cold War." *International Security* 7, no. 3 (Winter 1992–93): 5–58.

Gilpin, Robert. *The Political Economy of International Relations.* Princeton: Princeton University Press, 1987.

Government Accounting Office (U.S.). *U.S.-Japan Codevelopment: Update of the FSX Program.* June 1992.

—. "U.S.-Japan FSX Co-Development Program." May 16, 1989.

—. "U.S. Military Co-Production Programs Assist Japan in Developing Its Civil Aircraft Industry." Government Accounting Office, March 4, 1982.

Green, Michael. "Bōei zoku: Defense Policy Making in Japan's Liberal Democratic Party." MIT-Japan Program Working Paper, April 1992.

—. "Japanese Industry Views of U.S.-Japan Defense Technology Collaboration: Findings of the MIT-Japan Program Survey." MIT-Japan Program Working Paper, January 1994.

—. "Japan in Asia: The American Connection." *Global Affairs* (Summer 1991).

Green, Michael and Richard J. Samuels. *Recalculating Autonomy: Japan's Choices in the New World Order.* Seattle: National Bureau of Asian Research, 1994.

—. "U.S.-Japan Defense Technology Collaboration: Ten Guidelines to Make It Work." MIT-Japan Program Working Paper, July 1994.

Harries, Myron and Susie Harries. *Soldiers of the Sun: The Rise and Fall of the Imperial Japanese Army.* New York: Random House, 1991.

Havens, Thomas R. *Fire Across the Sea.* Princeton: Princeton University Press, 1987.

Holland, Harrison. *Managing Defense: Japan's Dilemma.* Lanham, Md.: University Press of America, 1988.

Institute for Defense Analysis. *Dependence of U.S. Defense Systems on Foreign Technologies.* Alexandria, Va.: IDA, December 1990.

Johnson, Chalmers. *MITI and the Japanese Economic Miracle: The Growth of Industrial Policy, 1925–1975.* Stanford: Stanford University Press, 1982.

Johnson, Chalmers, Laura D'Andrea Tyson, and John Zysman, eds. *Politics and Productivity: How Japan's Development Strategy Works.* New York: Harper Business, 1989.

Kaplan, Morton. *Systems and Processes in International Relations.* New York: John Wiley, 1957.

Katahara Eiichi. *The Politics of Japanese Defense Policy.* Ph.D. thesis, Griffith University, April 1990.

Katzenstein, Peter and Nobuo Okawara. *Japan's National Security.* Ithaca: Cornell University Press, 1993.

Keddell, Joseph. *The Politics of Defense in Japan.* Armonde, N.Y.: M. E. Sharpe, 1993.

Lincoln, Edward. *Japan's New Global Role.* Washington, D.C.: The Brookings Institution, 1993.

Liska, George. *Nations in Alliance: The Limits of Interdependence.* Baltimore: Johns Hopkins University Press, 1962.

MacDougall, Terry, ed. *Political Leadership in Contemporary Japan.* Ann Arbor: University of Michigan Papers in Japan Studies no. 1, 1982.

Mastanduno, Michael. "Do Relative Gains Matter?" *International Security* 16, no. 1 (Summer 1991): 73–113.

Middleton, Peter. "XT-4: Potent with Potential." *Flight International,* January 2, 1988, 24–26.

Ministry of International Trade and Industry. "Issues and Trends in Industrial/ Scientific Technology Towards Technoglobalism." June 1992.

Mochizuki, Michael. "Japan's Search for Strategy." *International Security* 8 (Winter 1983–84): 153–81.

—. *Managing and Influencing the Japanese Legislative Process: The Role of Parties and the National Diet.* Ph.D. Dissertation, Harvard, 1982.

Moravcsik, Andrew. "The European Arms Industry at the Crossroads." *Survival,* January/February 1990.

National Research Council. *High Stakes Aviation: U.S.-Japan Linkages in Transport Aircraft.* Washington, D.C.: National Academy Press, 1994.

Nau, Henry. *National Politics and International Technology.* Baltimore: Johns Hopkins University Press, 1974.

Neustadt, Richard. *Alliance Politics.* New York: Columbia University Press, 1970.

Nixon, Richard. *A U.S. Foreign Policy for the 1970s.* Executive Office of the President, 1972.

Noble, Gregg. "Japan, America, and the FSX Fighter Plane: Structural Asymmetries in Bilateral Negotiations." Paper prepared for the 1990 meeting of the Association for Asian Studies, Chicago, April 5–8, 1990.

Office of Technology Assessment, U.S. Congress. *Arming Our Allies: Cooperation and Competition in Defense Technology.* Washington, D.C., May 1990.

—. *Global Arms Trade: Commerce in Advanced Military Technology and Weapons.* Washington, D.C., June 1991.

Okimoto, Dan. *Between MITI and the Market: Japanese Industrial Policy for High Technology.* Stanford: Stanford University Press, 1989.

Olsun, Mancur. *The Rise and Decline of Nations: Economic Growth, Stagflation and Social Rigidities.* New Haven: Yale University Press, 1982.

Packard, George. *Protest in Tokyo: The Security Treaty Crisis of 1960.* Princeton: Princeton University Press, 1966.

Patrick, Hugh, and Henry Rosovsky. *Asia's New Giant: How the Japanese Economy Works.* Washington, D.C.: The Brookings Institution, 1976.

Pempel, T. J. "From Trade to Technology: Japan's Reassessment of Military Policies." *The Jerusalem Journal of International Politics* 2: no. 4(1990): 1-28.

Prestowitz, Clyde. *Trading Places.* New York: Basic Books, 1989.

Pyle, Kenneth. *The Japanese Question: Power and Purpose in a New Era.* Washington, D.C.: AEI, 1992.

Reich, Robert. "The Rise of Technonationalism." *The Atlantic Monthly,* May 1987, 62–71.

The Edwin O. Reischauer Center, The Paul H. Nitze School of Advanced International Studies. *The United States and Japan in 1991: Discord or Dialogue?* Washington, D.C. 1991.

Research Institute for Peace and Security. *Asian Security,* Yearbooks for 1989–1990, 1990–1991. Tokyo: Brasseys.

Roscoe, Bruce. *Defense: A Break with Tradition.* Stock Analysis Report, S.G. Warburg Japan, January 8, 1988.

Rubiner, Matthew. "U.S. Government and Industry Views of Bilateral Defense Technology Cooperation with Japan." MIT-Japan Program Working Paper, February 1994.

Sampson, Anthony. *The Arms Bazaar: From Lebanon to Lockheed.* New York: Viking, 1977.

Samuels, Richard. "Reinventing Security: Japan since Meiji." *Daedalus* 120, no. 4 (Fall 1991): 47–68.

—. *Rich Nation/Strong Army: National Security and the Technological Transformation of Japan.* Cornell: Cornell University Press, 1994.

Samuels, Richard and David Friedman. "How to Succeed Without Really Flying: The Japanese Aircraft Industry and Japan's Technology Ideology." MIT-Japan Program Working Paper, January 1992.

Sandholtz, Wayne, Michael Borrus, and John Zysman. *The Highest Stakes: The Economic Foundations of the Next Security Systems.* New York: Oxford University Press, 1992.

Schaller, Michael. *The American Occupation of Japan.* New York: Oxford University Press, 1985.

Schumpeter, Joseph. *Capitalism, Socialism, and Democracy.* New York: Harper, 1942.

Shear, Jeff. *The Keys to the Kingdom: The FSX Deal and the Selling of America's Future to Japan.* New York: Doubleday, 1994.

Snyder, Glenn. "Alliance Theory: A Neorealist First Cut." *Journal of International Affairs* 44, no. 1 (Spring/Summer 1990): 103–23.

Soderberg, Marie. *Japan's Military Export Policy.* Stockholm: Universtitet Stockholms, 1986.

TASC (The Analytic Sciences Corporation). *Foreign Vulnerability of Critical Industries.* Arlington, Va., March 1991.

Thayer, Nathaniel. *How the Conservatives Rule Japan.* Princeton: Princeton University Press, 1969.

Tolchin, Martin and Susan Tolchin. *Selling Our Security: The Erosion of America's Assets.* New York: Knopf, 1992.

Van Wolferen, Karl. *The Enigma of Japanese Power.* New York: Knopf, 1989.

Vernon, Raymond and Ethan Kapstein. "National Needs, Global Resources." *Daedalus* 120, no. 4 (Fall 1991): 1–22.

—. *The Technology Factor in International Trade.* New York: Columbia University Press, 1970.

Walt, Stephen. *The Origin of Alliances.* Ithaca: Cornell University Press, 1985.

Waltz, Kenneth. *Theory of International Politics.* New York: Random House, 1979.

Weinstein, Martin. *Japan's Postwar Defense Policy.* New York: Columbia University Press, 1971.

Welfield, John. *An Empire in Eclipse: Japan in the Postwar American Alliance System.* London: Athlone Press, 1988.

English Language Periodicals

NEWSPAPERS

Daily Yomiuri
Japan Times
Mainichi Daily News
New York Times
Nikkei Weekly
Wall Street Journal
Washington Post

MAGAZINES

Aviation Week and Space Technology
Defense News
Flight International
Inside Tokyo
Insight
Jane's Defence Weekly
JEI Report
Technology Review (MIT)
Tokyo Business Today

Interviews by the Author (1987–1993)

Agency for Industrial Science and Technology (MITI)
Allied Signal Japan
Army Materiel Command
The Asian Council
Boeing Japan
Chief of Staff's Office: Ground, Air, and Maritime Self-Defense Forces
Democratic Socialist Party (Staff and Diet members)
Fujitsu
General Electric Jet Engines Japan

Hitachi
International Institute for Policy Studies
Japan Defense Agency
Japan Defense Research Center
Japan Socialist Party [interviews with staff and Diet members]
Kawasaki Heavy Industries
Kayaba Industries
Keidanren Defense Production Committee
Liberal Democratic Party Headquarters (Policy Affairs Research Council staff and
    Diet members)
Lockheed–Fort Worth
Komeito (Clean Government Party) [interviews with staff and Diet members]
Martin Marietta Japan
Ministry of Finance (Budget Bureau)
Ministry of Foreign Affairs
Ministry of International Trade and Industry
Mitsubishi Electric Corporation
Mitsubishi Heavy Industries
Mitsubishi Research Institute
Mutual Defense Assistance Office (U.S. Embassy, Tokyo)
National Defense University of Japan
National Institute for Defense Studies, JDA
NEC
Nissan
Office of Naval Research, Japan
Pratt & Whitney Japan (United Technologies)
Science and Technology Agency
Sony
Technology Research and Development Institute, JDA
Thomson-CSF Japan
Tōshiba
U.S. Aerospace Industry Association–Japan
U.S. Department of Commerce
U.S. Department of Defense
U.S. Embassy, Japan
U.S. Forces Japan, Headquarters

Index